OUR
EMERGENT CIVILIZATION

OUR

EMERGENT

Planned and Edited by

Science of Culture Series

VOLUME I   FREEDOM : ITS MEANING

VOLUME II   SCIENCE AND MAN

VOLUME III   BEYOND VICTORY

(*Published by Harcourt, Brace and Company,*
New York, N. Y.)

HARPER & BROTHERS, PUBLISHERS

Science of Culture Series
VOLUME IV

CIVILIZATION

RUTH NANDA ANSHEN

NEW YORK AND LONDON

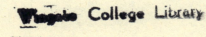

TO JUDITH

CONTENTS

PREFACE

During his brief existence on this earth, man alone is free to know, to examine, to criticize, to choose, and to create. In this freedom lies his superiority over the resistless forces that pervade his outward life. But man is only man, and only free, when he is considered as a complete being, a totality concerning whom any form of segregation and isolation is artificial, mischievous and destructive; for to subdivide man is to execute him. Nevertheless, the persistent interrelationship of the processes of the human mind has been, for the most part, so ignored, or forgotten, as to create devouring distortions in the understanding of man to the extent that one begins to believe that if there is any faith left in our apparently moribund age it clings in sad perversion, in isolated responsibility and with implacable tenacity to that ancient tenet: "Blessed is he who shall not reveal what has been revealed unto him." For when he does attempt to communicate his knowledge he is for the most part either misinterpreted or misunderstood.

The mutual unintelligibility among most contemporary thinkers, their apparent inability to communicate the meaning and purpose of their ideas to those of differing opinions, the paucity of their knowledge pertaining to the subjects and researches of others, all this has grown to be as profound as it is ominous for the future of mankind. And the possibility of clarifying the confusion, which is more than a semantical issue, and of dissipating the distortions seems remote. The subdivision, specialization, nay, atomization increasingly characteristic of religious, philosophic and scientific ideas, of political and social movements during the past two centuries, in spite of the unification of science movements, the decline and defeat of reason, have proved to be an almost invincible impediment to an adequate correlation of these very ideas and movements which, in truth, are in perpetual interplay. The postulates, categories, dialectical promptings, fecund analogies or decisive doctrines which first appear in one eminent province of human thought may, and frequently do, penetrate, through their inevitable divagations, into a diversity of other realms. And to be aware of only one of them is to misunderstand the character, kinship, logic and operation of the entire organism and to obscure and even eclipse the illuminating interrelations.

Human thoughts and knowledge have never before been so abundant, so kaleidoscopic, so vast, and yet, at the same time, never so diffused, so inchoate, so directionless. And human anxiety and restlessness, the dark loneliness and isolation of man amid hostile forces, exist commensurately. There has been little recognition of the importance of a synthesis, a clarification of modern knowledge on the basis of reason, and of the affinity of ideas, a kind of encyclopedic synthesis indispensable if in the future human affairs are to be handled with any hopeful freshness. We seem to have forgotten that all great changes are preceded by a vigorous intellectual reorganization and that nothing new can be attempted in collective human thought and action without a reinterpretation of the fundamental values of mankind. We have succumbed to a conception of nature and mind which has been determined by an incorrect analysis of the phenomenon of life, since it has been torn, isolated, from the whole to which it belongs. Is there no ultimate hope for man to live a well-ordered life, to be able to depend upon the help of his fellow beings, especially upon those who by their ideas direct and interpret the course of his existence? Will not the reality of fear and the equal reality of man's freedom to cope with it permit, in spite of danger, the actualization of human potentiality and the shaping of the world? And is the knowledge which man most requires, namely, the knowledge of himself, only to be found in terms of Delphic ambiguity or in erroneous and predatory understanding?

Out of such considerations as these and out of a concern for the integrity of the intellectual life, its moral and spiritual values, and a hope for the re-establishment of the dignity of man, the plan to bring about a correlation of those contemporary ideas which are not preoccupied with sense data and antiseptic, logical universals, but with the status of values, the bearing of these values on conduct, and the revitalization of reason, had its genesis. Those humanistic men, those men of reason in the various branches of scholarly inquiry (and the contributors to these books) with whom this plan was discussed were poignantly aware of the principal ailment of mankind—of the disjunction of empirical approach from theory, of methods of observation from speculative doctrine, and of the grave lacunae existent in the study of the nature of man. They know that values are eternally present, they persistently question how they may be discovered, they never cease to wonder why they are often confused, and they are anxious to determine in what sense these values are present when they are not recognized. These men are devoted to the rehabilitation of reason, reason which has suffered so many wounds during the past three hundred years.

It was considered desirable to establish a series of books, each devoted to the discussion, from diverse and important contemporary points of view, of a single, well-defined question, the object being to make clear first how much agreement there is, and on what specific points, pertinent to the question, and to make also as explicit as possible the points of disagreement and their real grounds. Such volumes (collectively known as the Science of Culture Series of which *Our Emergent Civilization* is the fourth book) seem to perform an indispensable function in clarifying the present situation with respect to the questions defined, and such clarification should be an aid toward eventual agreement. A co-operative effort to accomplish this, to exhibit with all possible clarity where representatives of differing schools of opinion agree and precisely where and precisely why they disagree, and to do this fairly concisely, is, we venture to say, of the utmost significance and importance. The Science of Culture Series is an endeavor to synthesize fundamental contemporary ideas which, by virtue of their dispersion, have been rendered comparatively ineffectual.

Although such a synthesis can have no judicial or political power of any kind, it can perhaps exert such an influence on the peoples of the world that no ruling caste could venture to defy the moral judgment of this "conscience" of humanity, living in the thoughts of the thinkers represented and expressed in these books.

One of the values of such a correlation of contemporary knowledge could be the formulation of a cultural directory for the guidance of mankind, the creation of a systematic circumspection compatible with democratic principles, the discernment of possible alternatives in a social crisis, leading to a genuine social democracy in which collective intelligence and collective conscience are so highly developed as to make individuality which includes personality not only possible but fruitfully effective and in which the antinomy of freedom and security may be resolved and *both* become at last the experience of mankind.

The material necessities of existence and the spiritual values of the contemporary world, which coexist in the same complex social totality are functionally dependent upon each other and must be co-ordinated to assure the stability of civilization. This work has been undertaken in the conviction that it will be the corporeal manifestation of the spirit of science and culture prevailing in the conduct of human affairs; that it will be a laboratory for the discussion of important contemporary problems—with an end to direct the thought and action of mankind; that by gathering in a synthesis, in a crucible, knowledge pertaining to values, knowledge which is being, not a mere methodological process of knowing, it may at least in part bring back into human society that humanity which has with such systematic contempt and cruelty been eliminated; and that, finally, it may, in the words of Bergson, help us to think as men and women of action and to act as men and women of thought.

                                                                    R. N. A.

New York, February, 1947

OUR

EMERGENT CIVILIZATION

Yea—for not Zeus, I ween, proclaimed this thing;
Nor Justice, co-mate with the Nether Gods,
Nor she ordained men such unnatural laws!
Nor deemed I that thine edict had such force,
That thou, who art but mortal, could'st o'erride
The unwritten and unanswering laws of Heaven,
Not of today and yesterday are they,
But from everlasting.

SOPHOCLES, *Antigone*

Chapter I

RUTH NANDA ANSHEN

THE DECAY OF THE OLD IDEALS

I look out on earth—lo, all is chaos,
I look at heaven—its light is gone,
I look out on the mountains—they are reeling;
And all the hills are swaying!
I look out—lo, no man is to be seen,
All the birds have flown!
I look out—lo, the sown land lies a desert;
And the towns are all razed by the Lord's rage.
For thus hath the Lord said:
The whole land shall be desolate—
And for this shall the earth mourn
And the heavens above be black—
I have purposed it and will not repent;
Neither will I turn back from it.
At the noise of the horsemen and the archers
The land is all in flight,
Men take refuge within woods and caves,
And climbing upon the rocks.
Every city shall be abandoned,
And not a man dwell therein.
You ruined creature, what will you do!

* * *

For the mountains shall depart,
And the hills be removed.
But my kindness shall not depart from thee;
Neither shall the covenant of my peace be removed,
Saith the Lord that has mercy on thee!

These portentous words from Jeremiah and Isaiah are no longer prophecy and vision. They have become scientific law; they have become the ineluctable truth of mathematics and physics. Man has always known that in the earth, in everything possessing form and structure, predatory forces abound. Man has known also that when the destructive power of even the smallest particles of the material world were governed and restrained, a place was provided on which life could take root and history develop, on which words could be heard, love and beauty experienced, truth discovered, reason esteemed and justice acclaimed.

But what has man done! He has discovered the secret which can liberate the forces hitherto restrained by nature. He has subjected the very foundation of life and thought to his will. And as a result, "gladness has gone from the earth, and pleasure is no more . . . For earth has been polluted by the dwellers on its face . . . breaking the Eternal Covenant." This is the experience of modern man. Is this to be the consummation of history?

Will man pursue his anthropocentric ways, seduced from reason by wily materialism, violent in greed, swollen with ambition, uncontrollable in lust, ingenious in his practice of greater and greater abominations? Or will he finally see through the crumbling of the world those immutable principles and values which alone can bestow upon humanity the intrinsic reality of existence? What will be his choice? How will he exercise his freedom?

The aim of this book is to point out the nascent forces in our civilization. Its purpose is to awaken the consciousness of modern man to the truth that knowledge in order to be effectual can never be made ancillary to merely biological or physical life and experience. It endeavors to evoke the recognition that man constitutes one substance which is both spiritual and material, soul and matter—two coprinciples of the same being, of one and the same reality. It demonstrates the sterility of the positivistic method in evaluating the nature and needs of man and society, a method causing the separation of analysis from synthesis, quantity from quality, phenomenon from fact, and fact from meaning and purpose. It considers the basic source of the aberrated existentialism of our time and points to its inevitable growth since its very seminal power lay in our theories of evolution and in our Hegelian emphasis on mere becoming, while repudiating our essence, our being, and thus inevitably leading to an apotheosis of absurdity and despair. It embraces that objectivity of reason in human affairs, in the organization of human communities, and in the establishment of justice which can never be considered mere intellectual achievements but moral and spiritual accomplishments involving the whole of man. And, finally, it demands the recognition that government is a function of the theory of the state, the theory of the state a function of the theory of knowledge, and the theory of knowledge a problem of metaphysics.

The importunate cry of Oliver Cromwell, echoing down through the ages, may well be repeated here: "My brethren, by the bowels of Christ I beseech you, bethink you that you may be mistaken." It was a plea that man refrain at last from deliberately avoiding existent avenues of knowledge, a plea that is palpably applicable to our pitiful modern society so richly inundated with the potentialities of a deeply moving, fulfilled life, and yet at the same time so desiccated, so impotent to make the leap from potentiality to actuality, to bring finally within the experience of mankind justice, peace, unchallenged liberty and the realization that God's will is at last being done on earth as it is in heaven.

What are the salient symptoms of our decaying ideals? By what signs do we recognize them? They reveal themselves in a boundless absence of any faith in a real order of existence independent of the opinions and desires of the national group; in a resulting scorn and contempt for rational intelligence, except as the contriver of technical instruments; in the abrogation of reason which alone can be a bulwark against a repetition of the errors of nineteenth century individualism and a totalitarian or "communal" conception of society. And, finally, the decadence of much of contemporary civilization is recognized by the irrational repudiation of the human person who uniquely possesses the rational faculty. Freedom itself is therefore stifled, the growth and expansion of the personality aborted, and life itself petrified. For, without freedom, the antinomies of thought and action can never be resolved, and the universe eternally defeats our aspirations and ideals. Unless we can transcend the practical antinomy of being forced by the moral situation both to assert and to deny a moral government of the world, we should be confronted with a universe that could not be moralized. On the assumption that freedom exists, the difficulty is overcome and the universe becomes an order in which the moral law has meaning and the attainment of the goal of our moral striving is guaranteed. In the conclusions to which we are compelled by logic and reason there is nothing to disprove the validity of this postulate of freedom, a postulate which is indispensable to moral action. Indeed, this very postulate is the heuristic force, the guiding ideal, of our metaphysical speculation.

Freedom, that strength which arises out of inherent human weakness, no longer can mean what the old theologians of Christianity intended it to imply. *Liberum arbitrium* is a liability and not an asset. It would perhaps be better if man were able to do only good; but his *libertas boni,* in spite of St. Augustine's affirmation to the contrary, eliminates human responsibility and with it the inner spring of moral life as a thing that flows from human conscience and human will. The whole dramatic sense of life that emanates from freedom disappears and man becomes but an automaton, a passive agent, like a worker in a modern factory who merely repeats automatically the gesture of fitting a screw into its preordained place. Thus man loses faith in man, he is no longer able to find rational justification for the truths for which he struggles, he abandons universal reason and the miasma of a mental and moral poisoning sets in, atrophying life and clouding the spirit. Instead of making use of all the potentialities he holds within him, his creative powers and the life of reason, instead of laboring to make the forces of the physical world the instruments of his freedom, man becomes enslaved, hemmed in by his unconditional devotion to a satanic image, his Self rejected and his soul deontologized.

The rebuke of Zeus to men in the *Odyssey* might well be the motto for contemporary man: "Lo you now, how vainly mortal men do blame the gods! For of us they say comes evil, whereas they even of themselves, through the blindness of their own hearts, have sorrows beyond that which is ordained."

The participants in this fourth volume of the Science of Culture Series are participants by virtue of their palpable awareness of the problems confronting our civilization, their ability to penetrate into the essence of these problems and evaluate them. They present with unfailing vision the future by virtue of their intelligent comprehension of the past and the present. They recognize the love and humanism indispensable to life on this earth by the wounds which this love and this humanism have received. They have crossed the dangerous zones where the spirit of despair might have seized them, as it has seized other men, distorting their vision, and they have arrived where they can point to a specific path for humanity leading to the great firmament, to the freedom of those who recognize the truth and are not reluctant to follow it, the truth that men must learn to live together or they will perish; the truth that international morality must be the only basis for human conduct, or there will be no human conduct for there will be no human life; the truth that the ghost of the atom bomb is already shaking its bloody locks in omnivorous greed for another bloody orgy and will yet feast on the bodies of men unless men exert their power of reason for their own vindication as men—the only power that can save them—and convert the deadly potentialities inherent in this instrument of man's ingenuity into its equally creative potentialities for human enrichment; the truth that the moral apathy of present society must give way to a revitalization of the spirit of man.

The participants in this book re-establish the principle of an all-equalizing justice of Being which can serve as a foundation whereon the sovereignty of intellectual and moral law can be erected; they recognize the depredations following the worship of a subjective self-preservation incompatible with society and man's essential nature; they see that each mind must be something more than a convenient implement in the unrestricted war of each against all; they insist that the state has another end than that of a mere tool in the hands of a temporarily ruling caste for the exploitation of all other men, and they indict that law which exists merely as the expression of the will of the strongest. They denounce those moral ideals interpreted only as a reflection of what society deems expedient, or accepted as a necessary fiction, a formidable façade behind which it can indulge without restraint those egoistic demands of its own existence. They demand a re-evaluation of the moral organism, of all ethical concepts for man and society, and a logic that is not mere formalism and devoid of content but which leads to ontology and the acceptance of the common good not only as a system of advantages and utilities but also a rectitude of life, an end, good in itself, the true *bonum honestum*.

This book finally warns man against the chaos that is his inevitable destiny unless he at last exerts his unique privilege as man, the privilege of choice. In him, one may say, lies the power of prophecy for the future. Every work of the mind and spirit of man, every work of art, of philosophy, of science, is the fulfillment of a prophecy, for it is but the volitional conversion of an idea into an image. So every human being is the fulfillment of a prophecy, for each human being is the realization of some ideal, either in the mind of God or in the mind of man.

The history of the evolution of life has revealed the manner in which the intellect, capable of conceiving the ideal, has been formed, formed by an uninterrupted progress, in a direction which has ascended through the vertebrate categories up to man. It has revealed in the capacity and faculty of understanding an appendage of the capacity and faculty of acting, an ever-increasingly precise, an ever-increasingly complex and supple adaptation of the consciousness of living beings to the conditions of existence. Thus it should, it seems, inevitably follow that man's intellect is intended to secure the most adequate, the most perfect, adaptation of his body, mind and spirit to his environment, to represent the relations of external things among themselves. But equally important also is a knowledge of man about man. In all the conflicts between the different and multiple schools of thought, this objective remains invariable, unshaken, undisputed. It is the Archimedean point, the fixed and immovable center, of all thought. Knowledge of the Self is the first prerequisite of the realization, of the fulfillment, of the Self.

What, however, during these many years of man's existence on this earth, has actually taken place? How much closer is man to the truth, or truths, about himself? Does he really *want* to know himself or is he possessed of an unfathomable "Angst" in relation to truth? Has he an *impulse* for knowledge, for truth, even a nostalgia for truth, and yet, at the same time and paradoxically, an anxiety and fear of understanding the truth, a desire to escape from it? At the beginning of Aristotle's *Metaphysics,* one reads: "All men by nature desire to know." It is true that man is impelled by some mysterious, centripetal power to submit to the law of truth in order to be free. Yet the authority of the evidence presented by experience frequently leads one to a conclusion directly antithetical to the Aristotelian position. For man seems to be hemmed in by a pitiful but inevitable dichotomy; on the one hand, he is motivated by the need of freedom and truth and, on the other hand, by the need of flight from freedom and truth.

Let us examine the evidence. The great majority of men are most secure among inanimate objects, where their action finds its fulcrum and their industry its tools. The concepts of men have been formulated on the hypothesis of solids, of tangibles. The logic of men has been established on the logic of solids, of tangibles. And the intellect of men has found its hitherto unquestioned sovereignty in the triumph of Euclid and his geometry, wherein has been revealed the kinship of logical thought with unorganized matter and where the mind must merely pursue its own natural movement, after the slightest and lightest possible contact with experience, in order to proceed from achievement to achievement, from discovery to discovery, in the implacable certainty that experience is inherent in it and will invariably vindicate it.

And all this has culminated in the almost incredible discoveries and achievements of science, the perhaps final chapter in the history of mankind, the most significant subject of a philosophy of man and held to be the summit and consummation, the "crowning glory" of all human activities. This much is true: Science is the last step in the intellectual development of man and it may even be regarded as the highest and most characteristic achievement of human culture. It is an achievement deeply refined and one whose multiple potentialities could develop only under the most special conditions. The conception of science in this specific sense did not exist before the Pythagoreans, the Atomists, Plato and Aristotle. And even such an apocalyptic discovery was forgotten and eclipsed in the ensuing centuries, only to be resurrected and rehabilitated during the Renaissance. From that period of the attempted revitalization of human reason to the last demonic acquisition of cosmic, atomic power, the triumph of science remains, alas, complete and uncontested.

Medievalism, too, made one of the greatest contributions to the formation of the scientific movement. That age was impregnated—in an all too alarming fecundity—with the inexpugnable belief that every detailed occurrence can be correlated with its antecedents in a perfect, definite and conclusive manner, exemplifying general principles. In fact, the incredible labors of science could not have existed without this hope. In it lies the motive power, the catalytic impulse, for research. In it is to be found the instinctive conviction, vividly poised before the imagination, that there is a secret in the universe—a secret to be unveiled, which can be revealed only through the methodologies of empirical investigation.

The medieval insistence on the rationality of God, exemplified as possessing the dynamic energy of Jehovah and the rationality of the Greek philosophers, found its vindication again and again in the belief that every detail of existence was supervised and ordered. There was faith, profound faith. There was faith in the intelligible rationality of a personal being, although the trust in the scrutability of nature was not always logically justified even by medieval theology. There was faith in the possibility of science, generated antecedently to the development and exposition of modern scientific theory. And this faith had its foundation, even though an unconscious foundation, in the theological hypotheses of medieval thought.

But a general sense of the order in things is not enough. Something more is essential. It requires but a brief paragraph to indicate how the habit of exact, definite thought impregnated the mind of man, especially European man, by the long and uninterrupted dominance of scholastic logic and scholastic divinity. The habit abided after the philosophy had been repudiated, which is the nature of habits, the exquisite habit of searching for an exact point and then adhering to it implacably when found. Galileo is indeed the ardent and unquestioned disciple of Aristotle (although profound influences of Plato also permeate his thinking) and owes infinitely more to him than appears in the *Dialogues*.

The progress of science has now reached a turning point. The spiritual revolution is here. The habit of analytical thought has been fatal to the intuitions of integral thinking. Science in its exclusively empirical form, just as thought in its purely logical form, is incapable of presenting the true nature of existence, the meaning and purpose of life, the full explanation of the evolutionary process. Created by life, in definite circumstances, to act on definite things, how can it embrace life, of which it is merely an emanation or an aspect? Deposited by the scientific movement in the course of its labyrinthian way, how can it be applied to science itself—to science in its etymological sense of knowing and being? For man in order to *know* must *be,* and in order to *be* must *know*.

Or, in the words of Eckhart, "people should think less about what they ought to do and more about what they ought to be. If only their being were good, their works would shine forth brightly. Do not imagine that you can ground your salvation upon actions; it must rest on what you *are*. The ground upon which good character rests is the very same ground from which man's work derives its value, namely, a mind wholly turned to God. Verily, if you were so minded, you might tread on a stone and it would be a more pious work than if you, simply for your own profit, were to receive the Body of the Lord and were wanting in spiritual detachment."

Knowledge for science in the Cartesian tradition has been a kind of knowledge that has a certain beginning and varies as it is associated with the things we call realities. But surely this is not all of knowledge.

As well contend that the part is equal to the whole, that the effect can re-absorb its cause, or that the pebble deposited on the shore can display the form of the wave that brought it there.

What has been the result of the blind and persistent worship of the ideals of science? Why has an inevitable decay of these ideals set in, metastasizing until the very soul of man is lost, bewildered, without hope? It is because mind has been separated from reason; because man has been confronted with a dualism incompatible with his nature: first, the dualism of the individual and the person, which has dissolved society to the advantage of its parts, overtly anarchistic, resulting in an individualistic materialism which bestowed upon the strong a pontifical freedom to oppress the weak, an individualism which accepted morally and politically Locke's theory that man is a mental substance, on the one hand, and, on the other, Hume's theory that man consists of an infinite association of sense data and sterile, logical universals; second, the dualism of thought and body. We have seen the results of this dualism in the second half of the seventeenth century. Then there was a theoretical contempt for the body and the senses. Nothing was worthy of man but the purity of thought. What did this mean? It meant the triumph and dominance of artificial thought and of false intellectualism; for human intellection can be living and fresh only when it is related to the vigilance of sense perception. The natural roots of man's knowledge were cut. There resulted the inevitable atrophy, therefore, in thought and in culture, a spiritual drought for which the sentimental, nostalgic tears were subsequently to provide a sadly ineffectual consolation.

We must at last concede that not one of the categories of science and of logical thought—unity, multiplicity, mechanical and physical causality—can precisely or exclusively apply to the things of life. Who is able to say where individuality begins and where it ends? Who can say whether the living being is one or many? Whether it is the cells that associate themselves into the organism or the organism that dissociates itself into cells? In vain does man force life into a multiplicity of forms, of molds. The forms cannot contain life. The molds crack and crumble. They are too narrow, too rigid, for what we try to put into them.

Affective life has been forgotten or has been disregarded. Feeling has been considered nothing more than a confused idea. The existence of love and of will as forming a distinct world, possessing its own laws in the life of the soul, has been relegated or has been radically misunderstood. And our intellectualizing, so sure of itself among things inert, begins to feel ill at ease, uncertain, without direction. It would be difficult to cite a biological discovery due to mere cerebration. And in the final analysis, when experience has revealed how life functions in order to obtain a certain result, we find its way of functioning is exactly the opposite of what we had thought.

Unfortunately, science received its inspiration and its derivation from the least significant aspect of the philosophies of Aristotle's successors. In certain respects, however, this was more fortunate than at first appears but only from a very limited point of view. For it enabled the knowledge of the seventeenth century to be formularized, as far as physics and mathematics were concerned, with a thoroughness and completeness which has its visible and felicitous manifestations today. But it did not hesitate to extend to the whole process and content of life the same methods of explanation which so eminently succeeded in the case of unorganized matter. By doing this, the progress of biology and psychology has been impeded by the uncritical assumption of half-truths. The lantern of science glimmering in the dark, tortuous passages of the life and spirit of man has been substituted for the Sun which alone can illumine the world.

The scientific disregard for the spirit and the essence of man's existence has resulted in many distortions, aberrations, and misconceptions, among them being one of the most formidable aspects of modern culture: Freud, with his engrossing, sadistic lyricism which has reduced man to sexuality, isolated individualism and the instinct for death. Life in the so-called unconscious presents itself, in accordance with Freud's conception, as dominated by drives, dominated in such a manner and to such a degree that it becomes the problem of life to obtain release from the inevitable tension these drives produce. This release epitomizes the desideratum of all drives, culminating ineluctably in the ultimate complete release or death; the final dissolution into the inorganic. Thus through an erroneous hypostatization of tension and release Freud, realizing that his concept of a libidinal impulse cannot account for all aspects of man's nature, postulates the inevitability of the death instinct. Life itself thereby becomes, in its very essence, unintelligible and futile. There can be no doubt of the genius of Freud in the realm of investigation and discovery. But his value as a psychologist has been adumbrated by a radical empiricism, a spurious metaphysics, and a too preponderant emphasis upon anxiety.

In no way can one insist that this "ordered" world, which culture represents, is the product of anxiety, the outcome of the impulse to avoid anxiety. And yet Freud conceives of culture merely as a sublimation of repressed desires. What does this imply if not an utter misapprehension of the creative direction of man's nature, of the primal tendency toward actualization! If this tendency were not inherent in man, the existence of the specific patterns of our culture would be completely unintelligible. They become intelligible and meaningful only when they are regarded as expressions of the creative power of man and of the tendency to effectuate a realization of his nature. In addition, for Freud, the unconscious includes all that is inaccessible to voluntary command and the term "preconscious" is employed only for those non-conscious aspects which voluntary command can draw into consciousness. What has been either repudiated or ignored is the life and dynamism of that entire region of the psyche to which consciousness is inevitably linked—the rational aspect of the spirit and the mind. It can certainly not be denied that the free decision of the will, the judgment of the mind, is in itself conscious and indispensable to man's true behavior as man. For Freud there is no free choice, no free will, and even the highest, most objective capacities and functions of the mind are fulfilled in the unconscious. The tragic result of this way of thinking has been a disintegration and dissolution of human personality and unity, of universal reason and objective truth, into a world of anarchistic instincts, sex and dream, animality and matter; in other words, into a ferocious and predatory acceptance of materialism. If science, of which the existential psychological values of Freud are but a few of the many effluences, could be correctly understood, if means were no longer confused with ends, a spiritual purification would ensue for man and a more adequate knowledge of himself, his world, and his relation to the universe.

As a further result of the passionate embrace of scientific empiricism, matters pertaining to social, economic and political life have been abandoned to their own secular law, depriving them of the light of reason. Nothing could be more opposed to the spirit of a social democracy for which the world is striving. Karl Marx did not err when he declared that capitalist society is in a state of anarchy where life is entirely abandoned to the caprice of particular interests and groups. Marx himself is the product of such anarchy, the epitome of modern society, which has failed in its duty to actualize in social, economic and political terms, in concrete, temporal experience, the truths of a social democracy. And by virtue of this failure, society is experiencing a sense of rejection of itself by itself, a profound resentment, a resentment and suspicion against those who failed to corporealize the truth of which they were the bearers and transmitters, a resentment which has created an antagonism against and suspicion of truth itself. Marxism has arisen from a perception of the importance and indispensability of material causality, of the significance of the role played by materialism in the course of nature and history. Such material causality Marx integrated with the dialectical process of history but it became for him unfortunately the source of all activity. The importance he attached to the economic interpretation of existence is indisputably great, but his limitation and his error lay in the principal role and exclusive power he attributed to it. Marx recognized the essential significance of material and physical causation, but he did not recognize its subsidiary, not primary, function in the life of man. He possessed a profound intuition. He saw with deep penetration the conditions of heteronomy and the annihilation of freedom experienced in a capitalist world by means of wage slavery and of subsequent dehumanization. But what he, with so much perspicacity, realized in the existential process of man's life, he failed, because of equal myopia, to understand in the essential, or ontological, process. He failed to see that the masses would one day oppress the masses, that they would be their own greatest oppressors. For if economic slavery and the social insecurity of the proletariat are to be abandoned, if the precariousness of life is to be assuaged, it must be in the name of human personality, human dignity, human reason and human freedom. The potent and compelling exigencies relating to economic life exist only because of man's essential need of transcendent rights and transcendent moral values inherent in natural law, the final source also of economic values. Economic liberty must not be cherished in the name of an anthropocentric collectivity or false communal demands but in the name of the spiritual, intellectual and moral dignity of the human race.

If science, which has made materialism possible, is not to degenerate into a quagmire of *ad hoc* hypotheses, it must develop a criticism of its own foundations, its own premises. It must become philosophical, endowed with an understanding and, more, a willingness to understand man's nature. The knowledge which man most needs is a knowledge of his own nature. At no moment, indeed, in the life of the race has the pertinency of the Delphic imperative been more tragically apparent. For it has, I believe, at last become evident that the problem of human nature is the gravest and most fundamental of our problems, and that the question which, more than any other question, demands an immediate and satisfactory answer is the question "What is the matter with man?"

It can no longer be said that the absolute is not within the province of science, that we must be content merely with a symbolical image, that the essence of things escapes us, and will always escape us, that we are brought to a stand before the Unknowable. For the human mind, after too much pride, this is nothing but an excess, an exaggeration of humility. It is true that all mental processes fail to grasp reality itself, that they are driven to the use of symbols. Yet all symbolism, it must be remembered, engenders the curse of mediacy and is ultimately destined to obscure what it seeks to reveal. If the intellectual form of the living being has been gradually molded on the reciprocal actions and reactions of certain bodies and their material environment, how can it not reveal something of the very essence of which these bodies are constituted? Action cannot move in the unreal. If man were born only for the purpose of dreaming or speculating, he might in truth remain outside of reality, he might even deform or transform reality, nay, even *create* reality, as figures of men and animals are created by the imagination out of the passing cloud. But man is intent upon the act to be performed. He is concerned with the reaction that must inevitably follow. The mind of man feels its object so as to receive its mobile impression at every instant. And in this way the mind of man touches something of the absolute, although the contemporary emphasis upon specialization tends to eclipse this fact.

The history of political events and social movements, of economic changes, of religion, of philosophy, of science, of literature and the other arts, of education and even of man's nature, has been investigated by distinct groups of specialists, many of them little acquainted with the subjects and the researches of the others. This specialization was in a certain sense indispensable to the progress of historical knowledge. Yet, paradoxically enough, the consequences proved to be also an ultimate impediment to such progress. For the departmentalization, whether by subjects, periods, nationalities, or languages, of the history of man corresponds, in a real sense, to the actual cleavages among the phenomena themselves. In this way a certain symbolism is obtained which is convenient and even necessary to positive science, but not a direct vision of its object. We must know how the frames of knowledge have been constructed, how we can enlarge and go beyond them. Thus, the mind can be turned homeward. Thus, there can be realized a true coincidence of the human consciousness with the living principle whence it emanates.

Certainly no one questions the indispensability of specialization. But we have come to realize more and more that specialization is not enough. A kind of new scholasticism has emerged as the result of this excessive specialization. We have forgotten that to know only one aspect of man is not to know man at all, and we have also forgotten that the totality of atomic facts is not the world. To be acquainted with only one aspect of man is to understand his nature and the affinities of this nature, its inner logic and psychological operation so inadequately that even *that* aspect remains opaque and unintelligible. Serious lacunae have resulted in the knowledge of man about himself, serious errors and serious distortions. We must destroy this new scholasticism that has grown with an ever-accelerated velocity around the hypotheses of Descartes even as the old scholasticism grew up around Aristotle.

The remedy for this division, subdivision and superdivision of man can only be found in a close co-operation among men at those points where the various provinces of thought and action overlap; in the establishment of more and better facilities of communication, communication containing substance; in mutual criticism and mutual aid; in the focusing upon what are, in their nature, common problems of all the special knowledges that are pertinent to them. The further remedy lies in the recognition that evil consists in the assertion of some self-interest without regard to the whole, whether the whole be conceived as the immediate community, the total community of mankind, or the total order of the world; the recognition that that form of culture which venerates science so exclusively, so ardently, as a substitute for the religious and moral spirit; which venerates natural causation as a substitute for God and for man's responsibility; which considers the systematic, sterile expediency and prudence of bourgeois man as morally more normative than knowledge and love, leads directly and inevitably to man's doom and destruction.

The remedy lies in the realization of the nature of contemporary thought, the realization that it is a speculative system-building which finds no reduplication in the life of the thinker, in the life of man himself, and which thus loses touch with Being. It is subjectivism and sophistry. It attempts to find substitutes for truth, such as tautology or systematic consistency. It fails to recognize the distinction between knowledge, algorism and opinion. It neglects with almost Machiavellian intent the directly intuited phenomena of personal existence. It inspires a category of thought which is sophisticated and nonontological, concerning itself with nonbeing rather than with being. It results in an abject uselessness of the moral command since it does not touch upon the ontological nexus of man's being. And its final consummation is a deep and unappeasable melancholy of all life.

Such emptiness can be traced to the incorrect hypothesis proclaiming the relativity of cultural values. Our very positive, anthropocentric and presumably scientific conviction that this world of matter and mind is the only existing universe, this conviction is nothing more than a cultural faith characteristic of our time and our civilization. We must remember that other civilizations lived under the equally unimpeachable and equally sanguine certainty that this is not the only reality. Could this have been a superstition? To declare in opposition to Milton that in his real environment there was not, and could not possibly be, such a thing as evidence of man's spirit not based upon empirical authority would mean presumptuously to render our behavioral environment absolute; to presume to have solved the whole question in advance; and to compel Milton to live in our "scientific" world. It is more than a possibility that a great part of our scientific world belongs to our behavioral, and not to our real, environment.

With all the stupendous knowledge of details with which science has endowed contemporary man, we are not brought one single step nearer to the fundamental knowledge of what matter is, or how matter is related to consciousness. It is merely a name indicating one of those methodological gaps in the world of existence which point in the direction of the world of essence. Once it is admitted and clearly understood that consciousness cannot be mechanically accounted for—not only temporarily because of the inadequacy of our information, but as a matter of principle, because consciousness is incommensurable with mechanical laws—the impediments to our knowledge of man may be greatly attenuated. We must be ready to admit the probability—not yet made manifest by empirical evidence—that every star has a destiny, that its burning matter is so constructed as to make life, consciousness and history possible. In other words, we cannot deny, on purely materialistic grounds, that the twinkling star, even though it be conceived as a mere machine, is in truth specifically adapted to produce or at least to prepare the ground for producing life, mind and spiritual values. The remote twinkling star may be pregnant with relations which lead to life, mind and history of man—of man as a cosmic entity, as the bearer of values, not merely as an atomized biped without wings or feathers, the collateral descendant of apes—a purely terrestrial, biological accident.

Man in his arid anthropomorphism has conceived the universe as a hierarchic order in which he occupies the highest place. In Stoic philosophy and in Christian theology man was considered to be the end of the historical universe. Both doctrines accepted the debatable truth that there is a general providence ruling over the world and the destiny of man. This concept is one of the basic hypotheses of Stoic and Christian thought. But all this has been called into question by the new cosmology. Man's claim to be the center of the universe has lost its foundations. Man is placed, man finds himself, in an infinite space in which his being seems to be a single and even, who knows, vanishing point. He sees that he is surrounded by mute nature, silent, implacable and impotent to his religious feelings and to his deepest moral and spiritual demands.

Man lacks direction. Contemporary culture is so devoid of unity of purpose, material and method as to be something of a heterogeneous mass of confused entities. Man is uncertain as to where he is going and where he wants to go, and why he is doing what he is doing. Unprincipled industrialism with its boast of liberty, of the autonomy of the individual, has precipitated a condition of society in which victimized men can neither do what they will nor will what they do. Life is overloaded, desiccated, congested, and requires simplification. There is a total absence of organic unity. There is incoherence, planlessness and suffering.

There is skepticism and finally cynicism, the predatory offspring of skepticism.

Skepticism has purged the idea of reason of so much of its content that today scarcely anything is left of reason, the only possible common ground for the solution of the problems of mankind. Reason, in destroying the conceptual fetishes by which it was dominated for a time, soon destroyed itself. At one time reason was the herald of eternal ideas which had only dim shadows in the material world. Then it was thought to find its vindication in the order of natural things and to discover the immutable forms of reality. And now reason is held to be a meaningless symbol, an allegorical figure without a function, and all ideas that transcend the banalities of a given reality are forced to share in the ignominious defeat and disgrace of reason. The synthesis of religion and culture has been obliterated, too. They both must be returned to their one theonomous essence so that the void which was inevitably precipitated by their separation may be filled, filled with a new theonomy. Secular culture has lost an ultimate and compelling *terminus ad quem* because it has repudiated the indeterminate, unconditioned and unconditional character of truth and reason. Unless this condition can be changed, unless a more valid evaluation of reason can pervade all strata of our society, it is futile to propagate freedom, the dignity of man, or even truth.

Society is suffering from the disease of recent history, the disease that has manifested itself in the substitution of politics for religion, power for love. Society has made such impossible demands for an immediate unmerited Utopia that man's dreams have turned inevitably into nightmares. Society is beginning to learn, at last, that there is more human history than nineteenth century materialism conceived. Society is becoming suspicious of the shallow optimism that stemmed from the unenlightened aspect of eighteenth century Enlightenment, of its ignorance of the dark, irrational forces in man. Society is beginning to recognize that man must recover what the spirit of religion has taught him; that there are two ways of knowing: the exploration of the horizontal, worldly planes and the contemplation of the vertical or transcendental order; and that these two ways are mutually indispensable, the one dependent upon the other for its validity and existence.

An unmistakable thread in recent thought and action weaving itself persistently through the crisis of our age and exploding in two world wars within the memory of most living men is that scientific pluralism and relativity of intellectual approach have rendered impotent most of the moral controls born of religious belief and have thereby given greater latitude to the bellicosity of men and nations. Both the cultural and the political revolutions of recent history were rejected by religion as the recalcitrant outpourings of a secular autonomy, while the revolutionary movements themselves abrogated religion as the arbitrary manifestation of a transcendent heteronomy. The wild tempest of war broke about us, with all its imperious fury and insatiable hunger feeding on the bodies and souls of mankind. Man was driven, is still driven, his brain mad, his heart wild and wordless. He became inarticulate. Now he is afraid. And somehow underneath it all is the pitiful cry surging from the thwarted dignity of his spirit, which demands some kind of redemption, that if he must be borne away, let it be by the glacier of life, not by its insidious lava flood.

But man need not be borne away. Reason can still be his salvation, his redemption, if he will but be realistic and unafraid. Man must realize in the light of contemporary problems that mutual understanding in the field of culture is impossible through means of mere cultural "reconstruction." Cultural disintegration reached such an abyss during the prewar years as to render mere cultural reconstruction an inevitable return to chaos. And cultural chaos is incompatible with mutual cultural understanding. Man is not faced with the reconstruction of those cultural conditions preceding the two world wars. Man is faced with the construction of the prerequisites for a new cultural equilibrium. Man must conquer reason, reason which has suffered and been lost in the wilderness of the past tragic years. Man has wished to forget that he possesses reason; that very reason which is the only thing that differentiates him from the beast and without which he becomes more bestial than the beast. Man has pretended not to understand any longer the meaning of reason. This has led to the destruction of culture by making him irresponsible for his thought and action. The contemporary contempt for reason has become the tragicomedy of our time. A life of initiative, of creativity, not impeded by ill-conceived and irrelevant planning, drawing its energies from reason in its fullness and richness—this is the first prerequisite for mutual understanding among men and the only way, if it is not yet too late, of preventing another war.

Reason must no longer be confused with efficiency as it had been by political fascism. When the dictators appealed to reason, they wished to imply that they possessed the most guns and tanks and ammunition. They were rational enough to build them; others should be rational enough to yield to them. In reality there is an intimate relationship between reason and efficiency, the causes being inherent in the basic structure of society itself. Only the sequence, however, is important. It is reason compatible with man's potential fulfillment as a being possessing dignity that must dictate the methods efficiency must adopt, and not vice versa. For man can fulfill himself and his natural wants only through social and spiritual channels. Use is a social category and reason pursues it in all the phases of competitive society.

The Revolution is here; and we hope with all the passion of our wills and being that it will not be bloody. There is still a chance that a true social democracy (not the aberrations of recent history euphemistically employing this term), which makes its means proportionate to its ends, may prove that there is a democratic solution for the issues of fundamental change which are emergent in society. To prove that this is so would mark an epoch in social thought as important in the imagination of man as the Reformation or the geographical discoveries of the fifteenth or the sixteenth century. It would drive forward the boundaries of freedom to an extent we cannot now conceive. And this is all the more urgent since man is clearly at one of the great turning points of history: the necessity for laying the foundations of individual liberty within the fabric of social justice.

Since the industrial revolution, which began approximately two centuries ago and has developed at an ever-accelerated pace, each great war has been more disastrous than its predecessors. But this fact has not prevented mankind from resorting to war for the resolution of differences. With the horrible prospect of utter annihilation presented by the atomic bomb, it is difficult to imagine that the people of any nation on earth can possibly consent to participate in another war. And yet this war seems to be imminent; nay, is imminent; is even inevitable, unless men experience a moral awakening and accept their moral responsibility for themselves and their children.

This war is inevitable unless man can mature quickly enough to win the race between civilization and disaster. Man has become scientifically mature but politically he is still infantile. And the most heinous sin of which man is capable is intellectual and emotional immaturity, the sin of omission. Tremendous tasks remain to be accomplished without loss of time. We must begin systematically to reduce, and ultimately eliminate, all the causes of war. We must revolt against the acceptance of international trade barriers and against the aberrated economic reasoning that leads to the creation of such trade barriers. We must extend the geographical and ideocratic radius of democracy. We must repudiate, by virtue of our moral strength and unity, dictatorships and despotisms wherever they may exist in the world. We must denounce the suppression of information and free discussion. We must not tolerate the feeding of people on a propaganda of lies. We must not prevent people from knowing the facts, else it will be too late. Wherever the press and information and discussion are free, wherever the facts are known and the government is really the choice of a liberated people, that people will want peace and can compel the government to maintain peace. Man faces, by virtue of the release of cosmic power, the prospect either of destruction on a scale which dwarfs the imagination and which quickens the dormant apprehensions and fears of what may happen in another war, or he faces a golden era of such social change and amelioration as would delight the most romantic utopian. Man is finally compelled to prove himself worthy of freedom and responsibility. Man is finally compelled to choose.

The first step to be taken by a social democracy in contrast to its hitherto laissez-faire policy consists in abandoning its complete lack of interest in values. The unifying elements in a democratic system and a progressive evolution of the social implications of democracy must be realized. This means that there is an inherent tendency in the present situation to bring to man's consciousness an awakening and appreciation of the values of a social democracy, of the democratic way of life, and a necessity not to discard this for any promise of a better world. Democracy does not mean a shapeless, inchoate society, a society without a value policy but one in which spontaneous integration of consensus on different levels continually takes place. Cultural groups, denominational groups, local groups, interest groups, professional groups, age groups, will develop a variety of approaches to valuations, but it is essential to supplement the divergence by a technique of co-ordination and value mediation postulated on the noumenal power of reason and objective truth which can only culminate in a collectively agreed upon and accepted value policy without which no society can survive, let alone fulfill itself.

The conception of history as a permanent class struggle is dead, is just as mythological as the ancient insistence that history is a struggle between ideas. That was a sort of economic Manichaeism declaring history to be a fight between the good and evil principles. Political and economic nationalism also is dead. This form of ethnocentric fetishism has been the feudal baron. Like the feudal baron, it has made laws for its own territories and there was no common, universal Law that transcended all territories and precluded individual tyranny. And therefore, in the absence of law, there was war, which always and inevitably occurs when nonintegrated social units of equal sovereignty coincide with each other on the basis of opposing ideologies and conflicting ends.

Law, as a conception of the restriction of human freedom also is dead. It is rather the instrument of freedom. Freedom within nations became possible when law reached the boundaries. It became impossible when industrialism wrecked the hope of national self-sufficiency and economic systems could no longer adequately exist except under a world-wide economy. Therefore, the achievement of freedom and the escape from tyranny become possible through the surrender of economic, and hence political, sovereignty. The citizen of an integrated society gains in freedom when a universal Law forbids war. And such a law can never be achieved by mere treaties or conferences. It can be achieved only by a legal order, by a sovereign source of law, emanating from reason; by a democratically controlled government which recognizes and accepts the necessity of sacrificing its political and economic ethnocentric sovereignty while retaining its cultural diversity and pluralism.

Because these questions have remained unresolved, contemporary man has been preoccupied with anxiety and guilt, a condition which contains an implied accusation against society's irrationality. Contemporary man has become a neurotic with a sapped will which is the result of a bad conscience and social insecurity. He has become helpless before society's habit of pyramiding one rationalization upon another in the ceaseless, shrewd explanation that gives the effect of actuality to the baseless and the nonexistent. Man's present condition is a societal phenomenon and society must be held responsible for it. This is the meaning of collective guilt. There must be a revolt, a scorn, and a defiance of the social structures which create these insecurities in man and incapacitate his sensitivity and conscience in dealing with these structures. The rights of all men must be defended by an attack against the political and economic, the reactionary cabalas that stifle man's development. As man has grown horizontally in broadening his world view, he has also, because of his feeling of isolation in a mechanistic and power-crazed society, extended himself vertically in his philosophy for better or for worse, reaching down into the wells of dream and myth. This much is clear: in other periods of history the categories of living, thinking and behaving were more strictly drawn and bounded. It was therefore easier to know the "right" way of life; whereas today everything is fluid and ambivalent, the "right" way far from certain in the minds of most men. Compromise is the general rule, compromise between idealism and realism, compromise which must inevitably lead to profound feelings of culpability and result only in moral irresponsibility, spiritual degeneration and intellectual degradation.

The cynicism and pathos of modern man may be traced to the dualism and ambivalence which are the result of a heightened skepticism and a heightened idealism, the result of a struggle between a more firm vision of the ideal, especially of the social ideal, and a growing despair of achieving it. Greater knowledge, by its expansion of conscience, involves the possibility of greater sin. Therefore, a deep sense of sin, of the repudiation of responsibility and culpability, is the salient characteristic of our time. Even love has been repudiated, and sexual promiscuity has taken its place. A scorn of love exists. The sexual freedom prescribed by the corrupt philosophy of a population policy or of mere sterile hedonism does not cure the anxiety of the world of sexual taboos but expresses a mere contempt for love. Love has become the irreconcilable foe of the prevailing rationality, for lovers preserve and protect neither themselves nor the collectivity of man. They throw themselves away. They degenerate into a state of instrumentalism. What has been encouraged as healthy sexuality is but an expression of the brutal, fiendish rationalism (not reason) that harries love, and the relationship between man and woman has become one of the saddest commentaries of our time. But all this has now reached an impasse. The progress of rationalism leading to the destruction of man has come to an end. And there now remains the choice between utter annihilation and true freedom.

All society is confronted by a mortal crisis, in all its institutions, organizations and associations. Coercion in the naked form of war is supreme.

Brute force is the only arbiter. Moral maxims and the norms of natural law are ignored. Instead of being an era of peace and order in international relationships, the present century has turned into the bloodiest, cruelest among the thirty centuries recorded by man. The time is tragic. The proud citizen of the nineteenth century finds himself deprived of all his values. His cherished individualism is trampled underfoot. He is an insignificant cog in a gargantuan machine operated without regard to his wishes, his needs, his essential being. His liberties and inalienable rights are gone. Thousands and millions of once proud citizens, heirs of the Declaration of Rights, are tossed hither and thither, pushed and pulled, more slaves than in the days of slavery. The contractual society of free men, with its contractual economic and free associations, has disappeared. The family is in a state of dissolution, of disintegration. With the frustration of man's most cherished hopes and aspirations, the tragedy of man's life is complete. Man is left aflame with sorrow and lamentation, with misery, grief and despair.

But out of the ashes the phoenix may yet arise. Man must know that justice, institutions of law, the growth of juridical processes and structures, and civic and international friendship which must also be embodied in institutions, all represent a principle of unification by internal, moral power, the only kind of unification that can have any meaning or any permanence. The divergence of the Orient and the Occident, that accident of history, is now recognized for the anachronism that it is. The impoverished reality, the epigonous determinism of the West must be re-evaluated in the light of first principles. For in the final analysis the differentiations of cultures may be compared with the multiplicity of dialects throughout civilization. The essential content of the language of the spirit is the same for all mankind. The only difference is that of the words employed, words expressing the same basic ideals and aspirations, frequently even in the same idioms. Verbal and visual language is universally intelligible and is fundamental alike to all civilizations of the world. Man must know that this is the only path that can lead to higher and higher degrees of co-operation, organization and unity— to higher and higher degrees of collective conscience and individual dignity. Man must re-evaluate and then accept the truth for himself inherent in these words—for in them lies his only redemption: "I am the Spirit and the Light." This is the meaning of the fulfilled personality. And this requires the communication of knowledge and of love. For it is the spirit in man that transports him, unlike other forms of life, beyond the sense of complete independence, complete "individualism," to a sense of personality and communion which unites man with man. Man cannot live in that isolated unity, lacking windows and doors, of the Leibnitzian monad. Each man is a person and by virtue of this fact expresses himself to himself as well as to others. Without this communication man inevitably slips into a preoccupation with death and the solipsistic solitude of the existentialist world. The ipseity of the human person is the tragedy of modern man, and the progressive, activated rationalism manifesting itself so ubiquitously as the modern substitute for knowledge and reason leads inevitably to the very obliteration of knowledge and reason in the name of which civilization is espoused. This subjectivity of reason which has culminated not in the preservation of the human person but in his disintegration, this prerogative (the offspring of subjectivity) of yielding to a partial inclination, a partial commitment resulting in the starvation of the mind and spirit, must now be transcended by the truth inherent in the objectivity of reason, in the existence of reason as a generative principle not only in the individual mind but in the objective world, in the relationship between man and society, man and man, man and nature. These are forever participating in the creation of one another while remaining solitary throughout. Although they are not one, they are yet inseparable, since there is a boundless manifold of universal potentiality perpetually actualizing itself and since there is a multiplicity of subjects. The objectivity of reason is the only force that can create concepts of knowledge, the greatest good, the meaning of human destiny, salvation, beauty and the way of actualizing ultimate ends. Such reason must be exhumed from the realm of myth and legend in which it has so irreverently been interred and must be restored to its rightful place with the great philosophical systems of Plato and Aristotle, restored to its hierarchical position of apostolic power in the history of mankind, a position which does not exclude subjective reason from playing its appropriate and logical role, but which recognizes that subjectivity is only a limited aspect of universal reason from which the ultimate values for men and things emanate. This alone can reinstate the dialectic of thought or eros without which experience degenerates into unilaterality and meaninglessness. Man must embrace at last the responsibility for himself and his fellow men that it is "your honor henceforth not whence ye come, but whither ye go."

Chapter II

BRAND BLANSHARD

CAN MEN BE REASONABLE?

1 One of the most significant changes that have occurred in recent decades is the decline of faith in reason. It is true that in the years before 1914, now so quiet in their appearance and so remote, there were deep divisions in most departments of thought, but it was not supposed that they were beyond remedy; it was taken for granted that there was an objective truth to be found, and that if it was looked for patiently and persistently it could be brought to light. However far men fell short of resonableness in thought and practice, they did not doubt that there was such a thing as a reasonable belief and way of life and that, so far as they could, they should make it their own.

In those days the dominant philosophy was idealism, which held that the real was rational and the rational was the real. The dominant psychologies were those of Wundt, James, Titchener and Ward, all of them brought up in this rationalistic philosophy and respectful of it even where they did not follow. The dominant logic was that of Bradley and Bosanquet, whose view was that thought in its very nature was an attempt at rational system. The dominant ethics were those of Sidgwick, Moore and Rashdall, who held that the test of right and wrong lay in the self-evident rational insight that x was better than y. The most influential political theory was one which found in a rational and general will the justification of the state. In religion the voice of the time was liberalism, which said that God revealed himself to men in the degree to which they achieved a coherent experience of goodness, beauty and truth.

All this has now changed. Reason has had a pelting from every side; even in its own field of philosophy it has been jostled and on occasion jeered at as if it were some rude interloper. The idealist systems, where they have not bowed themselves out, have become hesitant, vague and apologetic, and the splendid vision they inherited from Plato of a reason freely following its own law is put down by naturalists and pragmatists alike as a mirage. Psychology has been invaded first by Freud, who finds all rational consciousness to be controlled by reins that come up from an irrational unconscious, and then by the behaviorists, who profess to doubt whether consciousness exists at all. In logic, the most conspicuous present-day school denies that the sort of insight that rationalists have been seeking is even possible; no necessary connections exist except in logic, and there they are tautologies. The rising vogue in ethics is for a relativism beside which the relativism of Sumner and Westermarck is naïve; it holds that "moral judgments" are not judgments at all, but exclamations which, as expressing nothing but feeling, are neither true nor false. In the political sphere the theory that international differences are incapable in the nature of the case of any rational decision and can be settled only by force came within a very narrow margin of imposing itself on the civilized world. In religion, to name but one more province, the most striking of recent movements, the Barthian theology, represents the claim of reason to apprehend religious truth as an impertinence.

If these views were really acted upon, I do not think the results could be accepted complacently. For these results would include defeat in philosophy, an overstress in psychology upon the animal nature of man, a retreat toward verbalism in logic, a thoroughgoing skepticism in ethics, anarchy in politics, irresponsibility in religion. Just as there is nothing more practical than reasonableness, so is there no sphere of practice that will not have to pay a heavy ransom for the giving up of reason as its authority and guide.

But having pointed this out, I am going to pass it over. I do so partly for reasons of strategy. One of the things that must strike any student of the recent revolts against reason is the curious practical unconcern so often displayed in them. An acute young writer will propose an ethical theory from which, for example, it follows that the claim of democracy to superiority over nazism has no objective ground whatever, and being acute, he must have seen this; but it is apparently of small interest and receives no mention. It seems to be a matter of pride to leave all such things to others and to keep strictly to one's analysis, like a scientist perfecting his formula for botulinus toxin. That the sole practical importance of this toxin is its capacity to destroy one hundred eighty million lives per ounce is a consideration which after all is irrelevant to chemical theory. To anyone who works in this spirit, arguments from practical consequences cannot be expected to carry much force.

I do not find this unconcern about the human consequences of theory an attractive trait. But I suppose one has to admit that the implied logic of it is sound. To be sure, if the question were whether a course of conduct was right or wrong, the character of the consequences would be relevant in the highest degree. But if the question is whether a piece of analysis in logic or in psychology is correct, that is not to be proved erroneous by recounting the undesirable consequences that would follow if it were accepted. And the question whether reason is in fact the slave of the passions, or whether men ever do in fact grasp a necessary connection, is a question of this second kind rather than the first. The conclusions of the irrationalists do seem to me practically disastrous, and those who hold them ought to be alive to these. Nevertheless, if these conclusions are to be overthrown, it must be not by insisting that they are dangerous but by showing that they are incorrect. And I am convinced that, in the case of the irrationalisms most conspicuous today, that can be shown quite clearly.

But first as to the issue. The really pressing question raised by the attacks on reason is not whether the world is in the last resort rational or whether it is wholly open to human knowledge, or any other such tremendous question, but the nearer and comparatively humble one whether we ever can in fact be reasonable. If we can, there is hope for us, both in philosophy and in practice. If we cannot, the outlook is not bright in either.

2   What do we mean when we call a man reasonable? We mean at least this, that in his thinking and acting he shows objectivity of mind. And what is that? It means being realistic, impartial, just; seeing things as they are rather than as fear or desire or prejudice would tempt one to see them. The reasonable person will suit what he thinks and claims to the facts. He will be ready to give up an opinion if the facts are against it, and adhere to the opinion in the face of inner and outer pressure if the facts require it. His claims against others and their claims against him he will view impersonally and with detachment; he will not ask more for himself than is just

merely because he is he; nor will he allow himself to be put upon for the like reason; he bases his self-respect upon respect for the sort of justice that is itself no respecter of persons.

Now, if such reasonableness is to be possible, two further things must be true. In the first place, there must be a set of independent facts to be grasped. It would be senseless to try to suit our opinions to the facts of a case if there were no such facts to suit them to; and if justice consisted in following our own interest or desire, then, as Socrates and a hundred other philosophers have shown, there is no such thing as justice at all. To be reasonable either in thought or in act requires bowing to an authority beyond ourselves, conceding that there is a truth and a right that we cannot make or unmake, to which our caprices must defer. If I have a pet theory in science and am to be reasonable about it, I must be ready to trim it, recast it, or give it up, as an impersonal logic demands; noncomformity here is not heroism but suicide. As M'Taggart said, no one ever tried to break logic but logic broke him. It is the same, of course, with morals. Reasonableness in conduct implies wearing a yoke and walking a line; it implies that if you and I differ about our rights, there is an answer to our question waiting there to be found, and that we are doing what we can to find it and conform to it. To say that there is nothing right or wrong but thinking makes it so is to say that there is nothing for thinking to discover; and to say that is to deny all point in trying to be reasonable. If all our beliefs are reasonable, then none of them is.

Thus the first condition of being reasonable is that there be an independent common rule. The second condition is that this common rule should at times control the course of our thought. We must sometimes be able to say: If I thought as I did, it was because my mind was under the influence of an independent pattern, the pattern of an objective truth. This is only to say that thought, if it is to be reasonable, must be like perception when it is accurate. Suppose we look at a checkerboard. If there is to be any such thing as accurate perception at all, there must be, in a sense "out there," a certain number of squares related to each other in a certain way. That corresponds to our first condition. Secondly, we must be able to say: If I see them in this way, that must be because they *are* this way, because that independent order acts upon my mind and makes me see it so. If this arrangement presents itself, not because it is there but because my mind is being pulled about by wires from within, then there are no grounds for believing that we ever do or can see accurately; if we did, it would be sheer luck. I am happily not concerned with the mechanism of perceiving, but with a principle. If, when we perceive things, we never perceive them so because they are so, then perception is a cheat. Similarly in thinking, unless at times we think as we do because the real relations of things are controlling our thought, laying it under constraint, governing its movement, then knowledge must be an illusion from first to last.

Let us proceed with these two conditions in mind. To be reasonable implies at the least that there is an objective truth and right which we can at times apprehend and that, if our thought follows a certain course, it is because it is laid under constraint by the objective pattern of things. If these conditions are granted, reasonableness is so far possible. If either is denied, it is not possible. To show either that the pattern we seem to find in things is not there, or that, although it is there, thought can never surrender itself to the control of that pattern, is to put reasonableness beyond reach.

Now, it is by denying these conditions that the case against our power to be reasonable proceeds. They may be denied in many ways. They may be denied indirectly and by implication by persons who do not realize the bearing of their theories and who in most of their own thought and practice are models of reasonableness. Indeed this holds of all the theories we are to examine. They are not, as attacks on reason so often are, the manifest products of disillusioned or conceited crankiness; they are the considered views of men of distinction in both philosophy and science, to whom we owe much. But of course that makes them the more formidable. I propose to examine three current positions that seem to me inconsistent with one or the other or both of the conditions of reasonableness that have just been laid down. I choose them partly because they seem to me fundamental, partly because they are so ably advocated as to have received a wide assent.

The first of these positions is that the movement of thought is explicable in terms of processes in the cortex. This view is widely held among those who describe themselves as naturalists. The second is that the movement of thought is controlled by nonrational processes within the thinker's own mind. This is an ancient theory which has been given new life in recent years by the psychoanalysts. The third is that the very ideal of rationality, conceived as the following of an objective and neces-

sary truth and right, is an illegitimate one. This is the view of the logical
positivists. It is, of course, impossible to discuss these positions generally
or adequately within the compass of one chapter, and I make no pretense
of doing so. But I think it will be found in each case that the limitations
imposed on reason rest upon distinct and special grounds which can be
isolated without difficulty. Let us look at the three positions in order.

3 The first, or naturalist, theory rests on facts which physical
science has led us to accept as commonplaces. We are
asked if we do not concede these to be facts; we admit
readily that we do; and then, as we follow out the inferences from what
we have conceded, it begins to appear that we have conceded also our
rational birthright. How naturally we are led on from what seem to be
the most innocent facts to a conclusion that is far from innocent will
perhaps be clearer if we construct a little dialogue. The physiologist
interrogates us:

"When you step on a tack and feel pain, you would agree, would you
not, that stepping on it is the cause of the pain?"

"Yes, of course."

"The immediate cause?"

"No, a remote cause only. The change in the nerve ends, so I've been
taught, induces an impulse which is carried to the cortex and induces
a further change there. It is this change in the cortex that is the immediate cause of the pain."

"Correct. And you would take the same view, would you, about other
sensations, and about affections and emotions?—that is, that their immediate cause or condition is a cortical change?"

"Yes, there seems to be no doubt about that. It is true, isn't it, that
one can produce sensation artificially by stimulating the cortex?"

"Yes, and we are even learning what precisely to do to produce different kinds of experience; we can put the brain through its paces. We
can turn your world yellow by giving you santonin; we can increase or
diminish your anger by adrenal injections; we can lift cretinism into
normality by small doses of thyroxin; and if we reduce your body's secre-
tion of this by about a hundredth of a grain a day, you will slide down
into imbecility. It is true we haven't found out much about the cortical
correlates of ideas, but I don't suppose you would doubt that they are
there too?"

"No, there seems to be no escaping that. If sensations and affections are brain-conditioned, so must ideas be. One could hardly chop a mental state in two and say that half of it—sensation and feeling—is brain-conditioned, and the other half, involving the use of ideas, is a sort of will-o'-the-wisp, with no roots in the brain at all. If some forms of consciousness are brain-conditioned, presumably all of them are."

"Good, I'm glad you see that so clearly; we can't make an exception for ideas. Now suppose that one idea is followed by another; each of course is brain-conditioned?"

"Yes."

"And the thought sequence is conditioned by the sequence in the brain?"

"Well, since we have agreed that each thought is brain-conditioned, the explanation why one follows the other must lie, I suppose, in the explanation why one brain state follows the other."

"Obviously. And the reason why one brain state follows another is to be found, I suppose, in a physical law?"

"Since both are physical, that must, of course, be true."

"Then the reason why one thought follows another is also given in physical law?"

"Yes, that seems right enough."

"Thought, then, is under the control of physical law?"

"Yes, that does clearly follow."

"Well, we seem to agree perfectly. If you are a philosopher, you are at least an unusually sensible one."

I wonder if others have, as I do, a sense of doom closing in as this dialogue unfolds. The concessions do not seem extraordinary; nine out of ten natural scientists would grant them without hesitation, and, unless in a mood of unwonted suspicion, probably most philosophers too. That is just what makes this first argument so effective. You seem to be doing nothing more than conceding obvious facts and drawing obvious inferences. And yet I believe one can show, also by obvious reasoning, that this account cannot be correct, and that if it were, it would mean nothing less than disaster for our rational life.

Let us look at the matter more closely. I said a moment ago that, if we are to be reasonable, we must be able to follow the argument where it leads, which means that thought must at times be governed, not by secret strings within but by the pattern of what it knows. When we say that our thought is objective, we mean just that, that it is moving under the control of the object. Of course there are processes often called thinking that are not so controlled; I may sit down to a geometry problem and think first of the weather, then of my dinner, and then of my headache; but that is not thinking. Thinking proper means reasoning; and reasoning means surrendering one's attention to the logic of the case, moving to one's conclusion because the evidence is seen to imply it. Success here, as the experienced know, demands a wise passiveness; the best thinking is the least free, in the sense that it is most completely laid under compulsion by the course of objective necessity. If my inference moves from step 1 to step 2 and from step 2 to step 3, that is because, when I am really thinking, the facts that 1 implies 2 and that 2 implies 3 make a difference to the course of my thought; the inference takes the line it does because it is following, and is influenced by, a line of necessity that is there before it. This is what it does, for example, when, starting from the postulates of a logical or geometric system, it spins out the theorems that follow; and the account holds equally whether the necessity linking the steps is conceived as synthetic or analytic. Indeed this is what always happens when our thinking is at its best; its course is then governed and guided by the requirements of the evidence. Our conclusions are not arrived at by leaps in the dark, then checked against the evidence and found to hold by miracle; it is rather that, starting from the evidence, our thought moves to the conclusion it reaches because the evidence requires this, in both senses of the word; the objective entailment controls the movement of inference. If this never happens, then strictly speaking, we never reason. For if, when we pass from premise to conclusion, the premise's entailing the conclusion has nothing to do with our reaching it, then our reaching it as often as we do, indeed our reaching it at all, becomes incredible luck.

It will now be a little clearer why to explain thinking by cortical change is not to explain it, but to explain it away. The subjective process of deduction is, when really deduction, governed by an objective implication, but when one distribution of particles follows another in the brain, what we have, so far as can be seen, is not implication, but cause and effect. The sequence of brain state B upon brain state A is as little governed by any visible implication as the sequence in motion of Hume's billiard balls. I should not deny that between the brain states correlated with the steps of inference there is more than mere conjunction; but how far this is, as we know it, from anything like implication is shown by the facts, firstly, that, if for one of these states there had been substituted any one of a hundred others, we should have accepted the causal relation no less readily; and secondly, that between the sequence of states in the brain that serves as the correlate of a demonstrative process and that which serves as the correlate of the loosest association there is no detectable difference. Physical causality is one thing, logical necessitation another. If therefore you say that what controls the passage from A to B in inference is physical causality, you are saying that even in reasoning at its best and clearest, where we seem to see most plainly what we are doing, we are being grossly deluded. We suppose we think as we do because the evidence requires it; we now learn that this never happens. What really happens is that a sequence of distributions of material particles, or, if you prefer, of stresses and strains, or levels of energy, one connected with its successor by nothing nearer to logical necessity than the succession of waves on a beach, produces a series of mental efflorescences which turn out by some incredible chance to bear the relation, each to its follower, of ground to consequent. That this nexus among the objects of thought exercised the slightest constraint upon the course of our thinking must be set down as illusion. The fact that A is evidence for B had no influence at all in making us think of B, or in making us accept it. The purer reasoning seems to be, the deeper is the illusion, since, speaking strictly, we never reason at all.

Must we accept this view? I do not think so, and for two reasons. First, when our thinking is at its best and clearest, our certainty that it is controlled by necessity is greater than that of any physiological speculations that can be set on the other side. Take a simple train of reasoning and observe what goes on when you follow it. Two is to four as four is to what? Four is to eight as eight is to what? Eight is to sixteen as sixteen is to what? How do you manage to hit upon the answers as you move along this series? The natural reply is, Because the rule of the series logically requires that each successive proportion should be completed in just this manner. I believe that this, which is the natural account, is also the true account. There are dozens of directions in which thought could wander off at any step in the series, and I believe that if it declines these wanderings and remains in the groove, it is because there *is* a groove, because thought is laid under constraint by the logic of the process. We not only see when we reach the end that this constraint did operate; we may be aware of the constraint as we proceed. And to my mind there is something fantastic in brushing aside such empirical evidence for the sake of a flight of physiological speculation. Some persons, to be sure, are so much in the habit of prostrating themselves before physical science that they are ready to ignore their clearest insights if such science has shown itself cool to them. Let us recall, therefore, that what we are offered here is conjecture, not established fact. No competent physiologist professes to know exactly what happens in the cortex when any conscious state occurs, nor exactly how any cortical event leads on to another, nor exactly what is meant by parallelism between the two series—still less to have verified in detail any hypothesis about their relation. To set a theory at once so vague and so tentative against the clear, immediate assurance of the reasoning mind is not properly science at all, but the sort of philosophy bred by an uncritical idolatry of science.

But there remains a more cogent reason for denying that physical causation will account for the sequence of thought. The view is self-refuting. How is it arrived at? It is an inference from observed sequences of mental and bodily change. Now, the inference to this conclusion has either been constrained by the evidence or not. If it has, the conclusion is refuted by the mode of its own attainment; for something more than physical causality was at work in attaining it. On the other hand, if the inference is not under such constraint, why should we respect its result? For then nothing more is at work in it than in the equally good causal processes of woolgathering or derangement. It may be replied that, though rational and irrational processes are equally matters of physical causation, we can see by later reflection which are necessary and which are not. But this is again self-refuting. For even if I do, in a flash of later insight, see that the conclusion was required by the evidence, I do not have this insight because the necessity is objectively there, but solely because some change in my cortex has made it appear to be there. Given the physical change, I should have "seen" it whether it was there to see or not; and hence it is the physical change, not the presence of the necessity, that makes me think I see it. This is to make all apprehension of necessity illusory, and all attempts to prove anything vain, including this one.

It is curious that the disaster implicit in the physiological account of reasoning has been so seldom noticed. But there is one school of psychologists that has seen it and explicitly sought to deal with it, the school of Gestalt. They have said boldly that there are mental processes that cannot be explained in terms of traditional natural science; that it is futile, for example, to explain a course of reasoning in terms of habit or conditioned reflexes, or even association, and that if we complete a syllogism as we do, it is for the same reason that we complete an imperfect circle as we do, because the law of structure of what is before us makes its specific demand upon us. For this insistence, at a time when psychology is threatened with ruin by technicians without vision and without philosophy, we can only be grateful.

But their theory is now being developed in what seems to me a dubious direction. Having broken with a strong tradition of natural science by finding necessity in mental sequences, they make it up to such science by putting this necessity back into the physical realm. When we reason syllogistically, we *are* under the control of necessity, but this necessity is literally in the brain. They have argued with some cogency that when we perceive a square or a circle there is actually a field of similar structure in the cortex. They hold that when our thought is carried along the line of necessity there is a gradient of force in the cortex, a physical tension and its resolution, and that between the physical and the conscious necessity we can detect, if we look sharply, an identical "requiredness."

My chief difficulties with this are two: Firstly, try as I will, I cannot see that the necessity which moves us in reasoning *is* the same as physical compulsion, however abstract and schematic we make their allegedly common element. What the necessity is that links premise with conclusion I do seem to see; and I also seem to see that it is something different in kind from what the physicist means when he talks about a flow of energy from higher to lower potential. To say, then, that what moves me is really the latter is to say once more that when my thought is at its clearest I am under an illusion as to what is directing it. And I do not see how you can say that without discrediting reason generally.

Secondly, the Gestaltists would agree that between the conscious and the cortical state the parallelism is not concrete and detailed, but isomorphic merely, that is, identical only to the extent of a highly abstract and formal pattern. But is this the necessity that works in consciousness? The Gestaltists themselves have taught us that it is not.

They would hold, for example—and I believe with sound and important insight—that there is a necessity in music which constrains a composer to continue a melody in one way rather than in others. This necessity is one which holds among the sounds as heard; it takes its character from the terms it relates, namely, these phenomenal sounds in this concrete phenomenal field. But these sounds, as the Gestaltists agree, are not themselves cortical events. Any pattern, then, that is common to brain and consciousness would have to leave them out. But a pattern in which phenomenal sound plays no part is not the pattern that works within experience. Everything depends on which pattern is to control. To say that it is the first, the abstract isomorphic schema, is to say that what really governs the musician, the painter, the moralist, is not what he believes to govern him, but something extremely different; and this seems to me in effect to discredit our actual thought in the field of value. To say that what governs is the second pattern, the pattern that takes its character from the phenomenal sounds, is to concede control by what will never be found in the cortex.

4   It is time to turn to the second of the contemporary theories that imperil the life of reason, a theory that to most men is more familiar and more persuasive than the first. Even if our thinking is not in servitude to nonrational forces in the body, it is still, we are told, in servitude to such forces within the mind. Man is not primarily a thinker, he is an actor; for the reason that he is still an animal, with far more animal ancestors than human clamoring in his blood. His business, and that of his forebears, has been to fight for a foothold on the earth, first by instinct, then by cunning, then by intelligence; and of these, intelligence, the latest to arrive and not yet fully mastered, is as truly as the others a tool to ends selected for it and not by it. Man thinks to live; if he sometimes lives to think, that only shows that his mind, like his body, is subject to distortion. Thought sprang originally, and still springs, from practical need; it is maintained by a feeling—interest—and tested by another—satisfaction; its goal is not knowledge, for knowledge itself is only a means to survival and success. Little by little the beliefs that seemed to be the products of pure reason are being shown by subtle analysis to be the daydreams of frightened men who need to be comforted, or compensations for defects that cannot well be admitted, or rationalizations of the plainly irrational bribes paid

to the forces of unreason for letting us hug self-respect a little longer. Man likes to boast that he is a rational animal. How better disprove the claim than by pointing out that even in these latter years he has continued to make it?

There are people who believe all this to have begun with Freud. It would be less formidable if it had. The truth is that it is the undercurrent of all philosophic history, a strain in minor key that can always be heard if you listen attentively, even when the trumpets of reason are sounding most confidently. At the very moment when Plato was heralding a reason that was the impartial spectator of all time and all existence, Protagoras in the same city was declaring, "Man is the measure of all things," and Callicles was teaching that the doctrine of justice was convention only. While Plotinus was saying at Alexandria that reason was the highest emanation of Deity, Tertullian, farther along the coast, was saying: *Certum est quia absurdum est, quia impossibile est.* No sooner had St. Thomas completed the edifice of his rationalism than Duns Scotus was undermining it with the doctrine that even in God the will is primary and that it manufactures truth and right in accordance with inexplicable impulse. While one great Frenchman was building rationalism into the temper of France, another was protesting: *Le cœur a ses raisons que la raison ne connait pas.* Spinoza wrote a great book to show that the good life lay in progress in reasonableness; and before it was published Mandeville appeared in England to preach that goodness is the offspring that flattery begets upon pride, and to hear an echo from Scotland proclaiming that reason is and must be the slave of the passions. When Hegel announced at Berlin a series of five-o'clock lectures on reason in man and the world, a young gentleman named Schopenhauer set another series at precisely the same hour to show that in both man and the world the primacy belonged, not to reason, but to blind will. While Bradley in Merton was thinking out the dialectic of the *Appearance*, Schiller just over the wall in Corpus was teaching that "our knowing is driven and guided at every step by our subjective interests and preferences, our desires, our needs, and our ends." So it goes; so apparently it has always gone. And thus if Freud and McDougall and Westermarck have been teaching, each in his own way, that belief is the puppet of feeling, it is not as if their doctrine was something new under the sun; it is only a new form of one of the oldest protests against reason.

Before commenting on its claim to respect, perhaps I may be permitted a remark on its political relevance. No doubt the tidal wave that threatened recently to wash us and our studies into the discard is inspired by no one philosophy, if indeed it was tinctured by philosophy at all. But there are those who, to the amazement of some of us, have sought to link this movement in spirit to those who have made most of reason. The thinkers of the great tradition have held that our thought, if it was to be reasonable, must bow to a logic the same for all of us, absolute in its requirements and independent of desire; some of them have gone on and said that in such a logic we had the key to a world which, if we knew it fully, would be found intelligible through and through. This view is called at times absolutism. Perhaps for that reason some persons have professed to find in it the seeds of political absolutism. To set up logic as a final authority; what is that but authoritarianism? To bow to a truth that exacts recognition regardless of our desires—is not that surrendering liberty to a metaphysical Moloch? A philosopher of repute was advocating not long ago a view in which, to use his own words, "logic ceases to be a bully, and makes an appeal to our better instincts." The argument seems to be that rationalism appeals to a kind of authority, the authority of reason, that totalitarianism also appeals to authority, and that both are therefore authoritarian in the same sense.

On the virtuosity of this performance as an argument I shall not comment. What is important is that its conclusion is worse than untrue; it is the opposite of the truth. The authority of reason is about as congenial to authoritarianism of the political stripe as an atomic bomb; if it is brought home to this at all, it proves shattering. One feels that there is something absurd in calling the appeal to reason authoritarian; the term usually implies a claim to authority that is more or less arbitrary, while most men feel in their hearts that in the authority of reason there is no trace of arbitrariness; indeed the very meaning of "arbitrary" is found in divergence from its standard. Authoritarianism in all its forms distrusts the intellect and with a sound instinct fears it; for in reason it recognizes, and knows that the world recognizes, the most dangerous of its enemies, an authority without caprice, an absolutism that does not tyrannize, and a master in whose service there is freedom.

But to return to the argument: thought, we are told, is under constraint from within. It reflects not the outward pattern of things, but our hidden loves and hates, desires and fears. In *The Future of an Illusion* Freud explained religious belief as due to the persistence of the infantile need for a father. According to Westermarck, what is expressed by our moral judgments is no character in the act, but our emotional attractions and repulsions. In a recent book a distinguished psychologist, Professor Holt, has written: "The entire history of philosophy is little else than a tiresome and futile series of pictures in which each philosopher has imagined what he most yearned to have in his own 'best of all possible worlds.' This," he adds, "is levity." Such skepticism about reason, though anything but new, has perhaps never been more popular and more formidably supported than in recent years. What are we to say of it?

The first thing we must say of it is a commonplace. It is that if the argument is pushed through and made general, nothing further is called for; like so many other attacks on reason, it disposes of itself. If it is true that we are always governed by nonrational pulls, then of course our conclusion that we are so governed is also produced by nonrational pulls. But if it is, why should it have more respect than any of the other illusions produced by such pulls? Surely the attempt to prove by rational processes that rational processes are irrational is the last irrationality.

Perhaps the reply will be made: "I admit the inference; and hence I offer my theory only as one which expresses and satisfies my own feeling, and may turn out to have the advantage of rival theories in better expressing the feeling of others also." But the reply will not do. Firstly, to say, "I admit the inference" is to say, "I accept it because I see that it follows," and to say that is already to have abandoned the view that beliefs *need* be governed irrationally, since this one is not. Secondly, the theory is plainly not offered merely as something that pleases its maker; it is offered as true, as conforming to fact, and because it does so conform, as sounder than rival theories. If it is not so offered, why offer it? If it is, then the offer is inconsistent with the theory offered, for it offers as governed by fact the theory that, owing to subjective pulls, our theories are *never* governed by fact. And thirdly, when anyone says he is content to have his theory take its chances with other theories, it is hard to believe that he is really proposing to test it by its appeal to popular feeling. He is saying that as people come to know the facts better they will see that these facts exclude the other theories and require his own. That implies that the minds to whom he takes his appeal are not puppets of feeling, but are to this extent reflectors of fact.

The truth is that in this generalized form the theory does not make sense. It says that our thought is inevitably distorted by feeling, and it is ready to say pretty precisely, as Freud does in discussing religion, where thought goes off the rails. Now, you cannot recognize that another has gone off the rails unless you know what it means to stay on them. If Freud can point to the mote in other people's religious vision, it is because he is confident he has cast out the beam from his own. He is sure that in the main he is thinking straight when he thinks about religion and about the crookedness of most people's thought about it. What he has proved, then, is not that thinking straight is impossible— a proof that could not get under way without assuming the falsity of its conclusion—but only that thinking straight is hard, which we knew before. To say that we can never think straight is to expose oneself to that charge of fatuity which has now stood for some thousands of years against the sort of person who rises to remark that he knows he knows nothing.

I am, of course, not offering these few observations as an appraisal of the work that has been done by the students of man's irrationality. We owe them a great debt. McDougall has said that Freud threw more new light on the workings of the mind than any other psychologist since Aristotle, and I should not care to deny that he is right. All I am concerned to deny is the conclusion often drawn from these researches— that the mind is so controlled by pulls from within that it is never under the control of the objective pattern of things, or follows the thread of an impersonal logic. The observations I have offered, slender as they admittedly are, do seem to me to settle that point in principle.

5   We now come to the third of the current criticisms of reason. It is a far more technical criticism than either of those we have considered, and its importance is chiefly for the theoretical rather than the practical uses of reason. But it is a peculiarly formidable criticism, because it comes not only from within the camp of the philosophers but from a part of that camp in which clearness and accuracy are cultivated with laudable care. The attack is

formidable, again, because it calls in question the very end and goal of reason as we have described it. That end is to understand, and to understand is always to follow an objective pattern or order. What kind of order is this? If it is to satisfy reason, it must be an intelligible order, and what is that? It is an order that never meets our question Why? with a final rebuff, one in which there is always an answer to be found, whether in fact we find it or not. And what sort of answer would satisfy that question? Only an answer in terms of necessity, and ultimately of logical necessity, since of any answer that falls short of this the question Why? can be raised again. When we reach an answer that is necessary, we see that to repeat the question is idle. Of any statement of merely causal necessity, such as the law of gravitation, or Ohm's law, or Boyle's law, we can intelligibly ask why things should behave in this manner. But when we see that things equal to the same thing are equal to each other, we cannot sensibly ask why, because we are at the end of the line to which such questioning can take us. We have already reached the logically necessary.

Now, if the world is to be the sort of world in which reason could even in theory reach its end, it must be one in which intelligence finds an answering intelligibility. I see no way in which it can assure itself beforehand that this is what it will find; I only wish I did. It may be that when we ask such questions as Why does the sun attract the earth in accordance with the law of inverse squares? we are asking a question to which no answer that satisfies reason will ever be forthcoming, and this not because the answer is beyond our reach, but because there *is* no answer, because the connections of things and events are nonnecessary, and therefore in one sense nonrational and unintelligible. If this is true, the attempt to understand is doomed to defeat from the outset. But I see no way of proving this either.

Here is where logical positivism comes in. It claims to have evidence that in entering upon such a program reason is bound to fail. The argument is as follows: Thought must live and move among propositions, for it is intent upon grasping what is true, and only propositions are capable of truth. Since the material with which it directly deals is thus always propositions, a review of the kinds of proposition open to it will throw light on what we may expect of it.

Now, when we review the possible kinds of proposition, we find that they are all reducible to two. On the one hand are necessary propositions, such as those of logic and mathematics. Because of their necessity, they have always given delight to the rationalistically inclined. But unfortunately they are all tautologies; they unfold our own meanings only and give no knowledge of the actual world. On the other hand there are empirical propositions: this is a table; American robins have red breasts. These do assert of the actual world and, if they are true, tell us something about it. But then they are never necessary; they never report that S *must* be P but only that SP is the case. And if the positivists are right that these two are the only kinds of proposition that ever present themselves to thought, then the program of reason as we have conceived it is clearly impracticable. That program was to penetrate through into the intelligible structure of things. This we now see that we can never do. For though we can indeed know necessities, these necessities are never links that join actual facts; and though we can know facts, these are never necessary. The world of existence is unintelligible.

The positivist case against our program thus rests on two contentions: that all necessary propositions are tautologous and that all factual propositions are contingent. It is important to see more precisely what these mean.

It may be supposed that the first contention, all necessary propositions are tautologous, means what Kant meant when he said that analytic propositions were tautologous. These, he said, merely set out in the predicate what is already contained in the subject. Positivists reject this account of tautology as resting on psychological grounds; it places the test, they say, in subjective intension, in the accident of how one happens to conceive of the subject named. The test they offer instead is whether the proposition in question can be denied without self-contradiction; it is necessary if it cannot. Now, they admit that there are large numbers of propositions which are in this sense necessary; and if so, why should we take offense or alarm at their theory? Do not all these necessities stand for just so many intelligibilities in the nature of things, and are not these precisely what we are seeking?

Unhappily, the positivists will not let us read them in this way. They insist that the necessity here exhibited has nothing to do with the nature of things, that the contradiction involved in its denial means incoherence, not in nature, but in our own linguistic usage. Necessary propositions, writes Mr. Ayer, "simply record our determination to use words in a certain fashion. We cannot deny them without infringing the conventions which are presupposed by our very denial, and so falling into self-contradiction. And this is the sole ground of their necessity." [1] A necessary proposition of the form "S is P" tells how we propose to use S. A necessary proposition of the form "P implies Q" illustrates a definition of implication which has been adopted arbitrarily, and which stands, not for a nexus in nature, but for a convention of our own. Let us look at these two types.

A necessary proposition of the form S is P, which in former days would have been said to state a necessary relation between concepts, is now said to state how we use, or propose to use, S. I think that what this amounts to, after all, is that such propositions are analytic in Kant's sense; the predicate sets forth, in part or in whole, how one conceives of the subject; the addition to the older theory is that this predicate is arbitrary. Regarding this doctrine I should hold as follows: (1) the view that all propositions of this form are analytic is untrue and (2) the addendum that the predicate is arbitrary is equally untrue.

1. "Whatever is red is extended." This seems to me a necessary proposition, and most positivists would, I think, agree. By saying this they mean that its contradictory would be self-contradictory. Why would this be true? Because in our first proposition we merely set forth in our predicate part of what was meant by our subject. This analysis seems to me incorrect. What I mean by extension is not what I mean by redness, nor is it part of this; the two are quite distinct. If when I think of a billiard ball as red, the extension of that red is part of what I mean by red, then when I think of another billiard ball as white, the extension of the white will be part of what I mean by calling it white; and I shall then have to say that the balls are similarly colored, which is absurd. Being extended is, to be sure, so intimately connected with being red that if a thing is red it must be extended also; the one entails the other. But surely that is the way to put it. It is quite incorrect to say that when I call a thing extended I am defining the meaning of red. Though I am asserting a relation of entailment or necessity, it is evident from inspection that that relation is not one of identity, either in whole or in part. And if so, necessities are not always tautologies. I should myself maintain that in actual thought they never are, but that is another point.

[1] *Language, Truth and Logic,* p. 114.

2. To the contention that such propositions are analytic, the positivists add, as we have seen, that they are arbitrary, in the sense that they state or illustrate a convention which might have been different. Mr. Ayer writes as follows: "If I say, 'nothing can be coloured in different ways at the same time with respect to the same part of itself,' I am not saying anything about the properties of any actual thing . . . I am expressing an analytic proposition, which records our determination to call a colour expanse which differs in quality from a neighboring colour expanse a different part of a given thing. In other words, I am simply calling attention to the implications of a certain linguistic usage." [2] Now I suggest that when we call two differently colored patches of a rug different it is because we see that they are and must be different, and that this, which we mean to assert, is wholly independent of linguistic usage. If it were really a matter of usage, the adoption of a different usage would make a difference to what I assert. Would it in fact? Suppose we decided that when we saw two differently colored patches we should henceforth call them the same patch; would that which we meant to assert be different from what we meant to assert before? I think not. We should still be asserting the parts to be different, because we see that they must be, and if we used the word "same," it would now mean what we meant by "different." The fact is—to repeat —that we call two differently colored parts different because we see that they are so, and must be; they are not so, nor are they seen to be so, because we have adopted the convention of calling them so. Language adjusts itself to the observed nature of things; the nature of things does not wait on our language. These are truisms which I am almost ashamed to set down deliberately. And yet when we are offered statements of the kind I have quoted as the final result of exact linguistic researches, a few truisms may come as a relief.

I have been dealing with necessary propositions of the S-P form, that is, propositions which assert a connection between subject and predicate. I come now to assertions of the P-implies-Q type, which assert a necessary linkage between propositions themselves. The positivists treat these in essentially the same way as the others. They would argue as follows: when we assert that a proposition P implies another, Q, we are, in the first place, asserting what we have asserted already, and in the second place, asserting a relation to hold that belongs, not to the nature of

[2] *Op. cit.*, p. 104.

things, but to our own set of conventions. As for the first point, when we say that P implies Q, we find that we always know, or think we know, certain things about the truth of P and Q. Of the four possibilities—both true, both false, P false and Q true, P true and Q false—we know that one or other of the first three holds. But in knowing that, we know already that P implies Q, for that is what the statement *means.* At least that is what it means to us. For, secondly, say the positivists, you are at perfect liberty to mean by it something else if you wish. You may mean by it what, following the *Principia,* we have just offered, i.e., either P is false or Q is true, or what Clarence I. Lewis means by it, that P's truth is inconsistent with Q's falsity, or any one of a large number of other things. Which of these you choose is not determined for you but by you; it is a matter of convention. All that is required is that once you choose your conventions you adhere to them, that once you have defined implication in a given way you mean this by it consistently; otherwise you stultify yourself.

Now, the first of these points, that implication is tautologous, depends on the second, that it is a matter of convention; for, in the position we are examining, what implication shall be is conventionally determined. The question before us, then, is whether it *is* so determined.

It seems to me that there is one simple argument which shows that it is not. This argument is that of all the various definitions which are offered of implication, we can sensibly ask, Does this give what I really mean or not? We cannot only sensibly ask that question; we can see that the various answers miss or approach what we mean in various degrees. Thus we can see that the Russell-Whitehead formula of material implication misses what we mean by a wide margin, and that Lewis's strict implication approximates it much more closely. This shows that we have something in mind to which all the conventions must come for testing, a relation conceived as holding *independently* of our usages and conventions. When we say that the premises of a syllogism imply its conclusion, or that being extended implies being divisible, we do mean something definite, however difficult to hit with words; and this is what gives the target at which our definitions aim. If there were no target there at all, how could we tell, as in fact we can, that some definitions strike close to the mark and others go wide of it? Of course our definitions are arbitrary in the sense that to the word "implication" we can attach any sense we want. But to argue from this that any sense we attach to the word will equally fit what in common use we mean by it is surely confusion. When we dispute over the nature of "justice" or "number" or "truth," are we really free to define the term as we please? Do we not assume on both sides that we are trying to run down and capture the same thing? When we argue with each other as to whether an inference is to be admitted, is there no bar, in the form of a common understanding of what "follows" really means, to which both of us must take our appeal? If there is not, argument is futile. If there is, positivism is wrong.

This consideration is to my mind decisive, and those who hold logic to be conventional have not, I think, wholly escaped it. It is true that from differing definitions of "P implies Q" there follow "alternative logics," in the sense of differing sets of basic logical propositions. [If, for example, one defines this, not as meaning "material implication" (either "P and Q," or "not-P and Q," or "not-P and not-Q") but as meaning "either 'P and not-Q,' or 'not-P and Q,' or 'not-P and not-Q,'" a sort of logic would follow in which a true proposition implies and is implied only by a false one.] But so far as I can see, when one says that such things follow, one means by "follow" what all the rest of us mean by it. The concept of following is common to all the alternative logics; to that there is apparently no alternative. Once more, if logic is wholly conventional, there should be logics in which the principle of contradiction is replaced by an alternative. So far as I know, there is none such; without this principle the sort of distinction required by all logics in common would be impossible. But a convention that is necessary to make all other conventions possible is not in the same sense a convention itself.

I have been dealing so far with the first position of the positivists, which would make all necessary assertions mere statements about usage. It may be asked: If not about this, what else? You would not hold, would you, that they are statements about the actual world? I answer: Of course I should. "That apple yonder cannot, in the same part and under the same conditions, be colored in different ways." I believe that, when we say that, we are saying something about the apple. "X cannot at once have Y and not have it." The positivists take this as meaning, "I do not propose to *call* both that which has Y and that which hasn't by the name of X." Bradley takes it as meaning that nothing that is real is self-contradictory. Which is right? Of course if one says, as positivists do, that all assertions except those about usage are assertions about sense experiences, Bradley is talking nonsense. There is no space here to discuss this curious and interesting revival of sensationalism. All I can say is that after an inspection of my own meaning, I wish to make it clear that I am talking Bradley's kind of nonsense.

We turn now to the second position of the positivists, which must be dealt with in the briefest way: All factual propositions are contingent. What are we to say of it? I think that even if factual propositions are defined in the straitest positivist fashion, the statement must be set down as untrue. Before us, for example, is a series of colors arranged in order of their affinities. We perceive that in this series, orange falls, and must fall, between red and yellow. Is this an assertion about elements given in sense? Yes, and it is therefore a factual assertion. Is it a contingent assertion? No. Things are related contingently when they might be related otherwise than they are. But the relation I am here asserting could not be other than it is; if orange were not related as it is to red and yellow, it would not be orange. The Gestaltists tell us that when we "see," as we often do, that to continue a melody in the right key we must proceed thus and not thus, we are laying hold of a genuine requiredness; and I think they are right. Here again the *must* holds among the given sensory elements; the insight is at once factual and necessary. And if one breaks with the narrowly sensory interpretation of "factual," as one should, many other types of factual necessity are admitted. When I say that my present toothache is bad, am I saying that the badness is accidentally conjoined to it, so that the pain could be what it is without the badness? Clearly not; I am asserting a predicate that belongs to its subject necessarily, though that subject is an existent. When I say "I cannot doubt that I am now conscious" I am reporting that a present fact excludes, and necessarily excludes, a predicate suggested of it. Personally I should be ready to maintain, in respect to each of the positivist positions, not only that it is false, but that the truth lies in its contrary. I think that in the end all necessary propositions must be taken to assert of existence and that no factual propositions are altogether contingent.

But it is no part of my design to argue for these positions. My aim is sharply limited; it is merely to help clear the ground of some objections to our power to be reasonable, taking this term in one very important sense and of profound significance for the emergent civilization.

Is this all shadow boxing? It may be said that when people are moved to be unreasonable in thought or practice it is not because they have drawn irrationalist inferences from such theories as we have examined. True enough. But that is not the point. The point is that among present-day systems of thought some of the most widely influential would make the pursuit of the reasonable impossible, that if these systems prevail their implications will tend to be realized, accepted and acted upon; and that these implications are disastrous. If any one of the theories I have discussed is true, philosophy has no future except perhaps "the future of an illusion." If our reasoning is in truth the shadow cast by the irrational displacements of matter, if it is only the bobbing of corks on the surface, pulled about from irrational depths, if it is really a play with syntax, signifying nothing, then we should face the truth and, as Cromwell said to the cleric, we should "cease our fooling."

On the other hand, if these things are not true, it is the philosopher's business to brush them out of the way, not by alarms but by analysis, and so help men to get on with their work. If he succeeds, the first gainer will be philosophy, which stands in need today of some of the high and hopeful adventurousness of the great pioneers of reason. But the influence will not stop there. What the philosophers and men of science conclude today the public is asking about tomorrow and taking as a matter of course the day after tomorrow. There is such a thing possible as a "sentiment of rationality," a popular trust in reason, a pride in its private exercise, a general demand that the issues between man and man, race and race, nation and nation, be settled in accordance with it. Such a spirit is coming to seem less utopian than merely necessary, and to help prepare the way for it is the most practical service that any philosopher can render.

THE NEW BASIS FOR WORLD POLITICS

1   Every century has its own particular mental climate. The sixteenth century was dominated by geography and by the mood of the great discoverers who found the Americas. The decades of the seventeenth century, and those writers especially who took their intellectual lead from Descartes, were dominated by the recent developments in mathematics, particularly algebra. Hobbes found his inspiration when first looking into, not Homer (which he nevertheless translated), but Euclid.

Similarly, the sixty years or more after Adam Smith wrote his *Wealth of Nations,* this "post-Adamite" epoch was *ébloui* by the new science of economics, which so admirably fitted into a laissez-faire free trade which Britain then found profitable for her own economy and which she prescribed as a panacea to the world, as the United States very naturally does today. To urge social conduct which went contrary to the teachings of Ricardo and McCulloch was felt, and indeed pretty specifically said by Archbishop Trench, to be a flouting of the ordinances of Divine Providence as revealed to this new Adam and this other inspired Smith. Even the Catholic Church instructed confessors not to disturb the consciences of penitents about the complexities of interest-taking, *lucrum non cessans,* which the Church condemned.

In this world Karl Marx lived. It is true that Prussia, for her own national reasons, never fully accepted this economic teaching and was stanchly protectionist. But the country of List certainly did not neglect the new science or doubt it to be such. And when the refugee Marx came to live in London, and to study in the British Museum, he came to a land where Ricardo and Cobden walked as gods. His indictment of capitalism was an indictment of all that in which Liberal employers such as Bright believed. But Marx merely proposed to examine eco-

49

nomics from the perspective of the underdog and of labor, not of the capitalist. Here was no harking back to the "utopian" co-operativism of Owen or the working practice of the medieval guilds. It was out of the mouths of Locke, of Smith and of Ricardo that Marx quoted the axioms accepted by himself and opponent alike, and then with unerring logic (or almost unerring . . .) drew the conclusions, so unpalatable to employer, exploiter and capitalist.

Marx, however, did not question the axioms, and indeed it was not in his interest to do so. An expert who had written his German doctoral thesis on the early Greek hedonists, he accepted *a priori* the hedonistic and egoistic psychology of the early Utilitarians and economists, which traced from the materialists, Hobbes and Helvétius. Indeed by an odd paradox Marx remained throughout life in psychology a great deal of an individualist, although sometimes the individual units about which he speculated were classes. His appeal to the workers to "unite" was a Hobbesian appeal for a social contract in self-defense against the beasts of prey. And he remained, as Dr. K. R. Popper points out in *The Open Society and its Enemies,* a "utopian." Marx was this, not so much in terms of his "fading away of the state" into the classless society (after which the eternal dialectic ceased to operate by throwing up further antitheses), but a "utopian" in the bad sense of a doctrinaire who dealt in abstract entities and not in the positive and constructive remedying of actual situations by empiric (i.e., for the Marxist "opportunist") means.

Marx, in brief, did not break away either from the almost exclusively economic obsessions (which replaced the earlier "political institutionalism" of Hume) of his predecessors or from their egoistic psychological suppositions of "enlightened self-interest." In both points Marx, as a matter of historical relativism, is due to be superseded by a new basis for social science. Indeed, this would be the logical conclusion of his own historical dialectic. And if Marx is taken as the author of final pronouncements, upon which political systems have to be constructed, then, against such a nonempiric and antiscientific position, we have no option except to say that Marx is finally and dangerously wrong. Much has happened in psychological science and to economic science since the thought of Marx became set. To use an overworked cliché, "we cannot set the clock back." (Of course a wise timekeeper habitually does.) To use a more convincing phrase, we must not permit the advancement of the sciences or practical social change to be suffocated or poisoned by the incubus of Marxist dogma. We need a *novum organum.*

In 1929 I wrote a brief Discourse on Method in which I made the following suggestions: That politics, by every test including prediction and mensurability, was as much a science as economics. That it was an empiric and technical science of means to a variety of ends, not of itself requiring any teleology, and as such was distinct from political philosophy, and other "poetic," i.e. creative, studies. That the distinction between political science and sociology was a confusion and a name without a difference. That the unit of reference was the individual will (or "vote") in relation to other wills and the consequent structure of controls, aiming at assurance or security. That the best interpretative clue in politics was to regard it as primarily and in nucleus the abstract science (and all sciences *qua* sciences are abstract) of power, i.e., assurance for future liberty, power being both dominative and co-operative. That there was a political "market," in which the value men set upon individual "liberty" rose and fell with the times, in relation to the value they placed upon social "security," which was a species of guaranteed "liberty" for which other unguaranteed "liberties" had to be sacrificed. That liberty varied in inverse ratio to external menace or apparent menace. That the need for stability was increasingly to replace co-operative power with the administration of things for dominative power with the repression of men. And that this passed on into being a problem in education and even religion, or practical values, in which the issues of teleology, of the type of society required or normative, became all-important.

Since 1929 a great deal of literature, of interest both to students of political relations and to professional politicists, has been published. A group of novelists, Huxley, Maugham, Cronin, have depicted to us with remarkable unanimity their notion of "the good man," in the case of Huxley deliberately relating this to what he calls, quoting Leibnitz, "the Perennial Philosophy." Another group of writers, general and professional, Gill, Murry, MacMurray, Heard, MacIver, have deepened the meaning to be attached to the word "community." The educational psychologists, such as Susan Isaacs and Karen Horney, have explained, in terms of the school community and with a view to training good men and good citizens, what is meant by co-operation as against domination. Fromm has explained the limitations of the attractions of liberty, deplored by Decker and Hayek and refined upon by Mannheim. The academic psychologists and the psychoanalysts, such as Suttie, Harding, Ranyard West, Thouless, Glover, have carried further the ideas of Freud and Adler; have revealed the deep springs of the impulse to dominate, not unrelated to fear and frustration as well as to love of liberty (taken even, as by Pavlov, as a bare reflex against constraint); and have indicated how by analysis and then training these forces may be poured into social shapes or neutralized by other impulses not less basic. We are left with the structure of an elaborate discipline.

The anthropologists and sociologists, such as Benedict and Dollard, have shown how co-operation is inculcated in certain cultures, such as the Pueblo, and domination in others, such as those of the American Northwest, while Malinowski destroyed the myth that "men have always made war." The political philosophers, such as Bertrand Russell in his *Power,* have developed the precise theme mentioned in the above paragraphs, while broadly agreeing in their remedial approach with Einstein, Schweitzer, Gandhi, and Huxley in his study *Ends and Means*. Such theologians as Maritain have emphasized the elements of power and fear, in their realistic discussions, while Lasswell has drawn the conclusions in his discussion of *World Politics and Personal Insecurity*. All this has happened since 1929 and indeed most of it recently, since my *Principles of Politics* was completed and my brief article for the Aristotelian Society on ends and means. It leaves me with no reason whatsoever for retracting my original argument.

A new revolution is likely to take place in thought whenever one can descry an entire constellation shaping, with all the lights increasingly falling into pattern. One beacon, whether in psychology or in philosophy, would not be enough. But when we see the new teaching of psychologists, educationalists, philosophers, political scientists, anthropologists all pointing in the same direction, we may be sure that something will emerge as a new cast of thought as significant in its day as the work of Adam Smith and Bentham (or of Marx) was in theirs.

2 This new revolution is both negative and positive. Negatively, it calls attention to the profundity of the appetite for power, however shaped in expression by geography and other external conditioning factors. The nomad tribes did not invade the wealthy lowlands of civilization when they were stricken by famine. They invaded because as warriors, having always enjoyed fat, when they met overpopulation or shortage they proposed to recoup themselves by what, for them, was the cheapest means. The great revolutions of history have taken place under the stimulus of sudden injustice or incompetence but at times when, as in the France of 1789 and the Russia of 1917, economic standards were rising and men's expectations rising faster. The worker may be concerned with his security, in bread and butter, but he is concerned also (especially under a despotism) for his personal freedom and his life. He is under an oppression by no means merely economic nor mostly inspired by economic jealousy. It is a jealousy of power. The wealthy man is concerned to accumulate more wealth not for consumption but for power, of which wealth is a species. There is nothing in the nature of socialism or even of communism to prevent two Powers, significantly so called (not always Common-Wealths), from fighting for more power; or to prevent those who organize a classless society (howbeit in the U.S.S.R. with unequal wages, as Marx insisted in his *Critique of the Gotha Program*) from fighting to maintain their regime and position of control against the less privileged.

All our recent psychological knowledge warns us that, however important for justice economic readjustments may be, despite all merely economic rearrangements this will continue to be the case so long as the old politics remain the old politics. The cure must be more radical than merely talking about the "economic interpretation of history" whether as meaning "the material" (which is either mere dogma or means "the geographic," "the demographic," etc.), or as meaning that only the psychological "appetite for wealth" matters, which is again more misleading dogma. Economic change means social change; and social change (as no one recognized in practice better than Lenin) means power change.

The revolution of thought has a positive aspect. We are not left as by Schwartzschild, Spykman and even Lasswell with a mere negative power-analysis meaning a domination-analysis. This perspective which does not go beyond the domination-analysis is the point where the illusions of the old Geneva League, with its Liberal rationalism, faded out in gunpowder smoke, and which shows that the present United Nations as deadlocked in an embrace, not utterly fraternal, of the titans and apparently without hope of advance. Here is "realism" indeed, instead of Marxist myth and propaganda; but no new construction or shuffle of power factors indicates any way out of the problem, the social disease, created by the appetite for power. Merely one proceeds from war to war to settle these issues of power and of that sovereignty which is the jurists' expression of power.

The clue is to be found in the field of modern educational psychology; and in applying in the field of politics and of social relations, domestic and international, what is already appreciated adequately enough in the training of children. The desire to have the upper hand, to have prestige, to order the others is here well recognized. But recent research has shown that this deep unsocial impulse in part is the expression of fear, and indeed is an overcompensation for alarm lest one be found inferior; it is most marked in members of families characterized by a sense of inferiority; it can be not so much eradicated as healed (since it is but a frightened and perverted desire for liberty and its guarantees) by the proper educational treatment; but that this treatment requires that the educator shall be himself or herself in an unassailable position. As was said of the Papacy, *securus judicat orbes terrarum*. Here, if the conclusions of educationalists are to be accepted, lies the right prescription. It will be noted that the whole scheme of vindictive treatment finds no place here, just as Gandhi has suggested that it must not find place in penal reform. The issue is one of social hygiene. To punish the patient for having symptoms is a form of folly which assuredly brings its own nemesis. But it will also be noted that the New Method does not for one moment ignore the need for security or for a judge with executive and coercive powers.

The New Method involves a technique which Huxley and Heard would describe as charistic. It is indeed an old technique of which perhaps M. K. Gandhi and Albert Schweitzer are the greatest living exponents. It is the religious technique expressing what Huxley calls "the Perennial Philosophy." Further, if this be true, it means that a revised attitude must be adopted in "progressive quarters" toward that religious revival of which there are evidences throughout the contemporary European world, even in terms of electoral voting and the rise of new parties. An immense revival of Catholic Christianity is, in my view, to be anticipated. It also means that extreme importance is to be attached to that universal religious intuition which not only Huxley but an orthodox Catholic such as Maritain detects as being present, in different degrees of clarity, among the devoted men of all the great religions.

Because a technique is involved it requires training. Indeed what we are primarily confronted with here is precisely an educational technique. It does not follow that we should accept the classic criticism by Socrates of democracy; or abandon democracy along with the Communists to put a "vanguard of the more politically conscious" in power; or thrust technocrats into the controls of government. Gandhi seeks no such function for his ashram. What it does mean is that common people must be educated to respect those who are greater masters of the technique than themselves, a technique which involves, as with the monastic orders, deliberate training in detachment and disinterestedness. We have learned, not only in the U.S.S.R., to respect the engineer, the scientist, the technocrat. Men have to learn to respect the social physician, the trained expert in psychology. The capacity for such respect is the real meaning (as Marxists have rightly grasped, as touching this "vanguard") of "an educated democracy." The trouble with the "vanguard" is that it is still the bondslave of the old psychological techniques of suspicion.

I am more concerned here to stress the strictly scientific than the religious nature (so easily misunderstood) of the new technique, and also to stress its difficulty, since it certainly goes much beyond using the easy word "co-operation." It so happens that the psychoanalysts have shown to us part of the truth, so that the old dead bones take life, of the doctrines of original sin, conversion of the will, and grace. What here matters is that they have also shown us how deep in man are these drives to compensate for aboriginal fears by the seizure of power, and how thoroughgoing a conversion or education must be the technique that will correct this—not merely superficially and by force and more fears, as Hobbes recommended. Especially must it be thoroughgoing in a civilization which, owing to the reaction against religious forces, is soaked through with the acquisitive and dominative spirit.

As a practical matter, what is required is a great increase in the power of the religious spirit. This is the positive side of the matter. Only in this way can the right psychological training be translated into political mass terms. Historically this has to mean "organized religion," however imperfectly its own distinctive charistic technique may be grasped by its professors. On the one hand, it is empty to talk of an increase of the power of religion and then to divorce this from the millennial historical expressions of religion. This attitude is totally unhistorical, unpolitical and distorted in the direction of a false "otherworldliness," such as Marx denounced with some excuse. On the other hand, this stage cannot be final so long as religion remains not universal, resting on actual human experience, but schismatically divided, concerned to protest about differences or, if given power, to use this to apply indifferent techniques or to impose a rule of ignorant local prejudices and obscurantism. Such is not Augustine's City Pilgrim. It is dead in its conventions, incapable of withstanding persecution. Its concern is not to convert, but to argue. Instead we need stress upon the world-wide and essentially supranational character of religious experience.

In a conversation which I once had with Gandhi about the Christian communities of India, the Mahatma said shrewdly and wisely that "no truly religious man talks about rights and political guarantees. He is only concerned with the truth as he sees it, and to see it more fully. He is never a 'minority' because he feels himself to be with God. And he can willingly endure persecution to death for this truth because it matters more than, and overwhelms, all talks of 'rights' and 'guarantees' of this political section against that." The essence of religion is a coming together upon the basis of the *visio Dei,* the common mystical experience of men in charity; and in the external expression of this in the communion of saints, even under persecution of this one church of charity.

3   Even, however, with this new statement we are still left with a problem which has perplexed political thought since the days of Augustine—and indeed since the days when Aristotle propounded the problem whether a good man could be a good citizen in a bad polis. The problem is how far the sincere and single-minded adoption of the spirit of the traditional charistic technique is consistent with the maintenance of the law, and the order and authority, including the right to punish, which the law demands.

Walter Lippmann has pointed out, in *One World or None,* edited by him, that, whereas the association of sovereign nations in the United

Nations has bankrupted itself by reasserting sovereign rights through the veto power, at the same time at Nuremberg a principle of jurisprudence has been laid down which holds politicians and generals individually responsible for levying aggressive war contrary to the Kellogg Pact and for other offenses against international law. It is true that generals even of the victorious nations have been known to take all this with a grain of salt, but this has always been the case in the evolution of law. Looking back, any student of the evolution of domestic law will be aware that in the early stages not only the criminal but his whole community was held liable for his offenses against national law. This was done upon the not unreasonable ground that, even if in different degree, those who connive in breaches of law, as well as those who actually commit them, are guilty.

Are we, then, to hold the operations of the police and of the national criminal courts consistent with the adoption of the new psychological technique, which treats politics as a branch of social hygiene; and are we to hold an international police force, and world security council with world court, consistent with the technique of charity, cooperation and peace? Or must we, in the name of Christianity, abolish all police and all courts?

Gandhi has recently stated that he looks forward to the time when crime will be treated as a disease, and the criminal no more punished than the invalid, but the disease of violence or kleptomania cured by social medicine. While unreservedly sharing this hope and indication of direction—and increasingly we see how much of crime really shares the nature of disease and peculiarly springs from irrational fear and power-lust, curable at least in infancy—nevertheless, we still take the precaution of sending the medical man into the criminal lunatic asylum or mental institution accompanied by a warder. We make this concession to interim conditions and indeed hold it to be necessary. We do not, then, abjure the use of constraining force, even where the admitted object is to effect a mental cure. The balance of the mind is too affected for it to be left, unguarded, in charge of the physical machine of the body.

In the same conversation, above mentioned, with Gandhi, I inquired of the Mahatma what was his view of a world police force. All those acquainted with the most sacred book of Hinduism, the Bhagavad-Gita, will recall that it is specifically concerned with this issue of the use of force. It ends by authorizing it when it is exercised in the pure performance of a rational duty. Patently the issue of pacifism is, and always has been, not the preservation of the physical body from inevitable death but with the issue of mercy against the torture of war inflicted on others, and with the issue of the consistent exercise of charity.

Gandhi has always held that those who do not grasp the disciplined doctrine of *ahimsa*, or nonviolence, should not seek refuge in flight but should fight courageously for what conventional duty demands. His attitude here has been that of Christ to Herod's soldiers, and of Paul to the centurion. He is himself a decoré of three wars, who has never drawn the distinction between combatant and noncombatant service. The question for him has always been how far the general attitude, the exemplary and educational attitude, of nonviolence—and hence the cause of human charity—could be in effect best promoted. He has not been an absolutist of the letter in these matters, but of the spirit. In the recent conversations which I had with him, asking the Mahatma for his views on a world police force, Gandhi's reply was:

"We must proceed on principle in this matter. Who is entitled to be judge? If indeed we could get an impartial world police force we should all welcome it. But my instinct is to feel that, by the time when men had trained themselves to the point where impartiality ["disinterestedness"] is possible, they will also have trained themselves to the point where the use of force is unnecessary."

I would make only one amendment to this—and it is an amendment which, whether right or wrong, is entirely consistent with the Petrine and Pauline Epistles in interpreting the Christian expression of the charistic tradition, as also with the Gita; and is also entirely consistent with the later churchly doctrine of the subordinate and limited use of the secular sword. My concern is to point out that this canonical doctrine about force as a subordinate instrument is far sounder philosophy and far sounder science than any secular political philosophy which has replaced it. But it obviously involves the recognition of the position of the religions, *i.e.*, the church, not by tolerance but by right, in political society, not on the basis of sectarianism and of the "five and ninety sects," but of some common ground, including the ethnic religions. The amendment I would suggest is that, while men are training themselves for impartiality and disinterestedness, and while new values and a new moral standard are emerging in civilization, the historical need remains for a social force, increasingly subject to this standard, to restrain anti-social forces that make for aggression and the rule of the more aggressive over the less aggressive in a dominative world. In brief, a force sprung up in reaction to the dominative impulse, which in origin was only counterdominative (like Marx's "insurgent masses") and which did not originally leave the background of the dominative philosophy (as Marxism did not), can nevertheless be deliberately subordinated and utilized to police the world in order to produce the external conditions favorable to a charistic philosophy of which Marxism gives no insight. It can, in the words of Aquinas, secure the conditions conducive to the good life, without aspiring of itself to provide it, and destroy the destroyers.

This is the traditional position and I see no need to quarrel with it, although I see the gravest need to quarrel with nationalistic and state-idolatrous perversions of it. Its major objections lie in a defeatist scepticism concerning whether the human spirit is capable of creating an approximately impartial international tribunal. All alternative positions seem to me more difficult. But this position of Ayala, Vittoria and the first international lawyers seems to require vigorous restatement on its old natural law, *i.e.,* scientific, basis which rescues it from a position that identifies law with the mere opportunist convenience of the victors.

Where, then, are we left? There is a moral right to proceed against an aggressor, so judged by an impartial tribunal, by means of an impartial police force; and this moral right is also a necessary political safeguard for peace-minded people against war-minded people. The World Court offers an impartial tribunal in legal matters. It is to be regretted that it was not the source of authority of the Nuremberg Tribunal and has no power of judicial review of the United Nations Charter. UN offers an authority competent to decide on disputes affecting world peace and competent to take executive action against an aggressor. No one appears to be in a position to dictate either to the judges of the court or to the majority in the UN Security Council. They, therefore, achieve, if not abstract impartiality, at least as much impartiality as can reasonably be demanded by anyone with a sense for the evolution and imperfections of all historical processes. They have as much impartiality as was earlier achieved by the national and royal courts in their evolution.

Owing, however, to the veto power, at a critical stage the Security

Council is almost sure to be debarred from giving any decision at all, just as the League gave no decision in 1939. James Byrnes spoke in London of a route out of this dilemma when he indicated that, instead of admitting relapse into the international anarchy, the majority had a moral right to proceed by their own free will over the veto of the minority in matters affecting themselves. He has enunciated the same policy in connection with the making of the peace treaties. If we follow Kant and admit the moral obligation to establish an international tribunal with power, I believe that we must agree with this proposition and with the necessary means, that is, the right of majority decision.

If we do accept these three propositions—that there is a moral imperative to eschew aggression and develop a new technique of co-operation; that there is a moral right to establish a secular power (subject to the spiritual or educational power) to check aggression; and that a majority of states or peoples has a right, moral and juristic, to decide upon the exercise of such powers; then certain practical consequences seem to me immediately to follow.

The maintenance of peace depends, not upon such co-operation of a limited number of great powers as is decided by the minority among them to be co-operation, but upon the decision of the majority of the Council including those representatives elected by the Assembly. It is an insolence for the ambassador of any power to suggest that the United Nations is or is not "co-operative," since it is for the United Nations and not for individual powers to decide upon what constitutes co-operation. The history of the League shows the folly of not upholding, at need by full military force, the decisions of the League—even if this be done from fear of alienating some particular power, which (as in the case of Italy) has nevertheless to be fought in the long run. The incipient Federal Union has to be preserved against all comers. UN must necessarily exercise a measure of rule over the U.S.A., the U.K. and, let it be added flatly, the U.S.S.R.—a position which Soviet spokesmen such as Andrei Vyshinsky have themselves been disposed to accept in the cases of Spain and Java. The history of dealings in the past twenty years with Germany shows the extreme danger of ever beginning a policy of appeasement and departing from the principles that make an international authority operative and respected.

World War II need never have taken place if absolutely prompt action had been taken against the potential aggressor when he first showed overt signs of breaking his engagements. It is necessary that an international force should be competent to strike decisively, and prepared to strike instantly, upon any sign from an aggressor of defiance, whether by resisting a decision of the international tribunal, refusing due process of law, or taking action to secede from the international body for law and law enforcement. If peace is to be maintained, peace will have its costs from democracies in providing the full means of prompt action coupled with the will to be prompt.

The argument is often used that the United Nations is merely a gigantic fraud; that everybody knows that on decisive occasions it could not act to save peace owing to its deplorable constitution; that the expressions of hope for a supranational organization by Soong, Hofmeyer, Eden and Bevin remain mere pious hopes; and that the realities of power remain intertwined with the relations of the U.S.S.R., U.S.A. and U.K. This cynical "realism" is really a form of defeatism. It disbelieves that an international organization can be set up which, as a historical matter, can tend to the establishment of an impartial, legitimate and *de jure* world authority. It views everything as a conflict of units of power, while eluding any decision about which has the moral right to prevail over which. It weakens the moral right of those who wish peace as against those who do not, by refusing to make any *de jure* distinctions in a world of mere force, in which the most unscrupulous and ruthless in the jungle will have the advantage, owing to the timidity of others in finding a basis of co-operation. Such pseudo-realism, I suggest, should be condemned root and branch. This carries with it, as corollary, the shaping of all action, policy, and not least public announcements of policy, to the strict line of adhesion to due process of law, of adhesion to the tribunals that can render decisions in accordance with due process of law, and of determination to enforce, without flinching, the decisions of these tribunals against all makers of disorder.

4   There will always be some who press the claims of liberty against law—not only against positive law, where errors may easily occur and which is to be judged and abrogated by natural law, but against natural law itself. Such notions of liberty, founded on erroneous concepts, there is no time to discuss here. It is of a piece with a man's right to be unhealthy—which is certainly not a right he is entitled to impose, in the shape of a duty to humor him, upon

others. Similarly there are limits to the eccentricity which may lead certain people to prefer the international anarchy.

Again, there are those who oppose justice to law. It is true that positive law, if it is not to be the case that *summum ius est summa iniuria*, must be always subject to change. It must be this in order to bring it into accord with newly emergent conditions, and with the increasing sense for social justice which is a consequence of that campaign of radical educational conversion upon which we have based ourselves. If what we have said about the New Method is at all correct, then, not the mood of emulation but the mood of domination, including the acquisitiveness of economic domination of man over man, is unhealthy, and substantially founded upon irrational fear. It should be eradicated by proper education in youth, just as want should be eradicated by proper social readjustment and development of production in relation to population. Social change is the logical consequence of an inner change of approach, giving a new political basis (or, to be more precise, giving the reinforcement of a very old one).

Law, to be satisfactory, must keep itself in a condition of perpetual motion concurrent with opinion, which itself to be valid requires free discussion, free education, free press, as well as deference for the rule of reason and the judgment of those expert, not least in psychological matters. Natural law rests upon certain principles of nature and of human nature; but its application in positive law, although clear for the particular case, must never be static or show an undue cultural lag behind men's better social judgment. Social change may or may not take place peacefully (the history of religious change has been one of frequent persecution), but it can take place nonviolently; and it should take place constitutionally in any healthy condition of the law.

Similarly, in international law provision must be made for peaceful change. Although contracts or treaties must not be abrogated unilaterally, the corollary of this is that contracts must not be eternal, but subject to provision for termination or revision. New national movements, or other movements of self-determination, must have adequate facilities for presenting their case before the international authority and for moving the international conscience to legislative changes, even in abrogation of older established rights which are themselves relative to world peace and welfare, and not absolute. Constitutions which do not permit of internal change, in order to replace one regime or one economic system by another, must not be able to invoke the sanction of international law to uphold their unjust repression. But, whereas international law must be plastic to the forces of equity, nevertheless this law must be upheld against all international war-minded movements, whatever "dynamic" pleas they may enter, and against all regimes which in fact constitute a menace to world peace. The law must be improved but not in such fashion as to involve abandonment of the principle of due process of law. This peace takes a clear moral priority to all other claims on the secular plane, since alike a substantial freedom, an actual prosperity, and a reasonable justice are practicable only within a framework of peace and not of endemic war. Subject to this priority to maintain the highest liberty, which in the event of menace may as always involve restrictions on lesser liberties, the desirable peace is one of a democratic character which offers guarantees alike of minority liberties and of majority social justice.

To assert the priority of liberty—any liberty—to peace, as final rational priority, is to assert the right to dominate or to resist domination by counterdomination. To assert the priority of justice is, in effect, to claim the right to define our own justice by force, instead of submitting the decision to co-operation and persuasion. But the argument for the priority of peace does not exclude the organization of force to resist violence, aggression and the claim of a minority to dominate against those who are prepared to accept the rule of arbitration as selected by the majority.

In summary, world politics has often but not always rested upon the rule of domination. The idolatry of power-lust, especially at the national level but also permeating the entire civilization, has especially afflicted Western civilization since the sixteenth century. It has positive qualities making for technological advance which cannot be discussed here, but in the social sphere it makes for acquisitiveness and for a deterioration of civilization into violence. Just as religion was infected in the days of the Wars of Religion by this power-lust of the statesmen (often using religions of which they officially disapproved as their allies and tools), so Marxism was infected by this false psychological mood, and is unable by its very nature to provide an escape from it.

No escape is to be found save by a radical breakaway upon the basis of modern psychological and educational conclusions, which confirm the central findings of the great world religions. An adequate political force is to be found in appreciation of the common factors in religion and in co-operation with systems which today show a new life. There is a vast fund of religious life that can be liberated. Even in Russia there is certainly such a fund which can be utilized, despite repression. However, the adoption of the charistic method as a new education does not mean that it is just to decline to uphold the rule of such law as men have, even to the point of constraining the deliberate and forewarned aggressor. A United Nations, Kant's cosmopolitan institution, offers a just mechanism of constraint, providing a social life within which a charistic way of living may flower, subject to one condition. This is that the United Nations is interpreted, not statically, but dynamically as a new lawmaking body which is entitled to proceed, without impediment and overcoming deadlock, in accordance with the will of the majority. Such an organization is entitled to moral priority in its demand for support, and is supported by the teaching alike of the Gita and the Epistles in making this claim to the temporal sword. Its position is totally distinct from organizations seeking to use power or to make war for sectional ends, whose claims are totally incompatible with the charistic mood. Those who possess this mood may support, as Gandhi indicates, the first, although they may themselves have other vocations such as nonviolent nonco-operation as distinct from constraining force; but they cannot support the second, which are admitted selfishness and pure evil.

Political science is a study of means. The immediate need of our age is to take these simple moral judgments on ends. When this is done, the techniques are increasingly available in our day to realize these ends. This is true of production and prosperity, and it is also true in another plane of techniques of social well-being. Pursued with energy they will still enable our social sciences to overtake in their controls, and to harness to man's use, the discoveries of the physical sciences. These now, while the enmity of states is and has to be assumed, contribute to his ruthless destruction. The techniques are new but also old. What is lacking is the moral courage to choose them, and to discard clogging dogmas which, inspired by fear and suspicion, accept the fallacies of hate and mutual aggression.

Chapter IV

F. S. C. NORTHROP

TOWARD A REMOVAL OF THE IDEOLOGICAL CAUSES OF WORLD CONFLICT

Fear of a devastating world conflict has grown since the release of atomic energy. But even if the atomic bomb were never used again, the state of civilization upon this planet would be none the less desperate. For we are confronted in international relations with competition for the raw materials necessary to feed the industrial processes which natural science has made possible, while the social and human controls necessary to regulate this competition are lacking because of a continuous ideological war between the nations. This ideological war has its basis in the social sciences in conflicting conceptions of the economic and political principles upon which business practice and political policy should be based. It has its roots also in the humanities in different and often contradictory conceptions of the good, the ideal and the divine ends at which individual and social action should aim.

It is hardly necessary to point out that the fate of peace in our time rests in major part upon whether the ideologies of Russian communism and the Anglo-American democracies can be reconciled sufficiently to permit Russia, Great Britain and the United States to get on together. But even within the democracies there are the ideological clashes between the Latins and the Anglo-Americans, and within the English-speaking world between the more laissez-faire individualistic, or more hit-and-miss and conflicting pragmatic, conceptions of democracy of the United States and the more socialistic conception, on the one hand, or more Elizabethan imperialistic conception, on the other, of the British. And even more important in the long run, although less evident immediately, there is the conflict between Oriental and Occidental values, a conflict almost at the boiling point in India and already the cause of one major international explosion which found its outlet through Japan.

These facts make it evident that our difficulties center not merely in the failure to bring our social and humanistic conception of the ends of life into effective relation with its scientific instruments, but also and even more pointedly in a conflict within the social sciences and the humanities themselves concerning what the ends are. In other words, this world is in its present perilous state not so much because the natural sciences and their scientific methods have been pursued to the neglect of the social sciences and the humanities, but rather because the social sciences and the humanities have brought men into conflict with respect to the social policy and the religious and moral ends at which men are to aim.

But the purpose of this inquiry which I have been invited to contribute to *Our Emergent Civilization* is not to locate the blame but to seek out the cause of the trouble and to specify if possible the method for removing it. In the latter connection two things are evident: (1) The most pressing and inescapable social and humanistic problems of our world are ideological in character. (2) Neither our present moral philosophy nor our social science possesses an effective method for resolving ideological questions.

That the latter situation is the case is shown by the results. "By their fruits ye shall know them." Notwithstanding the idealistic moral philosophers' claim that their method of inquiry guarantees absolute moral standards the same for everybody and the similar claim of the naturalistic and pragmatic philosophers that they have a method for resolving problems of value which is scientific, these claims are patently false. The idealistic method has been available since Kant published his first ethical treatise in 1785. John Dewey's pragmatic method has been described for all to use since the beginning of this century. It is reasonable to suppose that were either of these methods effective, history should exhibit at least one ideological issue which had been at least in part resolved by the use of one or the other procedure.

Can anyone point to a single instance? One would suppose also, now that both idealistic and pragmatic ethical methodologies are known to all informed students in the social sciences and the humanities in the Western world, that were these methods worth anything, the ideological conflicts of Western civilization would be decreasing in number and intensity. Yet in the period between the two wars the exact reverse was the case, and it is doubtful even if ever in the past the value problems of civilization were as many in number or as acute as they are at the present moment.

It appears, therefore, that the time has come to reject the traditional preconceived methods with which modern moral philosophers and social scientists have approached the ideological issues of society and to begin instead with the specific ideological issues themselves, allowing an analysis of their specific content and character to guide one to the type of question which they raise, and the characteristics of this type of question in turn to guide one to the method appropriate for resolving it. In short, the concrete specific problems of value must come first; the method appropriate for resolving them must come afterward, as determined by the characteristics which each specific problem takes on when it is analyzed into its basic components.

Elsewhere [1] such an inquiry has been carried through for the major specific ideological issues of the contemporary world. Among the specific conflicts with respect to the humane ends of personal conduct and social action which were examined were the following: the Pan-American Issue between Latin-American and Anglo-American values; the Anglo-American Issue between traditional American and traditional British conservatism; the Western Issue between Medieval Roman Catholic and Modern Protestant conceptions of the good ecclesiastical organization and the good society; the modern ideological conflict between the Jevonean, or Austrian, and the Marxist theory of economic value and between the traditional democratic and the Marxian communistic theory of the state and that between the traditional East and the traditional West which could not meet.

In each instance the inquiry brought into the open the explicit economic, political, religious and aesthetic doctrines which together define the humanistic idea of the good of each party to any ideological conflict. It was found that for a given cultural ideology the economic, political, aesthetic and religious doctrines were not disconnected. Instead, all went back to a common set of basic assumptions. These assumptions by themselves constitute the philosophy underlying the eco-

[1] F. S. C. Northrop, *The Meeting of East and West: An Inquiry Concerning World Understanding.* New York: The Macmillan Company, 1946.

nomic, political, religious and other humanistic doctrines or practice of the culture in question. Thus, we arrive at the exceedingly important rediscovery of a truth noted long ago by Socrates and Plato in the middle books of the *Republic:* the criterion of the specific political, economic, religious and aesthetic principles which define the idea of the good of a given culture is the philosophy of the culture.

This essential connection between the cultural idea of the good made articulate in the doctrine of a given culture's economic and political theory, and envisaged in its humanities, and its underlying philosophy has been obscured because the people of a given culture fall naturally into the error of supposing that the observed institutions and behavioristic practices of human society are as objective and independent of one's theories about them as are the processes of nature. It is precisely the naturalness of this error of which Plato and Socrates were trying to make men aware, by their allegory of the den. The shadows on its end wall are the concrete introspections of conscience and the equally concrete institutions of one's own culture. These, as Socrates and Plato correctly saw, are not independent of one's theories about them, but are instead in considerable part the objective reflection of the philosophy underlying the specific culture in which one is brought up and embedded.

One has no difficulty in seeing this in the case of a foreign culture with economic and political institutions and religious and aesthetic conceptions and practices other than one's own. Contemporary pragmatists, for example, have no difficulty in recognizing that the Roman Catholic idea of the good for culture has its roots in the theology of St. Thomas and the philosophy of Aristotle. It is equally evident that the economic and political and antireligious ideology of the Communists is a similar expression of the combination of Hegel's dialectical theory of history and Feuerbach's epistemological realism and ontological materialism, which is the philosophy of Marx.

Nevertheless, so great is this error of supposing that observable social facts and practices in one's own culture are objectively independent of one's theories concerning them, after the manner of processes of nature, that even when we see this to be an error in the case of the Communists or the people of the Orient, we still persist in failing to see that the same error is occurring with ourselves.

For it is only if this error is committed that anyone would ever suppose that one's ethical or religious institutions would, apart from one's specific philosophy or the culture in which one is embedded, give one an absolute criterion of the good which is valid for everyone, as the modern idealists suppose. Similarly, it is only if the same error occurs that a modern naturalist or pragmatist or legal realist would conclude that one can find the correct normative social and humanistic theory of the good for culture by applying the methods of natural science to the facts of culture. It happens, therefore, that the connection between the normative social and humanistic theory of the good for a given culture and the underlying philosophy of that culture not merely specifies *in part* the method to be pursued in resolving problems of value, but also explains why the traditional modern methods for resolving such problems have failed.

The correct method is now in part clear. Since the economic, political and religious doctrines of a specific culture, which explicitly define their idea of the good or their theory of the ends of human and social action, and the arts of that culture which presents its social doctrines with the emotive meanings of vivid aesthetic immediacy necessary to persuade the hearts of men—since both the social doctrines and the arts of a culture have their source and the theoretical justification for their existence in a common, generally accepted philosophy, one must, in the methodological procedure for resolving any ideological conflict, proceed beneath the arts of a given culture and the normative doctrines of its social sciences to its philosophy. Always in the case of any specific culture with an ideology sufficiently universal to capture the support of a majority of the people of that culture such a philosophy can be found.

Thus the first principle to be followed in any ideological conflict is the following: bring into the open the rival philosophies upon which the conflicting cultural ideologies rest. This is done by examining the explicit economic, political and religious doctrines of the culture in question. The primitive assumptions and postulates of these doctrines will form a common system which is the philosophy of the culture in question.

A second question arises immediately: How are the conflicts between the different philosophies underlying the ideological conflicts of our world to be resolved? It would seem that when one has traced the conflicting social and humanistic ideologies back to a more basic conflict with respect to underlying philosophies, the problem of removing the conflict would be intensified rather than allayed, since basic philosophical differences of assumption seem more difficult to resolve than differences in the normative social theories with which we started.

Certain things are, however, to be noted at this point. The several philosophies which appear when differences in ideology have been traced back to differences in philosophical theory may be different but compatible, or they may be different and incompatible. If the former is the case, then the problem of resolving a given ideological conflict becomes that merely of enlarging the philosophical assumption of each party to the dispute to include those of the other party. There are many instances where this procedure is possible in the case of the ideological conflicts of the contemporary world.

The real difficulty arises where genuine contradictions occur between the rival philosophies at the basis of a specific ideological conflict. In this case, two procedures are possible, the one purely logical, the other involving an appeal from the philosophy of culture to the philosophy of nature.

The logical procedure is reasonably obvious. The physical sciences are confronted often with similar situations. For example, the Michelson-Morley experiment in 1885 verified a proposition which contradicted certain assumptions of the mechanics of Newton and the electromagnetic theory of Maxwell, Larmor and Lorentz. Einstein resolved this contradiction by passing to a new set of assumptions which provided deductively, without contradiction, for the validity of the Michelson-Morley experiment and the valid portion of the traditional Newtonian and Maxwellian theories. There is no reason why this same procedure should not be applied to the contradictory philosophies underlying conflicting ideologies. One should seek for a single set of assumptions, replacing the two conflicting sets of philosophical premises, which will have the merit of giving the valid consequences of each of the conflicting sets without contradiction. Not until we cease taking the validity for everybody of our own pet ideology for granted and proceed to give similar respect to rival ideologies, and then resolve the conflict between the underlying philosophies in the manner indicated, will there be any constructive move toward the removal of the ideological causes of world conflict.

There is also a second and even more effective procedure. Its appropriateness will be made evident by the following considerations. Resort to this procedure is necessary whenever the question of the validity of any specific ideology arises. Some ideologies should not be reconciled with others, but should be condemned. What is the criterion for deciding between an expanded toleration or the condemnation of a rival ideology? It is this criterion which our second procedure can specify for us.

Having traced the economic, political, religious, aesthetic and other humanistic doctrines of a given cultural ideology back to the underlying philosophy which defines its unity in several different cases, to arrive at several different conflicting philosophies, one can hardly escape asking what gave the people in question their confidence in this particular philosophy. A prevalent supposition is that one's own culture arrived at its ideology by scientific means, whereas rival cultures are governed by a dogmatic obscurantism. The investigations noted above indicate, however, that this is not the case. In fact, it can be said that unless one seeks out in the empirical knowledge of the founders of the philosophy of a given culture the empirical facts which led them to their particular philosophy, one will never understand the culture in question. More and more contemporary anthropologists are coming to this conclusion.

Furthermore, the founders of the philosophy of a given culture, in a large number of cases at least, took as the facts decisive in the formulation of their philosophy of culture facts from nature rather than from culture. It can be shown that this is true, even of the supposedly mystical culture of the Orient. It is certainly true of the ideology of medieval Roman Catholic culture. The religious doctrine of this culture was defined completely in terms of the metaphysics of Aristotle, and there is not a concept in Aristotle's metaphysics which does not occur in his physics. It is equally well known that the *Physics* was written before the *Metaphysics*. Thus the philosophy of natural science came first. This defined a metaphysics which was taken as a criterion of the good for the humanities. Similarly, the ideology of post-Kantian Germans, Hegelian Germans of the nineteenth century, and the Communistic Russians of the twentieth century rests upon one basic fact which is scientific in character; the fact, namely, that the pre-Kantian British empirical philosophy of Locke and Hume, which defines the philosophy of the culture of the traditional modern democracies, is incapable of providing meaning for the concepts of mathematics and of mathematical physics. In short, the Germans and Russians reject the ideology of the democratic cultures west of the Rhine because they believe that the political and economic ideologies of the latter cultures rest upon a philosophical theory which is incapable of accounting for mathematics or mathematical physics. They take it for granted that these two modern sciences entail a Kantian type of epistemology and philosophy of science, which in turn entails a Kantian and post-Kantian autonomous philosophy of the humanities, which with Fichte exhibited itself as grounded in the logic of dialectic.

All these considerations suggest that the philosophy of natural science to which the intellectual leaders of a given people are led by the empirical evidence available in their time is an exceedingly important criterion, although by no means the only criterion,[2] of the philosophy which defines the ideology of their culture. This suggestion makes it possible to use the philosophy of natural science called for by the latest advances of scientific knowledge as the criterion of the philosophical assumptions which, because of their greater adequacy for empirical evidence, are the most likely to possess the capacity to resolve the ideological conflicts of the traditional philosophies of culture. What this means, put more concretely, is that one's philosophy of the empirically verified for the natural man and nature becomes also one's philosophy of the good for the humane moral man in culture.

This has the consequence also of essentially relating the humanities and the normative theories of social science with the philosophy of natural science. Thus it happens that this final methodology for resolving the ideological issues of our world provides the clue also for the unification of the natural sciences, the social sciences and the humanities. Only when the primitive ideas and postulates of one's philosophy of the natural sciences are identical with the primitive ideas and postulates of one's philosophy of the normative social sciences and the humanities is the unity of the different phases of human experience and of culture made evident and realized.

It remains but to designate the two requirements of an adequate philosophy of the natural sciences. Such a philosophy must leave it to

[2] People arrive at philosophical conclusions for good, bad and indifferent reasons and by untrustworthy as well as trustworthy methods. All that is maintained here is that this is the procedure to be used if we are to have a philosophy of culture which may in truth be said to be valid for everybody.

the experts in natural science to determine what the verified theories are which are called for by the empirical data. Beginning with such theories when the natural scientists inform us of their verification, the philosopher of science proceeds by logical analysis, without the use of further hypotheses or speculation, to make articulate the ontological and the epistemological assumptions implicit in these theories. The ontological assumptions are given when the primitive entities and relations of the deductive theories in question are made evident. The epistemological assumptions are determined by analyzing the scientific method used in the verification of the theories in question to determine the specific character of the sources of the meanings of all the concepts involved and the specific relation between purely empirically given factors and theoretically designated factors in the method and theory in question.

Because of rival verified theories, such as relativity theory and quantum mechanics, the ontological portion of contemporary philosophy of natural science must remain in considerable part indeterminate. The epistemological portion can, however, be specified. This epistemological portion of the philosophy of contemporary science happens, by good fortune, to be sufficient to provide a criterion for resolving the ideological conflicts of our world.

It is the overlooking of the epistemological presuppositions exhibited in the verification of a given theory of natural science that *seems* to leave such a philosophy incapable of providing a philosophy of man as well as a philosophy of nature. Whenever the epistemological presuppositions of a given scientific theory as designated by the method by which the theory is verified are made evident, one finds oneself in one's philosophy of science not merely with a philosophical theory of nature as the object of scientific knowledge but also with an epistemological philosophical theory of the scientist in his status as the knower of the natural object.

It is because it asserts nothing more than is implicit in the verified scientific theory, both ontologically and epistemologically, that such a philosophy is automatically verified in the scientists' verification of the scientific theory in question. Since this scientific verification is of a character such that it gives the same verdict for one person as it gives for another, such a philosophy of science used as the philosophical theory which defines the idea of the good for culture provides a cultural ideology which because of the scientific roots of its verification must be said to be valid for everybody.

Our second procedure for resolving ideological conflicts rooted in rival philosophies which are not merely different but also incompatible now becomes clear. One identifies the philosophy which one uses to define the normative social theories of economics and politics and the humanistic doctrines of morality and religion with the philosophy of the natural man and nature at which one arrives by the mere logical analysis and articulation of the epistemological and ontological assumptions of the natural scientists' verified theories. This procedure has the merit of joining one's humanistic values and one's scientific knowledge and its instruments into a harmonious unity. One's scientific theory of man is not fighting one's humanistic conception. Also, by taking the latest verified theories in natural science as the subject matter of one's analysis, one gains a philosophy of culture with the most likely capacity to resolve the traditional philosophical differences underlying the ideological conflicts of our world. This is the case because the latest scientific theories have greater generality, accounting not merely for the empirical evidence leading to the traditional incompatible philosophies, but also for more recent empirical knowledge as well. At the same time one gains a philosophy of culture which, because it is verified by scientific methods giving the same results for one person that they give for another, may be said to be valid for all mankind.

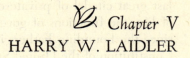
THE CHANGING FUNCTIONS OF THE MODERN STATE

In analyzing the changing functions of the modern state, the developments in the agricultural province of Saskatchewan and in other parts of Canada may be regarded as symptomatic of the changes now taking place in many nations of the world. The federal government of Canada, the provincial government of Saskatchewan, and the various municipalities of the Dominion have undertaken many functions which in former days were regarded as outside the scope of the political state. As a result of these developments, during my stay in Saskatchewan I found myself riding on the government-owned Canadian National Railroad, and in the new, attractive inter-city buses owned by the province; calling up my friends over the publicly owned telephones; hearing the latest news broadcast over the wires of the Dominion-owned radio corporation, CBC; catching a glimpse of the extensive forests and mineral lands owned by the province; eating and sleeping in Saskatchewan's most attractive hotel, run by the publicly owned railroad system; driving over the provincial highways; drinking of the water and reading by the electricity supplied by city governments; visiting the printing plant, the tannery, the shoe factory, the timber and fur marketing services, the woolen mill, the brick plant, the fish-filleting station, and the insurance company operated by the province; investigating the complete health services freely available to the old, the blind and other dependents; going the rounds of the schools, the colleges, the libraries, the museums, the parks and playgrounds conducted by local and provincial governments and listening to the plans of the provincial fathers for the still further expansion of state activities in behalf of the common man.

Even in the United States, regarded by the world as constituting the last great citadel of private enterprise and of the individualistic way of life, the functions of government have been constantly expanding since the Founding Fathers in 1787 appended their signatures to the Constitution of the United States.

In framing the Constitution these outstanding American statesmen of their day made little mention of any government functions outside of those connected with the protection of life and property within the country and the defense of the nation against potential enemies from abroad.

THE STATE AS DEFENDER AGAINST ENEMIES WITHIN AND WITHOUT

As a means of performing these functions, the federal government has through the years built up its armed forces on land, on the sea, in the air. It has developed extensive consular and military intelligence services with ramifications in every part of the globe. It has spent billions of dollars on the improvement of rivers and harbors, on the digging of canals, on the building and subsidizing of merchant marine, on the construction of highways and, during a major war, has mobilized a large proportion of the nation's material and human resources in a win-the-war program.

City, state and federal governments have likewise utilized police, constabulary and military forces and the vast and complicated court machinery for the protection of property and person at home. They have also exercised the manifold powers of the state to prevent the infringement of civil liberties and to preserve the vital freedoms of speech, press, assembly and religion guaranteed by the Bill of Rights.

THE DISTRIBUTION OF MAIL

The Constitution of the United States specifically gave Congress power not only over the nation's defenses, but over post offices and post roads. The postal services were a function of the central government even under the Articles of Confederation. During the last century the post office has grown into a gigantic industry employing a third of a million people and handling in a recent year over sixteen billion dollars of business. The Post Office Department has served the public not only as the main distributor of mail but has gone extensively into the express, the savings bank and other services, steadily improving its methods of delivering written communications with the passing years. Next to providing protection to life and property, all modern governments have regarded the development of a regular, inexpensive mail service as one of the primary functions of the state.

TAXATION

Another function assigned by the Constitution to the Congress of the United States was that of laying and collecting taxes.

The state has possessed the tax-collecting power from time immemorial. For the most part this power has been utilized primarily for the purpose of securing enough revenue to run the government and pay off the public debt.

As the country developed, as great inequalities of wealth and income appeared, and as the need for federal revenues increased, students of taxation urged increasingly the imposition of those taxes which would diminish income inequalities—notably the progressive income and inheritance taxes. The income tax law passed in 1894 was declared unconstitutional, but, following a constitutional amendment, another such law was enacted in 1913 during the Woodrow Wilson administration. Since then the mild rates in the first law have been gradually increased, and their imposition today results in definite shifts in the levels of income and wealth.[1]

HELPING BUSINESS

Since the beginning of the Republic, the federal government has also regarded it as one of its important functions to regulate trade and commerce.

Many an American today holds the quite unfounded belief that our Constitution-makers were faithful followers of Adam Smith and the laissez-faire philosophy; that they were all of the opinion that "that government governs best that governs least"; that they were convinced

[1] Senator Henry Cabot Lodge, of Massachusetts, denounced the 1913 tax as a war on wealth. A Congressman described it as "a tax of abominations." The 1894 tax imposed a normal tax of 1 per cent on net personal incomes in excess of $4,000 for a married couple; an additional surtax amounting to 1 per cent on the parts of net income from $20,000 to $50,000; and, by degrees, an increase to a 6 per cent surtax on incomes from $500,000 to any amount. By 1923, the top rate for the income tax was up to 50 per cent for incomes of $5,000,000 or more. By 1940, it was up to 75 per cent for $5,000,000, and 62 per cent for $200,000 incomes. In 1944, it was 91 per cent for all incomes above $200,000.

that the businessman should be able to run his business as he saw fit without any state interference.

While the delegates to the Constitutional Convention were, in considerable part, followers of the classical school of economics, they felt that the government had a bigger function to perform in the economic sphere than that of preserving order or of acting as an umpire. They were living in communities which had been profoundly influenced during their colonial days by the mercantilist philosophy of the early settlers and had been accustomed for years to lay down detailed rules for industry and labor alike.[2]

They were likewise living in a time when great chaos was resulting from attempts of individual states to enact and enforce tariff laws. During the years 1780 to 1787, businessmen in Pennsylvania, Maryland, New York and other states induced their respective governments to pass tariff laws regulating the flow of trade to and from their borders. Tariff rates on goods from abroad varied from 5 to 100 per cent, and British goods were constantly being shifted from port to port as import duties were raised or lowered.[3] At the time of the adoption of the Constitution, the lack of uniformity in tariff rates had become intolerable, and an examination of the writings of the delegates to the Constitutional Convention, as Daniel Webster later declared, showed that the main reason why many favored the adoption of the Constitution was that it would give the general government the power to regulate commerce and trade.[4]

Alexander Hamilton was indeed of the strong conviction that the federal government should foster, protect and even initiate economic enterprises through bounties, subsidies, tariffs and legislation—a point of view, as Beard points out, which constitutes a "strict denial of the axiom that men, if let alone, will make the wisest and best use of their material opportunities and effect a just and beneficial distribution of wealth." [5]

[2] See Richard B. Morris, *Government and Labor in Early America.* New York: Columbia University Press, 1946.
[3] Walter W. Jennings, *A History of Economic Progress in the United States,* New York: Crowell, 1926, p. 156.
[4] Charles A. and William Beard, *The American Leviathan,* New York: The Macmillan Co., 1930, p. 449.
[5] *Ibid.*

THE STATE AS PROMOTER OF BUSINESS ENTERPRISE

Following the adoption of the Constitution, the various governments in the country soon began to demonstrate their belief that one of the important functions of the government was that of strengthening the business interests of the nation. Congress early passed a tariff law to aid American industry in its competition with manufacturers and traders in other lands and provided for subsidies and bounties for American shipping on the high seas.

Later, during the middle of the nineteenth century, federal, state and local governments poured their treasures into the laps of the railroad builders of the country. So generous were governmental units with the people's land and money that by 1872 it was conservatively estimated that the federal government had assigned to railway promoters an area of land "almost equal to the New England States, New York and Pennsylvania combined"; that nineteen states had voted some two hundred million dollars toward the building of railroads and that the municipalities had contributed further large amounts.[6]

The American state, throughout its history, furthermore, has considered it an important part of its responsibility to look after the interests of American businessmen abroad. In the performance of this function, it has utilized the tax machinery, the Department of Commerce, the diplomatic agents of the Department of State, and the nation's powerful military forces. "We have extensive interests in the Near East, especially in tobacco and petroleum," ran one report of the United States Bureau of Naval Intelligence in 1919. "Early in 1919 several American destroyers were ordered to Constantinople for duty in the Near East." "The Navy," the report continued, "not only assists our commercial firms to obtain business, but, when business opportunities present themselves, American firms are notified and given full information on the subject. . . . One destroyer is kept continually at Samson, Turkey, to look after the American tobacco interests at that port . . . The American tobacco companies represented there depend practically on the moral effect of having a man-of-war in port to have their tobacco released for shipment." [7]

[6] Beard, *op. cit.,* pp. 398-399.
[7] Quoted in Beard, *op. cit.,* p. 481.

This is but one of a host of instances in which American business interests in the East, in Latin America, and in other parts of the world received the active support of the armed forces of the United States. It is an oversimplification to paraphrase Marx's statement and to declare that during certain stages of our history the American state seemed to function as an executive committee for the American ruling class, but time and again American business has brought tremendous pressure on government to use its good services in behalf of business interests, while protesting as contrary to the American tradition legislation enacted for the benefit of other groups.

A BIG BROTHER TO AGRICULTURE

The various agencies of the state have likewise frequently functioned through the course of the nation's history as a Big Brother to agriculture. From 1862, the year of the famous Homestead Act, to 1890 the federal government granted to individuals and corporations under various acts of Congress almost all the arable land that had come into its possession. From the early part of the twentieth century, the government, through the Department of the Interior, has engaged in extensive irrigation operations and by the end of World War II was supervising an irrigation area of four million acres.

Through its agricultural research services, its forestry, its reclamation, its soil erosion, its land utilization and its animal husbandry activities; through its Rural Electrification Administration, its Farm Credit, Farm Security, Production and Marketing administrations and many other agencies, the federal government has likewise striven on many fronts to improve the lot of the agricultural population.

THE STATE'S RELATION TO LABOR

The modern state has more gradually extended its activities to the field of labor legislation. When the United States Constitution was adopted, there was no organized labor movement. In the early part of the nineteenth century, when labor began to form trade unions in Pennsylvania, New York and other states, the police and the courts in many instances were used to suppress their activities. In the famous Philadelphia Cordwainers' case of 1806, involving a number of shoemakers who combined to raise their wages, the judge declared that the mere joining together of workingmen to improve their lot constituted an illegal conspiracy punishable by fine or imprisonment.

"What is the case now before us?" he asked of the defendants. "A combination of workmen to raise their wages may be considered from a twofold point of view; one is to benefit themselves . . . the other is to injure those who do not join their society. The rule of law condemns both. If the rule be clear, we are bound to conform to it, even though we do not comprehend the principle upon which it is founded. Hawkins, the greatest authority on the criminal law, has laid it down that a combination to maintain one another, carrying a particular object, whether true or false, is criminal."

The jury, after hearing the charge of the recorder, declared, "We find the defendants guilty of a combination to raise their wages." [8]

During the ensuing years, various agencies of government were used to suppress strikes, picketing, boycotting and even the mere organization of labor. The courts issued sweeping injunctions. The cities, counties, states and the federal government sent out armed forces against striking workers and legislatures passed laws to suppress their activities.

Labor, however, despite the application of the old English law of conspiracy and the use against it of governmental agencies controlled by business interests, organized increasingly, as the modern industrial system developed, into trade and industrial unions. As labor organization became stronger, labor began to exert increasing pressure on the state to wipe out its antilabor laws, to cease its hostile practices; to protect the labor movement and to advance labor standards.

Various agencies of the state have responded to the appeals of labor and social reform groups with the enactment of labor legislation. In 1840 the federal government passed its first law for the limitation of the working day of federal employees. In 1842 the state of Massachusetts declared that children under 12 years of age should not be compelled to work more than 10 hours a day in manufacturing establishments.[9] From that decade until today innumerable laws have been passed with a view to protecting labor against unsafe, unsanitary and

[8] *Documentary History of American Industrial Society*, vol. 3, pp. 233-234; Laidler, Harry W., *Boycotts and the Labor Struggle*, New York: John Lane, 1914, p. 208.
[9] See John R. Commons and J. B. Andrews, *Principles of Labor Legislation*, New York: Harper & Brothers, 4th Rev. Ed., 1936, p. 95.

unhealthy working conditions, and of guaranteeing to labor the right to organize and carry on peaceful activities.

One of the most important of these prolabor measures was the National Labor Relations Act, passed in 1935, providing for the suppression of unfair labor practices and for the right of collective bargaining. "Without genuine collective bargaining," read the preamble to this act, "the flow of commerce would be impaired, business depressions would be aggravated and unemployment would increase." This language is a far cry from that employed by certain Philadelphia judges of the early nineteenth century, who regarded collective bargaining arrangements as an illegal conspiracy which it was the duty of government ruthlessly to suppress.

THE GOVERNMENT AND CONSUMER AND INVESTOR

Increasingly governments in the United States have expanded their functions so as to include the protection of *consumers* as well as producers against undue exploitation. It was largely as a measure for safeguarding the interests of consumers and small businessmen that the federal government in 1890 passed the Sherman Antitrust Act, with a view to breaking monopoly control over industry. It was in considerable part to safeguard the consumers of transportation services, of electric power, of gas, of telephone, telegraph, radio and other services that the Interstate Commerce Commission, the Federal Power Commission, the Federal Communications Commission, and the various state regulating bodies were established. It was largely to protect the comparatively helpless consumer from unfair business practices that the government established the Federal Trade Commission. And it was likewise with a view to looking after the consumers' welfare that the Pure Food and Drug Act and numerous state and city statutes providing for inspection of all sorts of commodities have been placed upon the statute books and that numerous public utilities, especially in the field of electric power, were transferred to community ownership.

As the years have advanced, furthermore, the state has regarded it increasingly as one of its functions to protect the *investor* from flagrant abuses in the sale of securities. The creation of the Securities and Exchange Commission in the early thirties following the wild speculation of the twenties had as its object the giving of a degree of protection to the buyer of stocks and bonds which he had formerly sadly lacked.

EDUCATION

Under pressure of the consumer, of the businessman, of labor, of the investor, of the military forces and of the general public, the functions of government in the United States have been greatly expanded along other lines. The state has increasingly regarded as one of its essential functions the education of its citizens, so that they may participate effectively in the political, economic and cultural life of the community.

To educate its citizens was not always considered a legitimate function of government. In the beginning of the Republic, local, state and federal governments felt under no obligation to provide universal, free education. There were private schools for which a tuition was charged —schools attended by the more prosperous of the population—and there were "pauper schools" free for the indigent. A beginning was made in the system of free education in Pennsylvania when the delegates to its Second Constitutional Convention in 1790 inserted a clause in the state constitution for the "establishment of schools throughout the State, in such a manner that the poor may be taught gratis." [10] No action, however, was taken to provide for these schools until 1802, and for years little attention was paid to the education of those who were not included in the category of the indigent poor and yet were unable to pay the fees charged by private educational institutions.

During the next generation, workers and educators carried on a vigorous campaign for free, compulsory public education for all. In 1830 the Working Men's party of Philadelphia, in its campaign for such an educational system, maintained that "all history corroborates the melancholy fact that, in proportion as the mass of the people becomes ignorant, misrule and anarchy ensue—their liberties are subverted, and tyrannic ambition has never failed to take advantage of their helpless condition." "Let the productive classes, then," it continued, "unite for the preservation of their free institutions, and, by procuring for all the children in the Commonwealth Republican Education, preserve our liberties from the dangers of foreign invasion or domestic infringement." [11]

[10] See Seba Eldridge and Associates, *Development of Collective Enterprise,* Kansas: University of Kansas, 1943, p. 119.
[11] "Circular to the Working Men of the City and County of Philadelphia," issued by

The arguments of these workingmen from William Penn's state on behalf of a free public school system were, however, bitterly attacked by many of the conservatives of the day. The *National Gazette* of Philadelphia declared that "to create or sustain seminaries for the tuition of all classes, to digest and regulate systems, to adjust and manage details, to render a multitude of schools *effective,* is beyond their [the people's] province and power. Education in general must be the work of the intelligence, need and enterprise of individuals and associations." [12] At the same time the *Gazette* saw in educational opportunities for all the decay of business and the increase of poverty for the masses. "The 'peasant,'" it declared, "must labor during those hours of the day which his wealthy neighbor can give to the abstract culture of the mind; otherwise the earth would not yield enough for the subsistence of all; the mechanic cannot abandon the operation of his trade for general studies; if he should, most of the convenience of life and objects of exchange would be wanting; languor, decay, poverty, discontent would soon be visible to all classes. No government, no statesman, no philanthropist, can furnish what is incompatible with the very organization and being of civil society." [13]

Four years later, in 1834, however, as a result of the pressure of various groups in the population, a free-school law was passed in Pennsylvania and, during the next few years, a sound foundation was laid for a broad system of public school education.

During the past generation, greater and greater attention has been paid to the educational needs of the people by city, state and national governments and today over nine-tenths of the nearly thirty million pupils in elementary and secondary schools are in public schools— schools supported by public taxation and under public control. The rapid expansion of educational facilities in the nation is indicated by the fact that, in the seventy-year period following 1870, while the population increased by a little more than threefold, the value of public school property multiplied fiftyfold. It goes without saying that a repetition of the arguments used in the early nineteenth century that the education of its citizens is outside the functions of the modern state

---

the Working Men's Republic Association of the Northern Liberties, in *Mechanics' Free Press,* April 17, 1830; see also Commons and Associates, *History of Labor in the United States,* New York: Macmillan Company, 1918, vol. 1, p. 227.

12 Commons and Associates, *op. cit.,* p. 229; *National Gazette,* July 12, 1830.
13 *National Gazette,* July 10, 1830.

would be laughed out of court by the average wayfaring man in present-day America.

CONSERVATION OF NATURAL RESOURCES

Another field to which the various governments in the United States have been giving increasing attention is the field of conservation of our resources.

In the early history of the country the undeveloped natural resources were so vast and the population so sparse that the people and the government thought only in terms of the rapid exploitation of these resources to develop the continent and, incidentally, to carve out great fortunes for those fortunate enough to hold title deed to them.

As the years passed, however, the precious heritage of trees and minerals in the United States was exploited with such waste and ruthlessness that thinking people became alarmed concerning the future of the nation. Forests, like mines, were exhausted and abandoned. Private companies almost totally ignored the relationship of the forest to the soil and water. They not only sacrificed the timber, but destroyed or seriously impaired the recreational, wildlife and watershed values. The localities surrounding the cut-down forests, after a temporary boom, often found themselves facing bankruptcy.

Something had to be done about the resources of America. In 1891 the United States Congress inserted a rider to the agricultural appropriations bill empowering the president to set aside as forest reserves any public domains which were chiefly valuable for lumber growing. By the passage of this rider, observed Robert Marshall, the government, for the first time in the history of the country, "seemed to have conceived that it was possible to do anything with its land aside from giving it away." [14]

During the next fifteen years, in obedience to the 1891 act, Presidents Harrison, Cleveland, McKinley and Roosevelt—especially Theodore Roosevelt—set aside about 150,000,000 acres of public domain land for federal forest reserves. Under Theodore Roosevelt a million and a half acres on twenty-nine rivers were likewise withdrawn as powersites. The government set aside as permanent national property five million acres of phosphate lands and withdrew the resources of

[14] Robert Marshall, *The Social Management of American Forests*, League for Industrial Democracy, 1930, p. 18.

Alaska from the old-fashioned type of exploitation. Since those days, the federal government and the individual states have embarked on large-scale conservation plans in the fields of forestry, soil conservation, irrigation and flood control.[15] Conservation of our resources had thus become an accepted function of our governmental agencies.

CONSERVATION OF HUMAN RESOURCES

The various units of government in the United States have likewise been assuming, to an ever-greater extent, the function of conserving the *human* as well as the *natural* resources of our land. For decades following the establishment of the Republic health was regarded as a private, rather than a public, concern. With the congregation of large numbers of men and women, boys and girls, in city areas, and the opening up of mills and factories employing hundreds of working people, the health of the individual came to depend increasingly on his living and working environment.

To preserve and improve the health of the people, the government was compelled to step in. In the middle of the nineteenth century a Sanitary Survey of Massachusetts was conducted. Following this survey, a State Board of Health in Massachusetts—the first in the country —was organized. Similar boards were later organized in other states and in cities throughout the land. These boards engaged in quarantine activities, supervised garbage removal, sewage disposal and the community supply of water. Later the cities created sanitation departments, departments of water supply, etc., to take over some of these functions. In recent years municipalities have joined with other governmental units in the suppression of contagious diseases and have been successful in wiping out epidemics of smallpox, typhoid fever and other contagious diseases which swept periodically over community after community in the United States.

Today the public is engaged in many health services. It supplies about half the hospital income, conducts large numbers of hospitals, clinics and medical centers, supports an extensive health nursing service and provides free medical treatment to large numbers in the lower income

---

[15] See Stuart Chase, *Rich Land, Poor Land,* New York: McGraw-Hill, 1936; Harry W. Laidler, *A Program for Modern America,* New York: Crowell, 1936, chap. X; Eldridge and Associates, *Development of Collective Enterprise,* chap. VIII.

groups. The research activities of the Public Health Services have made great contributions to the advance of medical science.

RECREATION

As an additional means of conserving the human resources of the nation and of advancing its physical and mental health, public agencies have of late undertaken the task of supplying extensive recreational facilities to the people of the country. The play facilities in city parks have grown by leaps and bounds. Today these parks constitute the major source of outdoor recreation for the urban population.[16] City playgrounds, athletic fields, golf courses, tennis courts, etc., have likewise developed rapidly since the beginning of the present century, while state and federal governments have spent large sums yearly on the development of state and national parks. The magnificent tracts of land in Yellowstone Park, Yosemite Valley and a score of other national parks furnish vacation grounds for many millions of Americans. The schools of the country are also providing for expanding recreational facilities in connection with their educational programs. To supply millions of its people with play and recreational opportunities is thus a further recognized and evolving function of the modern state as well as of private enterprise and of voluntary service organizations.

HOUSING

As an additional means of conserving the human resources of the nation and of making life more livable for the masses, American city, state and federal governments during the thirties of the present century also began to assume the function of building decent and attractive houses for the lower income groups. The first venture in the United States in public housing was undertaken during World War I when a Housing Division of the Shipping Board and a United States Housing Corporation were organized. In the next year or two these public agencies built sixteen thousand family units.

During the postwar period of the twenties, hundreds of thousands of housing units were constructed by private builders, but few for the lower income groups. One-third of the American people remained badly housed. In the depression years of the thirties, when the construction of

[16] President's Committee, *Recent Social Trends*, p. 915.

residential buildings came almost to a standstill, the housing situation for increasing millions became intolerable. A demand that the public provide homes for millions of slum dwellers and others unable to pay the rents charged by private enterprise arose from all parts of the country. This demand was augmented by the fact that public housing would supply jobs to large numbers of idle workers. The result was the setting up of a Housing Division in the Public Works Administration to promote a program of low-cost housing and to help in the clearance of the slums.

In 1937 a National Housing Act was passed, creating the United States Housing Authority. The Authority was authorized to issue bonds totaling eight hundred million dollars to be used for loans to local public housing authorities, and to make annual grants of further millions to such authorities with a view to bringing rents within the reach of the poorer groups in the population. To secure these loans and grants and begin the clearance of city slums, hundreds of municipal housing authorities sprang up all over the nation. From that time on, the building of dwelling units for the lower paid workers became an accepted function of city, state and federal government in the United States as for many years it had been in many other countries. The public housing activities of the state are likely to become of increasing importance as the years advance.

SOCIAL SECURITY

Still another function of the state that has been assuming ever-greater importance of late years in the United States has been the responsibility of freeing the people of the nation from the fear of want.

The full recognition of this function has been slow in coming. It is true that even in colonial days the community accepted the concept that if a person could not support himself, and was not able to obtain help from his relatives, from his friends or from private charity, it was within the purview of the local government to provide public relief. But "with this concept went the conviction that the poverty of the poor was their own fault, and that they must be severely dealt with to prevent them from living in idleness at the expense of the workers who paid taxes." [17] Little attention was given to the causes of poverty, and the inclination

[17] Lewis Meriam, *Relief and Social Security*, Washington, D. C.: Brookings Institution, 1946, p. 8.

was to lump together all those who were in those days dependent on the community for aid—the morally weak with the physically and mentally ill.

In the beginning of the nineteenth century, public bodies began to establish almshouses in which the poor received a minimum of relief. During the hard times following the War of 1812, the movement for such almshouses, supported by state and local governments, gained in momentum, though these houses were often found to be crowded indiscriminately with the aged, the blind, the crippled, the feeble-minded and sometimes with criminals.

When the depression of 1929 came, large masses of workers never before on relief found themselves facing the alternative of accepting public relief or facing starvation. Increased demands were heard on all sides for the development of an adequate system of relief on the part first of local and state governments and, when tax revenues from these governments precluded further relief, from the federal government.

The national government assisted the local units at first through Reconstruction Finance Corporation loans and grants; later through numerous other organizations which, in 1939, were merged into the Federal Works Agency.

Then, in 1935, after the passage of old-age pension and unemployment insurance acts in several states, came the passage of the Social Insurance Act, and the acknowledgment by the federal government that one of its important functions was the safeguarding of large portions of the unemployed and the old from hunger and starvation.

Since then the social insurance system in the United States as in other lands has become a vast public enterprise, and the state has developed into by far the most important entrepreneur in the field of insurance in the country.

MAXIMUM EMPLOYMENT

Many are urging that the state assume still another function, namely, that of providing work to all able and willing to work and unable to secure employment in private or co-operative enterprise. The United States did much to provide jobs to the idle during the depression of the thirties. The Works Progress Administration alone gave temporary work to approximately seven million eight hundred thousand persons in an attempt to reduce the army of unemployed. The Employment

Act of 1946 went a step further, declaring that "it is the continuing policy and responsibility of the Federal government to use all practicable means . . . to co-ordinate and utilize all its plans, functions and resources for the purpose of creating and maintaining, in a manner to promote free competitive enterprise and the general welfare, conditions under which there will be afforded useful employment opportunities; including self-employment, for those able, willing, and seeking to work and *to promote maximum employment, production and purchasing power.*"

This act does not go as far as many have urged, but it places upon the government a responsibility which few were ready to call upon it to assume in the early days of the present century.

PUBLIC OWNERSHIP

With a view to advancing the interests of consumer, producer and the general public, the state in America has likewise conceived it as its function to undertake many businesses which at one time were regarded wholly or largely in the domain of private enterprise.

City, state and national governments have gone extensively, as we have indicated, into the business of supplying pure, cheap water to city consumers, and today about three-fourths of the nearly thirteen thousand water plants in the United States are owned and operated by the public.[18]

City and federal governments have entered the field of electric power. By the forties nearly two thousand municipalities owned and managed their own distribution systems. Partly in connection with its work of improving the navigation of streams and of controlling floods, the federal government has also vigorously undertaken the task of generating electrical power in the Tennessee Valley, at Boulder Dam, in the Columbia Basin, and in other regions of the country. Many citizens have urged such developments as pacemakers to private monopoly undertakings, believing that their example may induce private electric power plants to reduce their rates to consumers. Others would have this industry, which in most parts of the country is now controlled by private monopolies, wholly owned and operated by governmental units.

[18] Seba Eldridge and Associates, *Development of Public Enterprise*, p. 84.

ATOMIC ENERGY—WAR COLLECTIVISM

In the field of the most recently developed source of power and energy —that of atomic energy—the United States government has committed itself to a policy of public ownership and operation on a national and, as soon as practicable, on an international scale.

The country during the war spent over two billion dollars on the development under federal auspices of nuclear energy. In 1946 Congress passed an act creating an Atomic Energy Commission and giving this commission, as an agency of the United States government, power over the production, ownership and use of fissionable material.[19] This is a material, declared the Senate Report on Atomic Energy, the private manufacture of which is attended by enormous destructive potentialities, by serious hazards to public health and safety. "The responsibility for minimizing these hazards is clearly a governmental function."[20]

The future production of fissionable material, further, is closely interrelated with the possibility of achieving effective and reciprocal international safeguards against the use of atomic weapons. "It is undesirable, therefore, to permit private development in an area which may soon be placed under government control by reason of international agreement. The production of fissionable material is technologically in its infancy; unforeseen and unforeseeable factors may play a great part in its development. To permit decontrol and decentralization of this activity, and weaken continuing government supervision, would be contrary to the principle of prudent stewardship demanded of the government by considerations of national welfare. The technology of fissionable material production teaches that even a slight interruption in the manufacturing process may occasion great loss and damage to the entire operation. Government control is more likely to assure continuity of operation than is private control. However," declares the report, "wherever possible the committee endeavors to reconcile government operation of the production of fissionable material with our traditional free-enterprise system."

Representatives of the United States before the Security Council

19 See Public Law 585—79th Congress, 2nd Session (S. 1717), "An Act for the Development and Control of Atomic Energy."
20 "Report Submitted by Senator McMahon." From the Special Committee on Atomic Energy to accompany S. 1717, pp. 14-15.

also announced the government's desire to have this great source of energy controlled by an International Atomic Energy Authority so that this new discovery may lead not to the annihilation of our present civilization but to the advancement of mankind.[21]

BANKING AND CREDIT

In most industrial countries the central banks have long been governmental institutions. At the inception of the United States, Congress was given power to coin money and to regulate its value, with a view to putting an end to the chaotic monetary system operating during the days of the Revolution and under the Articles of Confederation.

A central bank, the Bank of the United States, was soon organized, and the first and second United States banks functioned until 1836. The refusal of Congress to renew the charter of the second bank in the mid-eighteen-thirties delayed the movement for a permanent central banking system for decades, until, in fact, the Federal Reserve System was established (1913) following the widespread depression of 1907.

Under the Federal Reserve Act, a governing Federal Reserve Board was created, appointed by the president with large powers of regulation and supervision over the banking system, a board which has been frequently referred to as the "supreme court of finance." While the ownership of the stocks of the twelve regional Federal Reserve Banks included in the system is still in the hands of private member banks, many students of the subject maintain that practically the whole of the control of the vast powers of the Federal Reserve System "has passed into the hands of the Board of Governors at Washington." "The Federal Reserve System," declares one group of students, "may now be said to be a government institution. Control banking in the United States is in fact under state control, and socialization here is a *fait accompli*." [22]

The United States government, during recent years, has not confined itself to the field of central banking. It has entered in one way or another into almost every portion of the banking field. In January, 1932, while Herbert Hoover was still President, the Reconstruction Finance Corporation was created as one means of fighting the great depression. Formed specifically to provide emergency "financing facilities for finan-

[21] See "A Report on the International Control of Atomic Energy," Department of State, March 16, 1946.
[22] Robert F. Wallace, Joseph H. Taggart and Ross M. Robertson "Credit and Banking" in Seba Eldridge, *Development of Collective Enterprise*, p. 308.

cial institutions, to aid in financing agriculture, commerce and industry, and for other purposes," by the end of World War II its loans and other authorizations to public and private institutions amounted to the vast total of approximately forty billion dollars.

The government since the early thirties functioned in the financial field likewise through the Federal Deposit Insurance Corporation, which insured deposits in banks; through the Export-Import Bank of Washington, which, as its title suggests, aided in the financing of imports and exports; through the Farm Credit Administration, organized to provide a complete and co-ordinated credit system for agriculture; through the Commodity Credit Corporation, created to finance the carrying and orderly marketing of agricultural commodities; through the Federal Home Loan Bank Administration, formed to encourage home ownership and economical home financing; through the Public Works Administration, the United States Maritime Commission, the Postal Savings Banks, previously referred to, and through many other governmental agencies.

During the years, bank credit for building construction, for agricultural improvement, for public works, for the expansion of shipping, for industrial development, particularly in connection with war industries, etc., was withdrawn and "the battalions of government credit" were steadily moved up.[23]

PLANNING

In addition to the foregoing functions, government in the United States is giving increasing attention to the general function of planning; particularly to the art and practice of city and regional planning.

An outstanding example of regional planning is the Tennessee Valley Authority, referred to previously. This federal authority was created in 1933 to develop the Tennessee River system, which includes land and rivers within seven southern states, in the interest of navigation, flood control, inexpensive electricity and national defense.

In the course of the co-ordinated attack on the resource problems of the valley, the authority has lowered the price of electrical energy to residential and industrial consumers. It has created a commercially useful channel on hitherto unnavigable parts of the Tennessee River; eliminated the risk of floods to hundreds of thousands of valley dwellers;

[23] See Harry W. Laidler, *A Program for Modern America*, p. 269.

conserved forest land; educated farmers in better agricultural methods; restored the soil and stimulated new industries through its varied experiments with minerals and food products. It has likewise brought distinct recreational, educational and cultural gains to the people of the valley.[24]

During the past twenty years hundreds of city, state and regional planning boards have been organized in various parts of the country. Some are still in the blueprint stage; others have succeeded in bringing about some degree of co-ordination between various departments of government in a common attack on the problem of how to bring about specific improvements or develop more livable communities in general.[25]

INTERNATIONAL DEVELOPMENTS

Following World War II, the federal government has regarded it as its function increasingly to give its aid to various international organizations designed to bring peace and a greater amount of well-being to other nations of the world. On all fronts the functions of the state in the United States have been steadily expanding as the country developed from an agricultural to an industrial civilization, as the village grew into the giant metropolis, and as we progressed through the steam and electricity to the atomic age.

Founded at a time when the main functions of a state were largely those having to do with defense from foes abroad and at home and with the stimulation of trade and industry, the local and national governments of the United States have added to themselves functions having as their object the protection of the consumer, the investor, the farmer, the worker. They have given increasing attention to the educational, the health, the recreational and the housing needs of the people of the country. They have sought to guarantee the necessities of life to those unable to work and have begun to apply themselves to the task of supplying work to those willing and able to work but unable to obtain

---

[24] See Herman Finer, *The T.V.A.: Lessons for International Application.* Montreal, 1944; David E. Lilienthal, *T.V.A.; Democracy on the March* (New York: Harper & Brothers, 1944; Pocket Books, 1944).

[25] One of the great leaders in the concept of planning for a number of years was the National Planning Resources Board. This board conducted numerous investigations into the natural and human resources of the country, and did much to encourage organs of the state on all levels to plan with foresight and wisdom for a better America. In the early forties the opponents of planning in Washington and others whom the board offended were successful in cutting off appropriations for the maintenance of the board, thus causing its death.

employment in private enterprise. In endeavoring to perform these tasks, they have imposed many regulations on private enterprise and have undertaken to own and operate some important industries as public ventures.

The purely police state, the laissez-faire state, as far as the United States is concerned, has dissolved in history. The transition from the laissez-faire state has not taken place primarily because of pressure from large masses of people imbued with a revolutionary social philosophy, but because groups here and there had specific real or alleged grievances which they wished to remedy or certain positive ends which they wished to attain, and they made their voice heard in the legislative and administrative halls in Washington and in local communities.

Most legislators, in urging that the city, state or federal government enter this or that new field of activity, have been at pains to argue that the steps proposed by them would strengthen, not weaken, "the American system of free enterprise." The same has been true in other countries controlled by supporters of the private enterprise system. In most of these countries, the state performs similar functions to those undertaken by government units in the United States. In many cases such governments have gone into the business of protecting the old, the unemployed, the invalided and other dependents and have entered the fields of banking, housing, etc., far earlier than has the United States. In a majority of capitalist nations, furthermore, the railroads and most of the other public utilities have for years been owned and operated in whole or in part as public enterprises.

STATE FUNCTIONS AND DEMOCRATIC SOCIALISM

While democratic states committed to the maintenance of private enterprise have been constantly driven by the pressing needs of the day to expand old functions and develop new ones in the directions indicated in the foregoing pages, other democratic states committed to socialism have been expanding the functions of the state in response to a conscious social philosophy.

In 1945 the government of Great Britain was added to the list of governments dedicated to the attainment of a co-operative social order. In its campaign manifesto, "Let Us Face the Future," the British Labor party declared to the electorate what steps toward democratic socialism it planned to take if and when it became "His Majesty's government."

On assuming the reins of office, it would, according to the manifesto, introduce measures for the public ownership of the fuel and power industries, of inland transportation and of iron and steel. Its short-term program likewise included the public supervision of monopolies and cartels; the planning of agriculture; the stimulation of home building and of town and city planning; the empowering "of State and local authorities to acquire land for public purposes wherever the public interest requires it"; the strengthening of the community's educational and recreational functions; the creation of a National Health Service for all and adequate provision against rainy days throughout the life of all of Britain's inhabitants—as its advocates had it—"from the cradle to the grave."

This program, the Labor party made clear, would be only a beginning. If re-elected to office after a five-year period, the party would continue to push for a more far-flung program of social change.

"The Labour party [declared the election manifesto] is a socialist party, and proud of it. Its ultimate purpose at home is the establishment of the socialist commonwealth of Great Britain—free, democratic, efficient, progressive, public-spirited, its material resources organized in the service of the British people.

"But socialism [it added] cannot come overnight as the product of a week-end revolution. The members of the Labour party, like the British people, are practical-minded men and women. There are basic industries ripe and over-ripe for public ownership and management in the direct service of the nation. There are many smaller businesses rendering good service which can be left to go on with their useful work," and there are some big businesses not ripe for public ownership which nevertheless require "constructive supervision."

No sooner did the party begin its term of office than it started by stages to enact into legislation its program of public ownership and expanded social services.

In a number of other governments in the world—notably in the Scandinavian countries and in Australasia—labor and democratic socialist parties have enunciated similar programs and have implemented these programs to a greater or lesser extent. In other countries where coalition governments exist, governments which include at times liberal, socialist and communist parties—France, Czechoslovakia, Belgium and Austria are examples—many steps have thus far been taken toward the nationalization of key industries. In many other nations where the socialist parties are now powerful opposition bodies, similar developments might be anticipated in the not distant future.

Under democratic socialism, now in the making, the functions of the modern state would continue to change. The type of state which was at one time defined by Marxists as an instrument of a ruling class for the exploitation of an oppressed class would, in the nature of the case, be a thing of the past. The state as visualized by modern socialists would have as its end the well-being, not the exploitation, of the vast majority of the nation's inhabitants.

In its more purely political functions, if the program of modern socialists was carried out, the state would protect life and property, guarantee free, democratic elections and preserve and strengthen civil liberties. It would preserve freedom of speech, of press, of assembly, of religion, of political organization, of unrestricted movement of person from place to place.

Many critics of socialism have frequently expressed the fear that civil liberties may be seriously restricted in a democratic socialist state. But it is not without great significance that for decades the foremost advocates of a strict observance of the Bill of Rights have been the labor and social democratic forces in the various countries of the world. Nor is it without significance that among the most democratic countries of the world have been the Scandinavian countries and the commonwealths of Australasia, which have long possessed labor and socialistic governments. To democratic socialists, democracy is an integral part of socialism and its preservation and extension are imperative in humanity's struggle for the attainment of the good life for all.

Under socialism, in the economic field, it will be the function of the democratic state to assume control of a major part of the industrial life of the country, not for the sake of superimposing upon the community a particular type of economic system but with a view to extending democracy from the political to the economic sphere and providing full opportunity for the physical, mental and spiritual development of all the people.

Democratic socialists, as is known, do not urge public ownership of all industry, but of the key or principal industries. They advocate, hand in hand with public ownership, the development of consumer and producer co-operatives in spheres of activity in which co-operatives have shown a special ability to survive and grow. They likewise favor the retention of private ownership under public regulation, in some sectors of the economy, particularly in the handicraft industries and the newer lines of industrial effort. In agriculture, they believe that private and co-operative, rather than state, industry should prevail. A large field should also be set aside for co-operative and private enterprise in the field of intellectual services, particularly in the agencies directed to the formation of public opinion.

Socialists do not advocate that the central government control all publicly owned industry. They urge municipal, state and regional, as well as federal, ownership and insist that in all public industries there should be as much decentralization in the management and control of these industries as is consistent with social efficiency and human well-being. They favor the wide extension of the public corporation form of government ownership, with general policies decided by the community, but with the day-to-day operation left to these semiautonomous bodies, managed by experts and representative of consumers, workers, technicians and other groups of interest.

It would furthermore be the function of the state under socialism, as under an enlightened capitalist order, to guarantee the rights of workers to organize and to bargain collectively, as well as to participate in industrial management.

The state would regard it as its duty to provide for all its people adequate opportunities for education, for recreation, for remunerative employment; to protect from want the old, the sick, the injured and others incapable of earning their daily bread; and to see that no one in need lacks competent services for the restoration of health.

In the field of international endeavor, the socialistic state would consider it its duty to co-operate fully with other nations in the task of raising living standards, uprooting the causes of international conflict, perfecting the machinery for the preservation of peace, and laying the foundation for a genuine world federation.

Thus we witness in the world today the functions of the state operating under a capitalist order of society changing and expanding with a view to ameliorating or abolishing a series of economic and social evils which have accompanied the development of a system of private enterprise in the machine age. We witness likewise the modern state enlarging its previously assumed functions and taking on other activities as the ownership and control of industry are transferred from private, community and co-operative groups; as the capitalist order is transformed into a democratic socialist order.

Under both capitalism and socialism, as they exist within the framework of a democratic political structure, wide scope is given to individual thought and action. Under both social orders emphasis is laid on the development of the individual, not of the state, as the goal of social action. Democratic socialism differs from capitalism, however, in insisting that the finest development of human personality among large masses of the people may be expected in a society where the criterion of success is not "How much wealth has a man acquired?" but "How large a service has he rendered to society?"

THE COMMUNIST STATE

The third type of modern state that is today competing for man's attention and acceptance is that found in Soviet Russia and in many of Russia's satellites. In the days of the czar Russia was controlled by a dictatorship—a dictatorship of the Russian czar and an inner circle of followers. Today that vast country still maintains a dictatorship—a dictatorship of an inner circle of Communist leaders—and it is a function of the Soviet state to exert such control over the political, the economic and the cultural life of the nation as is deemed necessary to ensure the continuance and the strengthening of that dictatorship. In exercising this control, the Soviets still refuse to grant freedom of speech, of press, of assembly, of organization, despite the provisions of their Constitution of 1936.

It is likewise the Soviet state's function to control through a myriad of community organs almost all of the economic and social life of the people. In the fields of social insurance and in educational, recreational and health services, the activities of the state are extensive. Its most distinct contribution in the economic life has, however, been the series of Five-Year Plans, under which the state has sought to lay down a blueprint for the future development of the economic and cultural life of the people for several years in advance. Industrial achievements under these plans have, in many lines of effort, been of a quite remarkable nature. Many plans of the Soviet Union, however, have required a terrific speeding up of production and distribution, and in numerous instances an entire revolution in traditional methods of work. In innumerable cases the Soviet citizens have been either unable or unwilling to carry out the tasks assigned to them and, as a result, have found themselves subject to arrest, imprisonment, exile and even execution.

The state under the Soviet economy has likewise assumed a variety of functions in the international field. At the inception of the Soviet government, one of the functions undertaken by its leaders was that of stimulating, through the Communist International, the development of revolutionary situations in other countries. According to the point of view entertained by Lenin and his followers during and immediately after the Revolution, the Soviet government would hardly have been able to survive against the attacks by capitalist countries, unless Soviet regimes were established in other European countries. Following the failure during the twenties of strong revolutionary movements outside Russia, however, the Soviet state apparatus laid less emphasis on the stirring up of revolution abroad and more on the strengthening of the Communist system within the Russian frontiers and, later, on the creation of a powerful military establishment.

The results of the feverish and concentrated efforts expended on these tasks during the thirties were strikingly in evidence during the progress of World War II. During and after the war, the Soviet government took advantage of every opportunity to incorporate into the Soviet Union a number of border states and to dominate the governments of other nations of Eastern Europe and Asia. At the same time the government became a leading member of the United Nations and pledged itself to international co-operation.

The future shift in domestic and international functions of the Soviet state is being watched with increasing eagerness by the nations of the world. The question is constantly being raised as to whether, now that Russia has become a powerful industrial and military nation, it will remain totalitarian in spirit and in fact or whether it will incorporate the democratic features of the 1936 Constitution into the daily life of the nation. A further question is being asked: whether Russia will insist on continuing its career of territorial expansion and its policy of domination over the political and economic life of countries outside its territory or whether it will withdraw from imperialistic adventures and concentrate its main attention on rebuilding Russia and co-operating in the rebuilding of the world at large. On the answer to these questions may well depend the future of our civilization.

THE FASCIST STATE

Today the chief forces in world politics are, as has been indicated, the democratic capitalistic states, as typified by the United States; the democratic states committed to a socialistic society, among them Great Britain, Sweden and New Zealand; and the Russian Communist dictatorship.

Prior to World War II, the fascistic states were likewise potent factors in world politics. Today, with the demise of the nazi government of Hitler and the fascist state of Mussolini, fascism is a discredited and, for the time being at least, an impotent international force. Yet fascistic states, as in Spain, continue to exist, states in which governmental agencies are geared to the suppression of the essential civil rights enjoyed in democratic countries, and where the government regulates in minute detail—but does not own—the major part of the economic life of the nation.

Will these states continue to exist? Will capitalist states which have failed to solve serious evils under democratic forms turn fascist in the blind hope that a dictatorship will offer the way of escape, or will the present fascist regimes, under the impact of democratic pressures from within and without, gradually swing over into the column of the democracies and cause a revolutionary shift in the functions performed by present-day dictatorial regimes? The answer to this question will depend to no small extent on the ability of the democracies successfully to meet the social challenges of the day and to provide an opportunity for a secure and satisfying life for all their people.

Whether under democratic or dictatorial regimes, whether under capitalistic or socialistic governments, whether with a view to "making capitalism work" or of ushering in a co-operative society, the modern state is today assuming increasing functions in the sphere of economic and social services. The great task before the world today is to demand in principle and in action that the state be controlled democratically by the many, not the few; that adequate democratic techniques be applied to each and all its manifold activities; and that the goal of social action be not the glorification of the state or of a small ruling group, but the enrichment of the lives of all.

In the past the state was regarded as something alien to the people and anarchists and others advocated its abolition. Today it is universally recognized that the state performs functions absolutely essential to the existence of civilized communities in our highly complex industrial age. If properly controlled, it offers undreamed-of possibilities for social advance. If controlled, on the other hand, by power-seeking groups, it may involve the world in adventures whose end result is death.

The harnessing of the modern state to the chariot of peace, of freedom and of the abundant life thus presents to our emergent civilization its supreme challenge.

Chapter VI
ROBERT M. MacIVER

THE NEW SOCIAL STRATIFICATION

1   In two lands the dream of a classless society has been dynamic. In both of them it has been expressive of social change in the present and of tendencies toward changes to come. But in neither has the dream been fulfilled in the goal of classlessness. Where the dream has been cherished social stratification has been transformed but not abolished, for, as we shall see, social stratification, though forever changing, is in some sense as inherent in society as society is inherent in man.

North America, or rather an important section of it, has cherished that dream. It was the dream of the pioneer West and it gradually took form in the processes of nineteenth century expansion. It was the dream to which Walt Whitman gave literary expression. In it there was something more than the older claim that men were born free and equal, for this was a social dream whereas that was only a political one. It was not content with the old vision that men were equal before God, or in some intrinsic sense apart from the realities that denied their equality. When the poet Robert Burns insisted that "a man's a man for a' that" he was not denying the existence or the operation of social distinctions but merely disputing the judgment that was based on them. The myth of North America went much further than that. Not only did it reject the titles and gauds of rank but it counted all the actual distinctions between men, station and office and wealth and power, as of no consequence in determining the attitudes of man to man. It admitted no deference, still less subservience, based on these distinctions. It called no man master. The man who served addressed on equal terms the man who employed. Office had no protocol. There was no class of human being named gentleman or lady in contradistinction to another class that could not pretend to the name. Wealth made a difference in what man could control but it won no higher respect on that account. The man in power was in no sense the superior of the man below him. The man of low estate had access to the seats of power no less than the man possessed of worldly advantage. The road from log cabin to White House was wide open. This dynamic myth of the classless society did not seek to level differences in wealth or in station. The buoyancy of its sense of freedom merely surmounted them. In this way it had powerful effects but it did not lessen the social stratification it ignored. Its weakness was that it denied the effects of the things it ignored. Thus it suffered contraction and partial defeat.

This North American myth did not fail of full realization merely because some parts of the land rejected it, because in the South social stratification assumed the ultimate form of caste, because New England maintained its reverence for the ways of the fathers, for family and name and ancient residence, because New York and the other great cities developed a new hierarchy of wealth and power. It was not realized in its own homeland, for class is a protean thing and when one basis of social stratification is destroyed others are subtly being formed. This fact made the western dream at length seem artificial. There was not a village in the Middle West or in the Prairie Provinces of Canada that was not in effect divided into at least two classes, separated by a river of social distance, even if here and there a shaky bridge was thrown across it. The dream had some effect. It set up new standards and sustained new values. But because it underestimated the effects of the things it ignored it lost its former power.

Social stratification did exist in North America even though the politician proclaimed its absence and although the historian and the social philosopher wrote with bland unconsciousness of its presence. But where the new myth was cherished it was a different kind of stratification. It was unstable, without deep roots, without claims to permanence. The dream did not destroy social classes but it destroyed the magic of class. It could not destroy status but it destroyed the reverence attached to status. The older social stratifications made certain extrinsic differences between men the ground of *social* distinctions. They admitted the right of one man to deference and honor because he was born in a palace and to another man because he was born in a home where his great-grandparents also had been born. In the last resort this is a belief in magic, for it did not ask whether such men were intrinsically better or wiser or stronger than the man who was born in a cottage acquired by his father's toil. The new social stratification rejected this magic. We do not at this point presume that magic may not sometimes have social functions; we are merely recording a fact. It is magic to do reverence to the extrinsic differences between men, the differences that are inherently irrelevant to their worth or function. By denying these grounds of distinction the American dream was moving toward other grounds, grounds that were more relevant or at least more meaningful, and in doing so it was moving in a direction which, as we shall see, is being approached by modern society everywhere.

The dream lost its first strength because it contained confusions, because it denied not only the extrinsic but also some intrinsic differences between men, and because in doing so it wore an aspect of over-optimistic and somewhat shallow individualism. It need not on these counts be underestimated, for it changed the whole land, as the potent dreams of men always do. America became very different not only from other lands but also from its former self because this dream had power. From the Canadian arctic to the Rio Grande men lived a different life because of it. Their modes of thought, their modes of expression, their customs and their aspirations were changed. Like other potent dreams it was made possible by conspiring circumstances. It arose in North America because there were no ancestral estates to dominate the landscape, no ancient privileges hallowed by tradition; because there were new opportunities for the common man, new life chances, and a new mobility; and because the people who enjoyed these opportunities and chances were themselves mainly derived from the same class sector of the peoples from which they had migrated. With these things went a breakdown of the ancient myths of authority, the clash and erosion of imported traditions. The new dream came to fill the vacuum thus created.

The other land where the dream of classlessness has been cherished is Soviet Russia. This was a very different dream. It was more dramatic, more revolutionary, more positive. It did not emerge from a social situation already congenial to it, but as a revulsion from a social situation that was rapidly dissolving. Hence it came as a revelation, as a grand new dogmatic faith. It did not merely ignore or deny social stratification. It conceived instead the sweeping abolition of class differences between human beings everywhere. It saw in the stupendous revolution that it worked the first and greatest stage toward total classlessness. Here the classless society was not construed as simply a matter of men's attitudes toward their fellows. Of course they were all equally "comrades," but they were "comrades" not because they thought of themselves as such but because they had abolished the foundations of distinction. They had abolished capitalism. By ending the private ownership of the means of wealth they thought they had destroyed forever the foundations of class. This dream also came short of fulfillment. Capitalism was abolished, productive wealth was socialized. The comrades began the triumphant transition to the classless society, but they were not moving toward the goal they dreamed. They were rebuilding society, it is true, but they were also building a new social stratification. Nor was it wholly new. The distribution of power had always made important differences between men. A few always ruled and the many always were ruled. It was still so here except that power was now stripped of its old concomitants. Productive wealth might be socialized but in that sense power was not, and never could be, socialized. A new social hierarchy had taken the place of an old one. Now as before the fate of millions depended on the decision of a few. Now as before one man's smile or frown could make or unmake the fortunes of other men. The new hierarchy rose as steeply upward as any the world had ever known.

A man no longer controlled his fellows because he was born to wealth or had inherited a title, but men controlled their fellows just as much as before. Just as before there were many grades of power, each subject to the power above it. Just as before there were more honorific and less honorific occupations. The most honorific occupation was political office. Below the immediate holders of government office, in their respective grades, came the elaborate hierarchy of managerial and bureaucratic functionaries. There were also the favored ranks of the artists, writers, actors and musicians, who enjoyed governmental favor. Then there came the labor élite, the higher paid Stakhanovites. The tendency to stabilize these grades inevitably developed. Educational opportunity and the command over material means varied with position in the hierarchy. The prestige and influence of the parent affected, to some extent at least, the life chances of the children. The disparity of remuneration among the working classes, not very dissimilar in character from that which exists in a capitalist country, could not help having some effect upon the status of their respective families.

In spite of their ardent dreams neither North America nor Soviet

Russia attained the classless society. The reason why in both cases the dream was unfulfilled is a simple and ineluctable one. Social stratification is a function of social differentiation. Whatever distinguishes man from man, or rather group from group, carries with it the implication of class. Marx erred if he thought that one particular economic disparity was the sole condition of social class. This economic factor was indeed an important determinant of the particular type of class structure that existed throughout the Western world. But it was not the *sine qua non* of class. Some of the most powerful class systems in the world, such as the caste system of India, did not depend upon it. Even where this factor was powerful it was far from being all-powerful. The magic of birth and of inherited status also played a part. The economic factor was important because wealth was also power. But there are other sources of power independent of the possession of wealth. Moreover, if wealth is a source of power, power is also a source of wealth. Wealth in the last resort does not consist in the possession of specific titles to material things but in the ability to control, to exploit or to dispose of these things. He who commands men commands also wealth. He has service where other men serve. He rides where other men walk.

In North America the dream of a classless society weakened the older bonds of class. It was a liberating dream. It was also a trusting dream, for it believed that progress was inevitable. Because it believed too easily it suffered disillusionment. In Soviet Russia also the dream was one of liberation. But here it was a swift and universal liberation to be achieved not through the quiet processes of providentially directed change but through an infallible system of action clearly expounded from the first. This dream was charged with the highest dynamism. It brought one form of liberation in a manner beyond the dreams of any previous age. But it brought also a new form of servitude. Revolution does not abolish social stratification; it only changes it, for better or for worse. What is new in a changing society is primarily the character of the social stratification. What is also new is the changing basis of power.

2 Social differentiation is not to be identified with social stratification. Social stratification expresses the relative values socially attached to different attributes or functions. But it is impossible to conceive different attributes or functions apart from some kind of social evaluation. The things men regard and the

things they strive after are attained in different degrees. Those who possess coveted social objectives in a higher degree tend to associate among themselves and in this respect at least to dissociate themselves from those who possess them in a lower degree. Social stratification may be sharply defined or it may be blurred at the margins. It may be rigid or it may be flexible. The stratifications characteristic of the older oligarchical society were sharply defined and rather rigid. The modern social stratifications tend to be less clearly demarcated. The lines are not so divisive. There is much more crossing back and forth. There is much more mobility up and down the scale. Class becomes competitive instead of being corporate. This feature is characteristic of democracy and it is peculiarly well developed in the democracy of North America.

It is generally true that when the magical element, to use an expression taken from Max Weber, is dominant, where a high social valuation is set on birth or tradition or long established privilege, there social stratification is sharp and hard. Where, on the other hand, the functional element dominates, there the class system is more complex, less abrupt and less determinate. These latter characteristics are congenial to a changeful society. Social stratification is responsive to every change in social evaluation, and social evaluation in turn reflects the processes of cultural, economic and technological change.

Social evaluation confers status on persons and on groups. Status is probably as old as society, as old as man. Man is not "born equal" in this sense. The very fact that he is born a helpless infant implies the status of the parents and the elders; that he is born of woman, the status of the male who provides the protection and sustenance of the home in the childbearing period. Inequalities of many kinds exist and develop everywhere; with them tend to go differences of status. Apart from social organization altogether, the differences of aptitude, skill, intelligence, cunning and prowess between individuals create relative position and the respect, deference or submission that goes with it.

But status, though it exists everywhere, does not always breed social class. Among very simple and small peoples it may remain personalized and free, without specific social establishment. Landtman in his work on the origins of social classes cites the case of the Kiwai Papuans, who have no system of social precedence, no ranks, no attributions of status other than those which arise directly from personal achievement or from the relation of the sexes and that of the younger to the older generation. It is noteworthy that this absence of social class is accompanied by an equality of property rights and a rudimentary stage of the division of labor. The only property that matters is property in land, and this is communally assigned to the various families or households on a basis of equality. Various anthropological investigations have shown that the absence of a class system is associated with the simplest forms of community life. In the more complex society the greater division of labor brings the distinction between the more honorific and the less esteemed occupations. The disparity of possession and of power leads to the formation of an élite, a hierarchy of rank. Inheritance confirms and hardens the difference between classes. The élite become the ruling class and entrench their own position against the less privileged orders. Thus government becomes wedded to a class system.

Once the alliance between government and class was established, all the forces of social control were enlisted on the side of the class system. Poets sang the virtues of the great and noble: they were the leaders of the people, the guardians of its ways, its champions in war, its authorities in peace, the patrons of the arts, the dispensers of bounty. The priest in his own way co-operated in mythmaking with the poet. The ranks of society were divinely ordained, and it was the will of God that the lower ranks should, as the English Book of Common Prayer expressed it, "order themselves lowly and reverently to all their betters." The upper classes took over all the mechanisms of control and all the avenues to opportunity and to power.

Thus all the great states of history came into being as class-bound states, organized and controlled by a ruling class. They became great by expansion, usually by the conquest of neighboring communities. The wars of expansion still further strengthened the position of the ruling class, giving them new agencies of power, new resources, new experience in government, and increasing the subordination of the subject classes under the more rigorous conditions imposed by the necessities of war and by the sharper differentiation of class from class. When that situation was reached the phenomenon of class struggle emerged and began to play its historical role. It is an exaggeration to say, with Marx and Engels, that the history of states has been in effect nothing more than the history of class struggle, that class struggle is "the immediate driving force in history," but it is the exaggeration of an important truth. The causes of social change are complex and hard to unravel and it is very beguiling to find some one "key cause," as Marx and Engels were prone to do. But the upthrust of subordinate or exploited classes was a continuously active factor in the unending transformations of the state. This is as true for the states of antiquity as for those of medieval or of modern times. Take, for example, the history of the Greek city-state. Aristotle remarked that every Greek city was two cities, one of the rich and one of the poor, and that "poverty was the parent of revolution." Thucydides gave an immortal picture of the devastation and corruption created in the Greek cities everywhere by the strife of groups claiming respectively to stand for a more democratic or a more aristocratic system.

Athens furnishes a crucial case. In the latter part of the seventh century B.C., Athens had a purely oligarchical regime, and "the poorer classes, men, women and children, were the serfs of the rich." There followed a series of convulsions, marked by the attempt of Draco to quell the revolt of the lower classes of the Athenian population—the slaves remained always outside the range of effective resistance; by the measures of Solon to diminish the severity of the exactions imposed by the richer on the poorer classes; and at length by the democratic constitution of Cleisthenes, which later was made even more democratic by Pericles. These successive reforms failed to achieve any lasting order, for the Greek city-states were torn by wars between one another no less than by the internal divisions of their people. Domestic order was always rendered unstable and precarious by this other source of conflict until Greece became finally the prey of more united powers. Thus its history illustrates both the truth and the exaggeration of the Marx-Engels thesis.

Rome offers an equally good illustration. The early history of the republic was checkered by the uprisings of the plebeians against the ruling families, during which, on more than one occasion, the plebeians undertook the unusual expedient of "seceding" from the city altogether. After the secession of 494 B.C. the plebeians were allotted magistrates of their own, the ten tribunes of the people each of whom possessed a veto power. From then on the struggle took a new character. The patricians combined with the wealthier plebeians to share the spoils of the growing empire, while below them lay a restless populace, including veterans of Rome's triumphant wars, husbandmen whose farms had been bought up to make estates for the wealthy, and new slaves from conquered territories. The culminating period of the strife began when in 131 B.C. a tribune of the people, Tiberius Gracchus, brought forward a law for the repossession of public lands and their redistribution in small holdings. Tiberius was killed, and presently his brother Caius took his place, proposing a whole series of more drastic measures. In the turbulent period that followed Caius Gracchus was killed, but from then on there was no stability in the Roman Republic. Successive contenders for power enlisted on their side the popular elements and became dictators. The line led from Marius and Sulla to Pompey and Julius Caesar, until Caesar's heir, Augustus, put an end to the republic and inaugurated the empire.

We need not continue the story. The struggle of classes was at times overborne by other kinds of struggle, wars between overlords and peoples, wars between powerholders and contenders for their power, wars of religion; and at times by the entrenched dominance of strong hierarchies, armed with all the apparatus of social control, over illiterate and dispossessed populations. But the grounds of class struggle persisted. The magic of the class myth could not wholly bind the minds of those who suffered exploitation and privation, "the oppressor's wrong, the proud man's contumely" and "the insolence of office." Sometimes there were doomed uprisings of the powerless against the powerful, revolts of slaves, insurrections of despoiled peasants. But these were intimations of a time when power would be less unevenly distributed between social classes.

Every social advance tended to hasten that time, every increase of knowledge, every gain in technology, every development of the division of labor. These advances brought men from the fields to the towns, where they founded guilds and asserted the rights of the new middle class. Their leaders learned how to govern. Their thinkers began to break the taboos of orthodoxy. Marsilio of Padua and others insisted that the common interest of all citizens, not the advantage of the powerful, was the end of government. Men began to appeal again from the law of the state to the law of nature or the law of God, thus undermining the myth of class authority. So began a new long struggle of social classes which leads all the way to the present world. In England, by the middle of the seventeenth century, there were already heard the voices of the Levelers and of the True Levelers (or Diggers), denying the right of class government. "I do not find anything," said William

Rainborough in the Putney Debates, "in the Law of God, that a lord shall choose twenty burgesses, and a gentleman but two, or a poor man shall choose none: I find no such thing in the Law of Nature, nor in the Law of Nations." The language is different but the spirit is that of the most modern advocates of democracy.

The relation of government to class has passed through many phases. As class lines became mobile and fluctuating, the whole structure of power underwent a continuous process of change. Status became partially dissociated from authority. In broad retrospect we can distinguish two main types of class structure. Under one type the status that determines class is rigidly defined, so that class approximates to or is identical with caste. Nearly all men live and die within the class into which they are born, and there is a social bar against intermarriage under any circumstances, since this would destroy the lines of authority, privilege and power. The status men enjoy is a *corporate* status, scarcely touched by the ambitions or achievements, the successes or the failures, of individual men. The population is divided into integral groups, each having its set limit of opportunity, vocation and social role, each regarded by or at least treated by the others as though it was a different species of the human genus. Under the other type status is variable and social classes are not demarcated by clear-cut lines. The individual is not identified, and exclusively assessed, by his social rank. The same culture is accessible to all and a rise in status, attainable in various ways, is one of the chief objectives of individuals, families and groups. Thus class, from being corporate, becomes in the main *competitive*. Government may then be in the hands of a class which lacks high status or of an ideological group (as under modern dictatorship), which may cut across prior differences of status, or it may be in the democratic sense a popular government, composed of elements drawn from various social classes.

3   Since social differentiation is highly variant, the class system is different everywhere, not only as between countries but also as between different areas of the same country. It has a different pattern in a North Dakota village from that exhibited in a Midwestern town. It is quite different in a Vermont community from that characteristic in a community of like size in Virginia. Sometimes, particularly in the smaller towns, the main stratification is

a simple dichotomy, often signalized by residence, as between those who live on the opposite sides of the tracks or between those who live on the hill and those who inhabit the valley. Sometimes the main stratification divides the community into three groups, as in a New England small town I have in mind, where there is an élite of the old residents and the upper professional class, a middle group of small traders and craftsmen, and a lower social level of millworkers and so forth. Not infrequently in such towns each class has a particular church associated with it. There are also other organizations that have a class significance. There are clubs exclusive to the élite and there are usually particular organizations representative of the middle groups. It is such facts as these that justify us in applying the term "social stratification." Although there may be a general air of pervading fellowship to the outside view, the more intimate relationships are roughly within the boundaries of each group. Within these boundaries the men plan together and play together and the women pay calls on one another. Within these boundaries, for the most part, they marry and give in marriage.

Over these local differences there is superimposed the broader pattern of national differences. We miss any appreciation of the character of social classes unless we recognize that it is both an intricate and an extremely variable phenomenon. Each country has its own distinctive type. It is idle dogmatism to conceive social stratification as the simple corollary of economic power or economic exploitation, to imagine that it arose solely out of a particular economic relationship, or that it exists only so long as that relationship endures. Within the great range of what is called capitalistic society there are many marked differences in the character of social classes. It is very different in the United States or in Canada from what it is in England. The English class configuration is very different from the French one. The French is very different from the German. We cannot know the pattern of any one country by studying that of another. Each has its distinctive system. If sometimes they approach fairly closely, often they show most significant divergences.

Beyond these differences, again, there spreads a still broader and perhaps somewhat more elusive pattern. Every civilization, every age, tends to create an appropriate over-all scheme of social stratification. The great secular trends of every age influence the modes of relationship between men and groups. With these trends go changes in the underlying schemes of valuation. As these changes are taken up into the living culture of the people they have their impact on class forms and class relationships. We shall now turn briefly to consider some of these broader changes in the scheme of values and in the conditions of social valuation and shall then proceed to consider how they have been and are at work to create a new social stratification.

4   If there is a new form of social stratification characteristic of the age in which we live or taking shape within it for the time ahead, it is because our age is itself subjected to social forces and cultural influences that differentiate it from the past. Thus our social valuations have undergone and are undergoing change. The direction of some of the major trends of our society is already clearly indicated, particularly in the economic and technological areas. Others are more obscure and more ambivalent. Some of these processes have already been operative over several generations; others are only slowly unfolding themselves.

Most manifest are certain economic and technological trends. These have a specific impact not only on the nature of wealth, on its organization and distribution, but also on the nature and the distribution of power. It is becoming difficult for us to realize that only a few generations separate us from the time when land was still the most prized and overwhelmingly dominant form of possession. With the growing competition of other forms of wealth went the decay of feudalism. Thus began the dissolution of class rigidities, a process greatly advanced by the later developments of capitalism. When land was the main form of wealth—land, that is, regarded simply as the storehouse of products, matured by nature and merely gathered or harvested by man—the essential division of mankind was that of the landed proprietor and the landless worker. This relationship was a relatively fixed one. Land in a feudal sense was the static, the one permanent good. It was not produced by the will of man. It could not be multiplied. It was inherited as a right or won as the prize of power. Authority went with it, authority as undisputed and as absolute as the right of possession. The landless man could rarely pass the barrier between him and the landowner. The lines of social demarcation were hard and fast.

Against this system the growth of industrial capital—as distinct from mere financial capital—began to assert its power. The new wealth, which unlike the old had the secret of reproduction, came into being through the enterprise and under the control of the middle classes, not of the landed classes; hence it had no relation to prior status. It was not associated with authority. Being itself a fluctuating and unstable, though mightily extensible thing, it was not inherently such as to command the reverence that went with a title to land. He who owned land owned what God had given. He owned part of the indestructible firmament of things. He had the authority that belongs to the eternal. But though industrial wealth carried no intrinsic authority, though the mode of acquisition was despised by the landowner, it was indubitable wealth and it could buy the landed poor and in the end the landed rich. Thus its status increased and it began to shake the seats of ancient power.

The new industrial wealth did much more than merely compete with and in the end dominate the old wealth in land. There were inherent in the economics and technology of industry forces which in various other ways brought profound changes in the relationships of men. For our purpose here we shall single out one of these. From the beginning of the industrial revolution *function*, in the first instance economic function, began to gain social significance. The function of landowning, being in itself static, was relatively passive, receptive and differentiated. The main office associated with it, that of social and political control, was derivative, not inherent. By contrast the function of industrial production was directly and continuously active. It was forever disposing, changing and establishing the relationships of men and groups. It operated through a network of interdependence. From any one focus it ramified to all the earth. It was not, like the function of the landowner, walled within the bounds of a self-sufficient estate. It created a whole series of contingent and intermediate functions. It made a society vastly more diversified than it was before. Gradually it brought a distinction between the owners of the new apparatus of wealth and those who organized or controlled it. Just as function became more complex, so did power.

There is a trend to consistency in the various changing components of a changing civilization. Each one operates to confirm and to sustain the rest. It would be one-sided to attribute the transformation solely or even mainly to technological and economic processes. These processes were themselves responsive to less overt changes. They fostered the cultural changes that in turn stimulated their own development. Social attitudes, religious doctrines, scientific perceptions, all the modes of thought and of belief, as they radiated from the centers of influence, also were undergoing congenial change. The whole complex of the new scheme of things was conspiring toward a characteristic social stratification. Before the industrial revolution certain profound political changes had already been responsive to new conceptions of authority. With the industrial revolution, or series of revolutions, these new tendencies were greatly enhanced. The middle classes were the bearers of the new order, and they carried through, first in England and then in other lands, an assault on the old establishment of power and therewith on the ancient entrenchments of caste. The nobility ceased to be set off as a race apart from the commoners. The men of means entered the portals once so jealously guarded. The nobleman found it expedient, and profitable, to join hands with the industrialist, and often to marry his daughter. Social mobility was everywhere on the increase. It penetrated line after line. The middle classes in turn found that the forces of which they were the beneficiaries were far from being exhausted at that stage. The hitherto powerless also learned to organize. Labor unions discovered the secret of modern power, the secret of function.

In our space we can give only a synoptic and simplified picture of the great transformation, so as to dwell rather more upon its effects on the system of class.

It is necessary, however, to stress the cultural concomitance of the new economic order. In the first place, the cultural gulf that had previously existed between social strata was gradually narrowed until the line of demarcation became blurred or wholly obliterated. Under the older oligarchical regime the culture of the gentry and the culture of the folk were far apart, save for such indoctrination of the latter as was congenial to the former. The different classes thought different thoughts and practiced different mores. Each had its own manner of speech just as each had its own garb. Since their life chances were totally different, there was a total difference in their outlook on life. The ruling classes had their own system of education; the lowborn acquired, apart from the localized traditions and customs of the folk, only the relatively unspecialized arts of earning a living. The vast mass of men were illiterate, as hopelessly cut off from knowledge as from power. In the industrialized countries of the world all that has been changed. The greater realm of human culture has been opened to the rank and file. The printing press and universal schooling and a thousand agencies of communication have broken down the barriers. Except where extreme poverty still prohibits it, the acquisition of culture has become selective, open to high and to low alike according to their fitness to receive it.

Under these conditions a sentiment alien to the class spirit and therefore scarcely known to the older world, that of nationality, has grown powerful. Nationality equalizes man. All alike, rich and poor, high and low, possess it in equal measure. It cannot be possessed in degree. Class, on the other hand, is based on inequality and on a sense of superiority which demands a corresponding inferiority on the other side. Class is exclusive, essentially hierarchical. So long as class was dominant nationality could not prevail. As the pretensions of class were challenged, the sentiment of nationality came in to assert the greater solidarity. It was not until the end of the eighteenth century that this new sentiment found its opportunity.

All other social values were at the same time in process of transformation, and not least among them the values of religion. In the old order religion was the strong buttress of authority, except in those instances where authority itself dared to challenge religion. Otherwise religion tended to give to mundane authority a supermundane sanction of the most impressive kind. It conferred on authority the aegis of eternity. The foundations of social order were divinely ordained. The religious hierarchy was prone to look on social change as dangerous. Those who rebelled against the social order were presumptuously resisting the dictates of an all-wise providence. On the whole, dogmatic religion tended to freeze the *status quo*. As it was expressed in one of the hymns sung in Anglican churches:

> The rich man in his castle,
> The poor man at the gate,
> God made them, high and lowly,
> And ordered their estate.

Even in our world today it is notable that systems of authoritarianism seek to confer a kind of religious sanction on their doctrines, seek to establish the sacrosanctness of their absolute power, although these modern equivalents are not nearly so enduring as the ancient faiths.

In broad terms this kind of religion has lost its hold on modern peoples. The character of religion itself has been undergoing a subtle and complex change. What has been most obviously challenged is the projection by the old faiths of a tradition of authority over the secular destinies of men. It may be that religion as a principle claiming ethical authority, as a guide of personal behavior, has not undergone much obvious change. It is hard in any event to trace, sometimes even to see, the influence of religion on the everyday behavior of men. But certainly the hierarchical principle of religion, as it bears on the stratification of men in society, has suffered eclipse.

Bereft of these cultural supports, the authority of man over man has lost its ancient anchorage. Authority is no longer viewed as predetermined, as given in the eternal order of things. Authority of some kind there must always be, but the new authority must find some other refuge than the ancient sanctity. There were now only two grounds on one or the other of which authority could sustain itself. The alternatives were either to find a new sanctity, no longer transcendental but immanent, in the social objectives proclaimed by government or else to make authority something that does not depend on the ruler at all but only on his relation to the ruled.

The choice between these two alternatives will be decisive and has already become crucial. The first is the way of dictatorship, alike in its reactionary forms and in the Marxist form. If we could afford to look at the choice *sub specie aeternitatis* we might regard this refuge of authority as merely a transitional one. For in the long run, and in the endless clashes between the new myth and the hard experience of reality, any sanctity not confirmed by a suprasocial sanction is not likely to endure. But that reflection cannot bring much comfort to those who may have to live through a new age of tyranny and who, besides, cannot possibly predict the manner in which such an age will channel the further processes of society.

The other alternative is the way of democracy. Its future will depend on the degree to which it can make its own new kind of authority secure, as the events of recent history have so amply shown. For it must be admitted that authority was an easier concept under the order of ancient sanctity. Then it was static, providentially assigned, inherited, guarded from above. Now it must be guarded from below. Now it is relative, with a relativity that belongs to our age. But this is another question not here to be considered.

5   It is not difficult to see how all these forces of change first loosened and then dislodged the magical attributes of class, the assumptions of social superiority and inferiority implicit in the ancient myths and rites of authority. But it is not enough to say that function has been substituted for magic as the new basis for social stratification. We still have to answer the question: What makes one function socially more honorific or more potent than another so that the lines of social intercourse are thus determined? Nor can we answer our question simply by scrutinizing the intrinsic attributes of one function as compared with another. A philosopher from Mars might reason that the functions which demanded the most rare capacities or regulated the more important or the most difficult tasks would be those which conveyed the highest social status. A materialist philosopher might conclude that the functions commanding the highest market value would win the greatest social esteem or power. Both would miss the mark.

Modern civilization involves a vast network of strategic controls over a highly complicated mechanism of interdependent functions. In some societies these strategic controls are unicentered. In other words, they are politically manipulated. The most complete embodiment of the unicentered principle is exhibited in Soviet Russia, where the political omnicompetence has wholly absorbed the economic function. There are also various approximations to this order in fascist types of states where the economic controls have been largely subordinated to politically conceived ends. In a much simpler fashion another approximation is found in such a country as Mexico, where since the antifeudal revolution the politicos somewhat freely manipulate the economic processes of the country. In these very diverse instances the division of classes becomes wholly or in large measure the simple one between the ruling class, with its inner clique and its outer cohorts, and the class of the ruled. The traditional social classes, relying on tradition, inheritance, birth, sanctity or other magical properties, have in these countries fought generally a losing battle against the new political hierarchy. They tend to disappear as coherent classes. They are either liquidated or else they somehow merge into the new order of things. It is noteworthy that the new political hierarchy in these countries is not determined by prior status. The Georgian peasant or the Austrian semi-skilled worker or the Italian journalist or the Latin-American adventurer, may become the apex of the new pyramid.

A quite different picture is presented by those areas which maintain some kind of socio-capitalist system, including a considerable majority of the greater industrialized countries. Here the restratification of society is much more complex. Here there is some kind of moving adjustment between the still-expanding domain of government and the increasingly centralized systems of corporate enterprise, financial and industrial. Here too the function of control has in great measure severed itself from traditional limitations, from the older determinants of status. The divorce is by no means complete, since a minor type of traditionalism develops within the new order. Wealth to no inconsiderable extent tends to confer higher function, particularly with respect to the economic controls. The executive is increasingly likely to be the son of an executive. But since there are practical tests that must be met to hold the more exacting jobs, there are important limitations to this tendency. As for the political bureaucracy, a different test must here sooner or later be met: the capacity of its heads to make the effective kind of competitive public appeal. Hence the new stratification remains mobile. It cannot harden to anything like the rigidity of the older stratification.

In a broad sense we may perhaps think of this transformation as the "managerial revolution." But we must then include in the category of managers the upper political leaders, the party manipulators, and various other kinds of "social engineers." We must include, for example, the heads of the great labor organizations. The relative domain of one type of leadership or another, or of one group or another, fluctuates. The socio-capitalist order, unlike the socialist or the fascist order, is multicentered. There is much stress and strain between rival controls. The spheres of control are differentiated but by no means separated. While the political control always claims over-all authority, that is only the formal aspect. What the voice of that authority proclaims depends on the changing relations of various economic and politico-economic forces. Moreover, the source of power is often disguised. The great cartel runs a secret imperium of its own. The consortium of finance pursues its particular ends through devices the outsider cannot fathom.

The organizations of industry on every level muster power against power, control against competing or opposing control. The bureaucracy of government is subject to the coalitions and the conflicts of these various interests, while at the same time it struggles to maintain its hold on office against ever-renewed insurgent political movements. Everywhere, however, it is the control function, the larger organizing function, that according to its scale holds or seeks the primacy in modern society, creates the relations of subordination and superordination, and thus presides over the stratification of the modern world.

This statement may somewhat oversimplify the complex and ever-changing fact. There are other determinants, but they are subsidiary. The ancient magic of class is not wholly dissipated. There are foci of reaction or resistance. There are also forces inherent in the creative culture which exercise great influence on social standards and convey status on their exponents or interpreters. It is indeed conceivable that with the permeation and diversification of new cultural movements, within a society that produces a sufficiency for the material needs of all and that is moving at the same time toward the abolition of abject poverty and economic insecurity and toward the conferment of new leisure on all the people, there will come a time when the increased ranks of the groups that minister to cultural needs will possess a much higher role than now exists within the social order. Here one important difference between the wholly socialized system and the socio-capitalist system is apparent. In the latter the creative culture is not subject to the direct control of the political function. It can follow its own spontaneity, subject no doubt to various economic pulls but nevertheless inherently free. Since in the last resort the stratification of society expresses the prevailing social valuations, this kind of system is much less restrained from following new paths and seeking new goals.

Before we conclude this brief survey we should point out the main factors that in the socio-capitalist order resist the processes of restratification we have sought to indicate. It may well be that the fate of this order itself, over against the new authoritarian order, will depend on the success with which it is able to overcome these resistances. For the factors to which we refer are not merely unreconciled with the spirit of the new order, the emergent civilization. They generate types of hostility within it which if unchecked may well cause its overthrow. We place first the struggle for dominance between nonfunctional groupings, in particular between the various ethnic groups that compose many of the larger societies. The extreme type is the dominance of group over group in the name of racial superiority. This type of dominance constitutes the most formidable obstacle to the trends of modern civilization. Not only does it assert the primacy of class distinctions that have no intrinsic relation to function but it turns the classes thus distinguished into castes, the ultimate form of dissociation between members of the same community. This, for example, is the bitterly inflexible class structure that comprises the white and the colored groups of the United States. Another form of the assertion of racial supremacy, that which distinguished the Nazi regime, identifies race with nation and in a different way resists the whole trend of modern civilization. In this form it devotes itself to military conquest and to that end superimposes another stratification altogether. The myth of race and that of ethnic superiority combine to create one of the last strongholds of traditionalism, one of the last defenses of the ancient magic. A further limiting factor on the processes of restratification is the existence of great military establishments. Not only do they also claim a functional superiority that is utterly irrelevant to all the functions characteristic of modern civilization but also, because they divert the energies of peoples toward the preparation for war, they blunt the efficacy of all other social tendencies. In the older times the ruling class was also a warrior class and the fusion confirmed the social distance between this class and the rest of the people. When modern civilization has not been threatened by war it has worked toward the reduction of the status of the military class, since the function of that class is alien to the whole functional scheme of things. Thus the decline of the influence of a warrior class on government has been an important development of modern society. Consequently the measure in which the new stratification will proceed to its complete evolution, whatever that may be, depends to no small extent on the chances that a more peaceful world will emerge out of the convulsion through which the whole world has been passing, perhaps in the last resort as a result of the appalling agency of annihilation that science delivered to the world at its close.

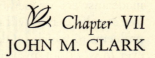
ECONOMIC PRINCIPLES OF THE NEW CIVILIZATION

THE BASIC IMPORTANCE OF "PROBLEMS"

Conventional economics is divided into principles and problems. Originally, in the case of Quesnay, Adam Smith, Malthus and Ricardo, the principles were themselves derived from, or closely bound up with, consideration of problems of economic policy which were live issues in a given historical setting. These principles were presented as general laws, thereby gaining a peculiar academic dignity; and in time their relation to their original practical setting grew dim or was forgotten.

In the future economic students may rightly insist that their study be focused around the major problems of their own time and place. They will also crave, consciously or unconsciously, some orienting framework of ideas which can give coherence to the whole picture, provided this framework is relevant. The traditional treatment of numerous special problems too often gave the student a multitude of trees and no forest: disconnected cases unrelated to common principles or common criteria of judgment. The present generation has two dominant sets of principles: those of war and peace, and the overshadowing domestic problem, which may be given decidedly comprehensive scope if it is defined as the problem of energizing the economy to a high level of employment of its resources, in the creation of products having the largest practicable amount of service value.

Consideration of problems in such a framework, by deeply inquiring minds, will lead to theoretical questions, just at it did with Ricardo. Therefore, pedants need not be unduly uneasy for fear theoretical problems will lose their importance. It is only the traditional ready-made answers—or methods of evading the need of an answer—that will lose standing. This will make trouble for the pedant who is faced with problems to which he does not know the answer. But if a new age is ever to work out answers to its urgent problems, pedants must necessarily suffer from obsolescence of their intellectual capital goods. By way of example, one of the most vitally important theoretical problems for the future is the problem of the approximate elasticity of demand for labor, both in particular industries and trades and in the market as a whole. Can or will employment be stimulated by reducing wage rates or curtailed by increasing them? Is the answer different for very low wage rates and for very high ones? Is it different for a self-contained economy and for one heavily dependent on exports? Popular thought implies quite contradictory theories on this point, while academic literature is almost barren.[1] To take another illustration, one way of approaching the theory of the market as an organizing force is to ask why we do not let it run a war on supply-and-demand principles, as we let it run ordinary peacetime affairs.

RELATION BETWEEN ECONOMICS AND POLITICAL SCIENCE

Using the method of projecting observed trends, one would easily reach the conclusion that politics will soon finish swallowing up economics. Economists used to have a comfortable amount of the feeling that politics proposes but something called "economic law" disposes. Nowadays they are forced to entertain an uncomfortable suspicion that economics proposes and politics disposes. Market forces operate on sufferance, and the "economic law" that decides what happens consists largely of things like the policies of the Triple-A and the decisions of the Federal Trade Commission, whatever qualms that may give some economists.

However, the economists' trade union has a keen eye for its jurisdictional vested interests, even if it has not been able to define their boundaries; and we may expect economists to go on dealing with wage

[1] Pigou's analysis in his *Theory of Unemployment* is impressive but can hardly be accepted as definitive. Pigou's basic assumption that wages equal short-run marginal productivity seems inescapably contrary to fact. On this basis most businesses would be "in the red" most of the time. Moreover, his treatment is obviously unteachable except to the limited fraternity of mathematical specialists. Keynes's defense of wage rigidity deals with general movements in one direction (downward). Thus it is not a rounded theory.

adjustments, including the politics of unions and the jurisprudence of wage boards. In return, they may look the other way when political scientists show an awareness of the economic grist that is ground in the political mills. Much economics may go into administrative proposals, to be killed by the economic forces in Congress. This an academic economist may regard as a political act of God, though the Washington administrator is not likely to look on it with the same detachment. In short, our politically determined economics and our economically oriented politics may maintain academic separation if they try hard enough.

More seriously, however, if education responds to the needs of the age, it seems fair to expect that the relation between economists and political scientists may become less and less that of custodians of insulated disciplines with academically defined boundaries, and more and more that of partners in attacking problems of policy which involve both economic and political or administrative aspects and cannot be finally settled from the standpoint of either discipline, taken by itself. We shall not get far if we stick to the attitude in which the economist regards his part of the job as done when he has decided what would be desirable from an economic standpoint alone, while the political scientist is busy studying the workings of political machinery which, from the economist's standpoint, seems to have a habit of grinding out measures of just the wrong sort. Or we shall not get far in resolving the political difficulties if the students of politics take refuge in the idea that these are rooted in the ills of the economic system and cannot be cured until the economic system is reformed, regardless of the fact that reform of the economic system requires political action.

Political proposals cannot be properly settled by merely asking, for example, whether they agree or conflict with our traditional conceptions of democracy. It is equally important to consider the economic job that the government has to do and to adjust our mechanisms so that they may be able to do the job while preserving the democratic principle, in some practicable form and in such degree as the people are currently capable of achieving.

For example, control of inflation and reduction of business fluctuations require a coherent economic policy rather than piecemeal measures; and some parts of this policy require prompt and flexible administrative action in response to changing conditions. This needs to be combined with democratic accountability; but if the machinery of accountability hamstrings administrative unity and flexibility, the government cannot do its job.

MARKET VALUES VS. INDEPENDENT APPRAISAL OF OBJECTIVES

It is impossible to look realistically at the problems we shall face in the future without realizing that traditional conceptions of economic objectives and standards of value are bound to be disturbed, and in some respects reversed. The overwhelming preoccupation of those who are looking forward to the domestic future adjustment is not goods as such, but jobs. The typical calculation starts with an objective of, let us say, fifty-seven million jobs in 1947 and goes on from there to the volume of production that must be created and disposed of if that many workers are to find employment. The answer takes the shape of a finding that we must produce a certain volume of real output—say, for example, the equivalent of a real national income of one hundred forty billion dollars in 1943 prices—not because we calculate that that is the amount of goods needed or the amount that will be demanded, but because that is what fifty-seven million workers could turn out. This flatly reverses the ordinary economic way of calculating whether a certain commodity, or a certain volume of commodities, is worth producing. It means that, regardless of conventional economic yardsticks, people have decided that a reasonably high level of employment is a paramount necessity, in its own right.

Of course, World War II has given us a great deal of experience with standards of value independent of those of the market. Materials and manpower were allocated among industries according to a rating of the essential or nonessential character of the products as aids to the war effort. Now, after the war, military considerations demand a hearing with respect to the location of certain industries, or the decision whether or not to maintain them in this country by protection or subsidy. In such decisions, the word of the General Staff should have weight. But we should not stop there, because the State Department, for example, may offer testimony to the effect that, while a protective policy might give us an industry of some slight military value, its reactions on other countries would be such as to endanger the willingness of those countries to co-operate—a willingness on which the chance of future peace depends.

Furthermore, we have been forced to treat our working manpower as a national asset, and the need of conserving this asset will not be forgotten completely. Therefore the policy of the "social minimum" is undoubtedly receiving a great impetus, both as a measure of conserving manpower and as a measure of reducing unemployment by maintaining diffused purchasing power. It could, however, be self-defeating in several ways. Liberal benefits might make some workers prefer unemployment. Idleness would outbid employment in marginal industries struggling to get on their feet after a depression, which can offer only part-time employment. This would be especially true in regions where the scale of money wages and living costs is low.

We have entered the postwar period, having demonstrated to ourselves that we possess vastly more productive power than we have ever before utilized. Approximately five years' accumulation of increased productive power has been suddenly released for civilian uses, making available at one stroke a standard of living considerably beyond the highest we have ever realized (even if it is substantially less than the most optimistic estimates). Many of the things we want are things individuals buy in markets, but many are not—improved services of public health and public recreation, for example. And many are things vitally needed by people who do not have the money to buy them. It seems inevitable that there should be a searching reconsideration of the question of what we want an economic system to do for us in the light of this vast increase in potentially available productive power and altered social and national objectives or requirements. I am not suggesting that final answers will be easily and quickly formulated. What I am suggesting is that economics will need to raise this question and that if it is answered by conventional formulas based solely on satisfying commercial dollar demand, it will not be facing the realities of the time.

One of the things that are wanted is something called "security," including greater security of employment as well as compensation if employment fails.

Back of this are still more basic questions. What are the economic roots of war and the means of protecting peace? What is there in our economic system that is worth fighting for? What basic attitudes are fundamental to a workable system? How do self-interest and loyalty combine in a workable system? What kind and degree of loyalty does a system need to command in order to be sound, and does our system meet that test? These questions go far beyond the ordinary conception of the mechanics of the system of business enterprise; but they are coming to be integral features of the mechanism, in the sense that unless they are answered passably well in practice the mechanism may break down.

The fact that we cannot give neat and definitive answers to all these questions does not excuse economists from raising them, and from recognizing that they are integral concerns of the system of business enterprise. The academic economist is equipped with traditional devices to excuse him from grappling with such questions, but it seems likely that these escapist devices will not hold against the pressures of our emergent civilization.

AN ECONOMICS OF RESPONSIBLE WORKING TOGETHER

Some are saying nowadays that we cannot solve these questions, because we do not have a "unified culture." Therefore the only basis on which a working economy can be organized is either the valuations of the market, with its well-known biases and blind spots, or the outcome of irresponsible political pressures, with their equally well-known tendencies toward sacrificing the good of the whole to the temporary or apparent selfish interests of organized groups. And these will lead us into chaos. With due respect to the exponents of this doctrine, I shall contend that this is a half-truth, both important and dangerous.

The fact that we have embarked on the adventure of liberty and democracy is sufficient reason why our culture can never be unified to the degree and in the sense that the European culture of the Middle Ages was a unit. Medieval culture was regimented—regimented by material penalties, in this world and the next, wielded by a church which had power over the dispensing of penalties in both worlds. The ideological machinery was in the custody of a minority of scholars, trained in prescientific mental disciplines. It would be a waste of time to discuss whether we should go back to that kind of unification. What we need to do today is to find a basis which will appeal to millions of people, with varied cultural origins and social backgrounds, who do not think like medieval schoolmen, who are free to disagree, but who disagree less in their codes of feeling and action than in the intellectual creeds or reasons, or rationalizations, with which they support these codes. We need to find a basis on which people of this kind may find enough sense of common interest and enough basic like-mindedness on which to build a workable world.

One idea is that scholars should find unity among themselves, and then pass the results down to what Veblen called the "underlying population." This appears to be going at it wrong end to, displaying an unconscious arrogance and failing to recognize that, whatever the modern American cultural unity may be, it will be democratic. The scholar can play an important part if he will accept the more modest role that the democratic principle assigns to him: that of interpreter and catalyzer; of leader in the democratic sense, but not dictator. The task is both greater and simpler than that of achieving unity among scholars. The closer all scholarly disciplines get to the underlying springs of action of the common man the nearer they will be to unity among themselves.

This attitude should come naturally to economists, who have traditionally worked in the spirit of Bacon's dictum: "While philosophers are disputing whether virtue or pleasure be the end of life, do you furnish yourself with the instruments of either." They have been content to let the market decide the uses to which economic goods should be put. I am suggesting that they make a declaration of partial independence from the market, which is a biased instrument for recording values, though an indispensable one. But I am not suggesting that they abandon the attitude of "decent respect" for the underlying standards of the people at large.

According to the dominant philosophy of the nineteenth century, not much unity was required in order to build a workable economic world. In theory, our system was one in which every individual looked out for his individual interests to the best of his ability, and he was prevented from doing serious harm by the natural checks of an individualistic system, centering mainly in universal competition. This gave the individual what was often wrongly construed as a license for irresponsible self-seeking. This spirit of irresponsible self-seeking persisted into a new age in which the competitive checks are vanishing or being progressively weakened, and in which group organization is taking the place of the competing individual. These group organizations have power, for good or for harm, which the simple individual did not possess. As a result, irresponsible self-seeking can no longer be trusted (if it ever could be) to build a scheme of voluntary working together. But this system of group organizations is animated to altogether too great an extent by a spirit and philosophy suited to the individualistic era of one hundred years ago. This "cultural lag" is one of the most threatening features of our whole situation.

A similar change has taken place in the matter of international trade policy. New and more powerful methods of interfering with the free course of trade have been developed, and irresponsible use of them can be increasingly destructive. Part of the change is in economic theory itself. Economists used to teach that mercantilist policies were self-defeating; but the newer economics has rehabilitated some mercantilist principles. For example, it is admitted that an underactivated economy may gain by establishing an export balance, by excluding imports which compete with home production, or in other ways. What is the conclusion: not to accept an inevitable trend toward autarchy, but rather to combat it in the face of the fact that single countries may gain by single acts of exclusive trade policy. If international trade is to work in the future, it must be because nations recognize the necessity of making it work to the sound advantage of all, and of making some beginning toward renouncing policies that would sacrifice a workable world system of intercourse for the sake of temporary national advantage.

If a spirit of irresponsible self-seeking remains dominant, then our choice is between regimentation and chaos. If we are to have liberty—which means fairly orderly working together by free men—it can only be on the basis of a spirit of teamwork and a recognized responsibility for working together. Among all the uncertainties of the future, this one principle stands out as one of the greatest certainties on which we can build. It will stand comparison in that respect with most of our so-called "economic laws," either traditional or modern. It does not deny self-interest or set up altruism as the rule of economic life; it merely recognizes the obligation of each self-interest to accommodate itself to the others, on some basis that will stand common scrutiny. Fairly crude levels of this virtue may suffice to keep the economic system from falling apart; but more advanced levels are necessary to build a satisfactory economy.

CONTENT OF ECONOMICS

The foregoing remarks may seem to have wandered far from the matters with which economics must necessarily be mainly concerned. I am contemplating, among other things, a growing tendency toward treating the problems of a civilization; not being confined within the boundaries of the traditional disciplines. But even within the sphere of economics, if the pressure of the future age works in the way suggested it will mean that we shall not be satisfied to start with the conventional treatment of human nature, which separates out certain supposed economic motives for purposes of specialized study. We shall need instead a more rounded treatment which gives us some basis for judgment as to what the needs of human nature are and the relative importance to the community as a whole of meeting these various needs in varying degrees. This needs to be maintained in the face of the inevitable and valuable tendency to make economics increasingly statistical.

Going on to matters more directly concerned with the economic mechanism, there appear to be three major areas of theoretical analysis, all of which need to be adequately dealt with. Traditional economics is concerned with one, the modern or Keynesian type of economics with another, while the third remains so inadequately treated that it is almost fair to call it a blind spot or a no man's land. The first is the study of the relative structure of prices and incomes, and its job of allocating resources between different uses. This is the main theme of the traditional economics, and it does not deal with the question of the total amount of economic activity, either "taking full employment for granted" or avoiding the problem in some other way. The second type of study is concerned with the flow of income and expenditure as a mechanism determining the total rate of economic activity. This relationship has been studied for a long time—since the time of the mercantilists, in fact. Numerous writers have contributed to it, on penalty of being treated as heretics. But it remained for a group including Lord Keynes, D. H. Robertson and others to give it a formulation and a sponsorship which secured its admittance into the recognized academic discipline, and in this country the Keynesian form appears to hold the field.

The current generation of young economists has in "Keynesianism" a new and powerful orthodoxy, which threatens to displace the old. This new orthodoxy is a tremendously important fact. Not since Ricardo has the stream of Anglo-Saxon academic theoretical economics been refreshed with such a major current so resembling Ricardianism in that it grows out of and interprets new and dominantly significant problems and conditions, and is embodied in a formula both academically satisfying and offering a basis for policy in action. It expresses elements long neglected because of the too-implicit acceptance of some of the formulas of Ricardian orthodoxy.

What is the moral? I suggest that it is that we give the newer orthodoxy its due as a great reorientation and a great contribution to our tools of thinking, without repeating the former error of too-implicit and uncritical acceptance. Orthodox Keynesianism, with orthodox imperfect-competition theory added, does not answer all questions or foreclose diverse major lines of inquiry. We shall need fresh jobs of constructive heresy, and this time they had better not wait for over a century to be developed and to gain acceptance.

The third area, or no man's land, contains the problems of the relation between the structure of relative prices and income, on the one hand, and the total amount of economic activity, on the other. The older economics dealt with putting resources where they would do the most good, assuming that they would be used somewhere. The newer economics deals with ways of maintaining a flow of income and expenditure in terms of money, but with no guaranty that faults in the pricing structure will not prevent the money flow from being realized in a flow of real production and real income. The connection between the two remains sketchy. There is much discussion of it, but there is not yet an adequately grounded body of theory establishing necessary relationships. And there is every likelihood that groups with monopolistic or partially monopolistic power would be able to pervert any program for ensuring full operation of industry via maintaining an adequate flow of dollar income and expenditure, by simply raising their own price, or wage, and corralling an increased amount of the dollar flow for themselves, at the expense of reduced physical output.

In general, the future seems likely to call for increased realism. The economist will have a duty to resist the hypnotic effect of abstract formulations with their tendency to anesthetize the critical faculties as to the degree of resemblance between the symbols and the reality they are supposed to represent—a reality which is usually rough-hewn and frequently paradoxical. Perhaps the main temptation in the near future will be to deal with lines on statistical charts and forget the reality that lies behind them. I hope that in the treatment of imperfect competition economists may make use of realistic cost curves, with special attention to the difference between short-run and long-run variation of cost. This would tend to a truer gauge of the relative importance of different departures from theoretical "perfection."

The widely held theory of competition is tending toward a condition in which there is, by definition, no such thing as competition in quality, per se, and in which there may soon be only two groups of cases: less-than-pure competition (classed as a form of monopoly) and approximately pure competition (which appears to mean a "sick industry"). If this describes industrial conditions fairly, something should be done about it: our policies should be changed. If the fault is partly or wholly with prevalent concepts of competition, something should be done about that, and the concepts overhauled.

I also have hopes that the stage may be set, as I have elsewhere suggested, for a revival of objectivity and impartiality, at least among economists not definitely attached to some special-interest group. This might occur by way of reaction from a condition which has swung rather far in the other direction. Whether this comes about or not, and whether or not economists live up to their responsibilities as teachers or formulators of teachable doctrine, there has never been a time when the profession bore a greater responsibility for realism, for objectivity, and for relevance to issues of policy which will be vital in the coming decades. These decades can easily be disastrous and are pretty certain to be stormy.

THE CHANGING KEYNOTE

The past fifty years—in fact, the last thirty of those fifty years—have witnessed a transition in the key and tempo of our life, thought and feeling, from an atmosphere of easy optimism, confident in assured progress within an established social framework, to a state of supreme emergency in which everything we stand for is fighting for its life, including the spirit of reasonable co-operative readjustment, on which evolutionary progress depends. The relation of government to the economic system has been revolutionized in an even shorter time—little more than a decade.

The dominant economic fact of the nineteenth century was the amazingly rapid development, by private enterprise, of the powers of production inherent in machinery and applied science, with the aid of a progressively growing equipment of industrial capital. In this process private enterprise displayed abundant, if irregular, energizing force. The task of government was to restrain abuses incidental to this exuberant expansion.

In contrast to this the dominant economic problem of the present generation arises from failures of the energizing forces generated within the system of private enterprise. Further growth of productive power is still an important matter, but the crucial limiting factor is the incapacity to activate the forces we already possess. These failures have taken the form of intermittent cyclical depressions, culminating in an unusually long and stubborn period of semistagnation, suggesting a new and more serious form of the disease. The past defense boom of World War II was an interlude, proceeding from an extraneous stimulus. In the long run, barring unforeseeable good fortune, this problem of stagnation will be the dominant preoccupation of government in relation to the economy. Political government, accustomed and adapted to restraining incidental abuses without fear of unduly weakening the main forces at work, now faces the very different task of strengthening those main forces. For this new function its adequacy remains to be determined.

It is also rapidly acquiring the task of umpiring the distribution of the nation's product between farmers, laborers and various business groups. Here again the government is grappling, not with incidental abuses, but with the central features of the economic system. These, then, are the keynotes of the relation of government to the "economy of the future."

Obviously, the possible outcomes are too numerous to be exhausted in a volume, let alone a chapter. I shall assume that we start out with the existing system, using measures the purpose of which is to make it work more steadily and nearer to capacity and which do not have the conscious and definite purpose of uprooting the system of (qualifiedly) private enterprise and replacing it with something basically different.

These measures will presumably include provision for those who cannot find a self-supporting place in the system, and also continued efforts to reform particular abuses.

Such a policy presents grave difficulties, and success will not come easily. In order to show how important it is that we do succeed, even though this requires us to readjust rights and sacrifice privileges, I will first consider the alternatives that face us in case of failure, with an eye to their consequences and their costs.

SOCIALISTIC POSSIBILITIES

One outcome which I shall spend no time considering is a chaotic breakdown, leading to a violent totalitarian revolution, replacing democracy with a communist or fascist dictatorship. Not that such an outcome is unthinkable, but there is no need of laboring to convince the reader that it would be the worst possible disaster from the standpoint of those values we all hold supremely important. But one cannot dismiss so lightly the possibility of a more orderly shift to a collectivistic system which would be, in its original conception and purpose, democratic. This might come as a result of a deliberate change of policy due to growing dissatisfaction with the results of the more limited methods. Or it might come as the result of a breakdown, necessitating the taking over of industry by the government or under its sponsorship. Or it might come from a mixture of reasons, including the possible sabotaging of less radical policies by those who do not want them to succeed.

Suppose for a moment that a socialistic system is to come by deliberate democratic decision and planning. It has been pointed out that such a far-reaching program requires a substantial term of years to show the kind of results that might afford a fair test of its success. The same would presumably be true of a decision by an established socialistic government to return to private enterprise. Private enterprise could not show its capabilities if it was exposed to a heavy probability of being resocialized in two years or in four. Therefore a new system of either sort needs more security of tenure than is possessed by an administration in a responsible popular government, which must bend its policies to the need of winning the next election in the face of terrific efforts on the part of the opposition.

This suggests that the decision to adopt an outright socialistic system is of the order of constitution-making. The issue should be opened and the decision made only at fairly long intervals, and a change should not be undertaken unless it has support assuring greater continuity than is afforded by a bare momentary majority. This issue is hardly suited to be the continuous football of current politics. This carries the further suggestion that if the administration wants this decision made, and the formal constitution is not sufficiently responsive, the change is likely to be made, and stable administrative tenure secured, by extra-constitutional methods. This would mean, in effect, a dictatorship.

This may not, however, be inevitable. Let us suppose that this hurdle is safely passed, and also the further hurdle of maintaining an adequate flow of investment and efficient operation in those sectors of industry which have not yet been socialized but know that they soon will be. We assume, then, that a socialistic system is set up, with central administrative authority resting in a government which, as far as political forms go, remains democratic. Will it have the conditions necessary for genuinely operative democracy?

One thing which is, I believe, too easily taken for granted in discussions of socialism is that, because the original conception of socialism is democratic, the working reality will embody democratic conditions and display democratic tendencies. This idea needs to be most searchingly scrutinized.

The basic condition of democracy is that the official is responsible to the citizens and that the citizens have ultimate control over the official. This requires that the official shall not meanwhile have the citizens at his mercy. They must have some kind of independent status which the official cannot destroy. In an economically simple democracy this is roughly secured by individual rights of property and contract, defined and protected by an independent judiciary. Where many citizens are hired employees, the key to the situation is the security of the job against interference for political reasons; and this hinges largely on the existence of many employers, themselves independent. Where every employing unit is an agency of the state, the power of administration to punish political opposition and criticism becomes a thing of sinister possibilities, even if hedged about by formal constitutional restraints. Too many subtle forms of pressure are available, and an administration needing continuous tenure (as already mentioned) will itself be under tremendous pressure to use these leverages. Workers who expect to own the government after the government has taken over industry should think further.

Again, the organs for the formation of public opinion must be independent; and this includes the publishing of newspapers, periodicals and books, the stage, the motion picture and the radio. It is hard to see how state control of these can be consistent with freedom of political criticism and opposition. Nor is it exactly easy to see, although it is not an impossible conception, how healthy private enterprise can be maintained in these fields if they stand alone as the only forms of private enterprise.

All in all, it seems likely that an established system of centralized administrative socialism would tend powerfully toward making us, not independent citizens of a truly democratic community, but subjects of a nonresponsible bureaucracy, without effective rights of criticism and opposition. (Unless, of course, the sanctity of individual conscience and autonomy in relation to the good of the entire community were preserved.) If bureaucracy is axiomatic, however, to such a system, we should think more than twice before adopting this solution to the dilemmas of private enterprise, and we should be prepared to do much and endure much in the search for some less stereotyped answer.

Another suggested form of socialism is one in which the economic units would themselves be democratic—let us say, a producers' co-operative for each industry—and these would be joined in a system which would be federative and not centralized. The difficulties here are different but no less real. They sum up in the proposition that this system would still exhibit most of the characteristics of the present system which are now responsible for its failures to operate steadily and close to full capacity.

Single industries now have the incentive to time their investment outlays in a fashion which makes them go by irregular spurts. They also have the incentive to limit output in order to maintain price at the expense of other industries. And the government is handicapped by having to act on these industrial interests from outside, and largely by indirect means. A system of federative socialism would still exhibit all these characteristics. In fact, the incentive to restrict output in order to maintain price might be stronger than before, since each industrial group would be acting, not simply to increase profits, but to "maintain an American standard of living" for its workers; and it might defend this aim more stubbornly than profits are now defended. On the other hand, such groups might have more respect and sympathy for one another's self-seeking ambitions if brought face to face with them, with the suspect claims of the separate profit-taker removed. But it is not safe to trust to this when the pinch comes.

So far as depression is rooted in excessive saving, due to an unprecedentedly large national income and aggravated by a too unequal distribution, a socialism of federated co-operatives would make some difference, in three main ways. It would presumably reduce the inequality of distribution and extend the application of the social security principle. Also, if the past history of producer co-operatives means anything, this system would probably mitigate the embarrassment of a national income larger than private enterprise has lately succeeded in using, by reducing the productiveness of industry. As to this last, it is doubtful whether we are exactly ready to welcome this type of remedy. And as to the other two, progress in these directions is almost certain to occur in any case.

Without developing the argument in detail, it seems probable that the federative type of socialism would either tend to be transformed into the centralized-administrative type, via a victory of the central government in its inevitable struggle with the constituent bodies, or it would bring us no nearer to solving our central problem. If this problem could be solved by the federative type of socialism, there is every reason to suppose that it could be solved by essentially similar means under a system developed out of the one we now have, since the elements of the problem and the means by which it would have to be attacked would be basically alike in the two cases.

THE ECONOMY: DETERMINANTS OF ITS RATE OF OPERATION

The actual approach to this problem will be nonrevolutionary. Since the defense boom of World War II has tapered off, government has been searching for substitute stimuli growing out of its past experience. This implies that it has an understanding of the specific causes of depression in the existing economy, or at least has theories about them, on which it is willing to act. These causes are many; but they may be brought to a focus in the fact that in our economy income arises from the spending of funds, for consumption or for capital outlays, and the income is renewed by being respent. If present income is not fully spent, future income will diminish. No one individual can make himself rich by merely spending; but his income depends on the spendings of others, and theirs depend in part on his spending. In our system the most sensitive and crucial sector in the flow of income and spending consists of capital outlays by private business enterprise. When these outlays exceed the income not otherwise spent, expansion or boom follows; when they fall short, there is depression.

But the flow of money incomes is not the whole story. The important thing is real incomes and the volume of real employment. An increase in the monetary flow may be wholly or partly absorbed in increased prices and wages, as wartime inflation should teach us, and may mean little or no real economic expansion. In respect to this feature of the system, one of its outstanding characteristics is the extent to which effective resistance to deflation of wages and prices is becoming general, even at the cost of idleness for labor and capital. Most commodities and services are felt to have a relatively inelastic demand, so that a reduction of price or wage will not increase the physical volume of sales, or employment, sufficiently to increase total money receipts, let alone net receipts above costs of production. Adjustment of supply to demand via the mechanism of prices is becoming increasingly sluggish and incomplete.

Among economists, also, there is doubt whether general upward and downward movements of prices and wages are effective instruments for countering pressures toward increasing or decreasing total demand. Sharp and general price declines involve business losses, and their net effect is likely to be a contraction of total real spending rather than an expansion. And wages, for example, have a twofold role, being at once the cost to industry of employing labor and an important source of income on which the sale of most classes of products depends. Given existing productivity, higher wage incomes mean also higher wage costs. Thus there must be some point beyond which increased wages would be an obstacle to full employment. But the nature of this point is obscure, and it is impossible to prove whether it has been reached or passed at any time by wages as a whole. Under these circumstances it is the line of least resistance to accept the "administered" character of wages and prices, and to focus on the flow of money incomes and spendings as the main determinant of real economic activity. This is natural but not sufficient. Government cannot well underwrite a continually increased monetary flow which is destined to be continually gobbled up by inflation of prices and wages, before it can lead to "full employment." This aspect of the problem will refuse to be permanently ignored.

THE GOVERNMENT: STRONG AND WEAK POINTS

The government that has this economy to deal with has both strong and weak points for the task. It is one in which economic pressure groups are more systematically organized and represented than ever before; and its habit of settling one question at a time affords wide opportunity for single groups, or groups of groups, to secure their ends and less opportunity for the integrating of all interests in a comprehensive settlement. The tendency is for government to give each interest a considerable measure of what it wants; and these wants are likely to be cast in the mold of promoting group interests at the expense of those of other groups, in those crucial matters in which conflicts of interest are an essential feature. This may be called the grab-bag conception of government, and until we can improve on it our civilization will remain in danger. It is most earnestly to be hoped that the compulsions of the present exigency will lead to some real advance in the art of composing pressure-group conflicts in the common interest.

Along with the growing influence of pressure groups is another growing influence of a different sort: that of the expert in the administrative departments. The pressure groups also have their experts, and the governmental experts are not all insulated from pressure-group interests; nevertheless, many are disinterested, and they introduce the element of objective analysis of economic problems. They have their biases, their theories and their intellectual vested interests. Some are visionary or lack balanced judgment and some are unduly dogmatic, and their technical vocabularies make it hard for the man in the street to find out what they are driving at and to check their reasoning. Hence arises some natural distrust. Nevertheless, the corps of experts includes a large amount of ability and good judgment; and its members are, to an unusual extent, incorruptibly devoted to the common interest as they see it. And it has at its command a growing equipment of statistical data and techniques, which are becoming more and more indispensable.

The logic of events is on the side of the expert; the job of governing a complex and technical economy cannot be done without his services. And to those who claim that this is not democratic, because the people cannot keep their attention constantly focused on all the things that all the different experts are doing or proposing, the answer is neither to get rid of the expert nor to surrender to him unconditionally, but to devote some real effort to devising ways of keeping track of him. The methods of democracy must be adjusted to the job that has to be done, and this job now requires the expert. The people have ultimate power over him if they can use it; but it is not always easy to find out where his policies tend (something which he himself may not fully know) before it is too late to alter the course. This is one of the dangers we run.

Another danger consists in the fact that policies aimed to stimulate industry will continue to be mixed with attempts to reform particular abuses, some of which attempts are likely to have restrictive rather than stimulative effects. And these will be divided among many agencies, each of which is zealous for its particular reforms and subject to a bias, all the more powerful for being unconscious, toward regarding these reforms as essential to the cure of depressions, whether the facts justify this view or not. Even more serious, perhaps, no one of these agencies is effectively responsible for the resulting aggregate of public action, or for its total impact on the system of private industry.

Another matter of some moment is the fact that we have departed from the older standards of legal justice, before which all men and all groups were equal, and are well embarked on a system of unequal legal obligations for members of different groups. This has been an inevitable result of the realization that formal legal equality does not produce substantial equality as between groups whose powers and positions are different. But it lays on us the obligation to work out the much more difficult standards of substantial equity and reciprocity appropriate to the differentiated type of jurisprudence; and with this task we have hardly made a beginning.

The government will some day face the necessity of a renewed attack on the problem of depression. The experience of the defense drive of World War II revealed the stubborn character of unemployment when it has been long continued, and the virtual impossibility of eliminating everything that is classed as unemployment in the statistical estimates. As to just what the lessons are there will continue to be disagreement; but the experience also revealed to us how much we could accomplish under an all-out stimulus. This will increase the intolerance with which the people will view the prospect of a return to the conditions that marked the decade of the thirties.

THE PROGRAM OF DEFICIT-SPENDING

The government's experience during this decade has left it with one outstanding remedy in which it has the greatest confidence: public spending of funds that would not otherwise be spent. Of this, the most "obvious and simple" form is deficit spending. The defense boom of the war fortified confidence in this remedy, despite lingering doubts on the part of some as to whether the mere fact of spending was the sole and sufficient factor and whether any other kind of spending could have been counted on to have fully equivalent effects. The defense experience also brought into the foreground one further problem in connection with this form of stimulus, since it resulted in inflationary pressures on prices and wages long before any level of general "full employment" had been reached.

Here, again, there will be disagreement as to what has been proved, since a peacetime drive may be better balanced in its demands on different parts of the economy; and the bottlenecks revealed by the defense drive for the most part have been broken sufficiently to meet the requirements of full production for normal civilian needs. Whether the state of world commerce will impose new bottlenecks, no one, of course, can say. If it does, the difficulty will at least be less urgent than that of the past defense bottlenecks, and there will be more time available for the development of substitutes.

The transition to a peace economy is inevitably cushioned by the accumulated "backlogs" of unsatisfied demands for consumers' durable goods and for the re-equipment of industrial plants for civilian production. For a time we shall continue to furnish food and other needed supplies to the war-shattered areas of the world.[2] And there are other "backlogs" in the shape of deferred rights to purchasing power, accumulated in the hands of those who will spend them when they get them.

If, by the time these temporary demands are filled, private industry

---

[2] This phase may be extended if arrangements can be worked out permitting some resumption of export of capital, under sounder conditions than prevailed in the improvident twenties.

has found fields of investment which will maintain full production, well and good. There will still be fluctuations, but the most threatening danger will have passed. However, it is not safe to rely on this, and I shall assume that a time will come when total spending will lag and the government will face a demand that it make a determined drive to maintain full production. Its first line of defense will be the planned reservoir of public works projects which it has been accumulating for just this occasion.

But these proposals for more spending will be made in the face of a public debt of stupendous proportions; and the prospect of further annual deficits will generate stubborn opposition to the resort to mere deficit spending as a continuing policy. People will ask insistently what is to be the end of it—a question the serious study of which has been strangely neglected by both advocates and opponents. I anticipate that, when such a study is made, the answers are likely to be disquieting. One may conjecture that, at about the time when drafts on the reserve of public works projects reach formidable proportions, the conclusion will be reached that deficit spending is a temporary palliative and that enduring success depends on other measures. At this point will begin a crisis which may not be the least vital of the various crises the coming generation will have to face. We shall then be grappling with the really hard problems of our economic order.

ELEMENTS OF A DIFFERENT PROGRAM

There may possibly be a wider reaction not merely against deficit spending, but against governmental controls in general. In that case, depression policy may for a time take on the character of encouraging private industry to do as well as it can, mainly by removal of restraints and furnishing relief for those it does not succeed in employing. Such a limited policy, however, can hardly be permanently satisfactory, and, even temporarily, it would not be likely to succeed in radically reducing the amount of public activity. In short, there is no chance of a real return to laissez faire, requiring as it would the impossible achievement of breaking up all economic interest groups and making the system genuinely individualistic. This would, in fact, require perhaps more drastic controls than any other course we might follow.

Moreover, this in itself would not solve our main economic problem. It might give us shorter depressions and quicker recoveries and be to that extent an improvement on the conditions of the past decade; but it is inevitable that more than this will be attempted. Some relaxation of controls, in some fields, may be consistent with a positive attack on depression, if we come to appreciate the importance of dealing effectively with the main problem and not cluttering up our efforts with attempts to do everything at once, as bureaucracy tends strongly to do. A move for the reduction of controls might usefully accomplish this much; it could hardly accomplish more.

We return, then, to a positive attack on depression by other means than deficit spending. It will not be necessary or possible for deficit spending to come to an end suddenly and completely. In fact, if the basic rate of interest should decline to little more than a nominal level, as might happen, it would be possible to go on increasing the public debt for some time without incurring an altogether prohibitive burden of debt charges; though the likelihood of rising interest rates would always be a threat, and there would be other complications. Deficit financing might still be sanctioned as a regulator of cyclical depressions, with intent to balance the deficits with surpluses in active times. It would not be necessary or practicable to require that the surpluses should precisely balance the deficits. I am assuming a really determined effort in this direction, but I am also assuming that the attempt to find other stimuli will be a fumbling affair, with errors of forecasting and failures of performance, and that there will be further demands for deficit spending to make good these lapses. For example, under certain possible plans government might undertake guaranties in order to induce private production and incur contingent liabilities which would materialize if the plan failed to produce the hoped-for effects. It seems fairly sure that the budget will not soon be neatly balanced over the term of each business cycle. We shall need all the latitude the situation is likely to afford us.

The basic requirement of the program I am now contemplating in considering the economic principles of the new civilization is the accomplishment of readjustment such that the income resulting from reasonably full production—a larger income than has ever been available to the people in the past—shall all be spent, either for capital outlays or for consumption, in order that it may continue to renew itself. Or, to focus on the critical point, savings must be utilized to pay for currently produced goods and services and utilized to a large extent privately. Assuming that such full use of savings does not occur automatically, the problem is one of increasing capital outlays or of decreasing free savings and increasing the proportion of private income which is spent for consumption, or both. Capital outlays may be private or public, but the success of the program hinges on the extent to which they are self-liquidating.

If the basic interest rate goes to extremely low levels, as already suggested, this will have some effect on the balance, though not a decisive effect. It cannot be expected to stimulate private capital outlays very greatly, though under favorable conditions it might have some stimulative effect. More important, probably, will be its effect on private savings, though most of this effect will be fairly long delayed. It will not prevent people from saving to provide for their future needs, and possibly saving about as much as they would at higher interest rates. But it will prevent most of them—those with moderate incomes—from receiving a liberal enough return to take care of their future needs out of interest alone. They will be forced to follow methods which involve ultimate consumption of their principal to a much larger extent than at present; for instance, by the purchase of terminable annuities. Ultimately, this will mean that while some are saving, others will be spending principal, and the total fund will not increase as fast as if only the interest was used. But the most troublesome effect of extremely low interest rates will be to make it less expensive for the saver to hold his savings idle. Owing to this, if to nothing else, low interest rates alone will not solve the problem.

One thing which will almost certainly happen is an increase in self-liquidating public investment. This could be made to include low-cost housing; and the term might also legitimately cover the public production of munitions which would otherwise have to be purchased. This kind of public investment will help the whole situation only if it is so handled that it does not displace or discourage an equal or larger amount of private investment. To this end it will be important to keep the public investments within a well-defined field, in order that private investment may know what it has to expect in the way of competition. The existence of an established field for public investment will afford increased opportunity for a cyclically flexible program of self-liquidating public construction. It might also make some net addition to the sum total of public and private investment, though not a decisively large amount.

Measures aimed to reduce the volume of savings, or of idle balances, will presumably also be tried. Present proposals of this sort are too numerous to consider here, and some of them are too complicated and ingenious to command confidence easily. Despite this, they will have to be carefully scrutinized and fairly considered. But one implication seems clear. To the extent that deliberate discouragements may be applied to private saving on the part of that great majority of the people who need all the protection of this sort which they can now get, such a policy carries with it an obligation to provide substitute safeguards for the future needs of these people. It is a question not simply of penalizing saving but of altering the mores and institutions by which the future needs of the people are provided for. Extension and modification of the principle of social security seem to be implied.

One of the simplest factors bearing on savings is the distribution of incomes. For this reason the striving toward more equal distribution, which has long figured as a mild humanitarian aspiration subject to more or less indefinite postponement, may come to be viewed as an immediate necessity for the continued full operation of industry. The simplest instrument for reducing inequality is heavy and steeply progressive taxation, definitely aimed to alter the distribution of free income, reducing those incomes from which substantial portions are saved and falling lightly on the smaller incomes most of which are spent for consumption. Something of this sort will happen almost automatically if the emergency rates of taxation on personal incomes are retained or only slightly reduced, while taxes bearing on consumption are repealed. Heavy taxation of incomes will be necessary to finance the large public expenditures which we shall certainly continue to make. But it will not do to dismiss this question with the easy assumption that we can tax that third or quarter of the population whose incomes are largest, and from whom most of the savings come, and that this will mean taxing only the well-to-do and the rich. We have learned that this upper third of incomes begins in the neighborhood of two thousand dollars per year, even under past conditions of defense-induced prosperity. We shall be taxing very modest incomes, and, if savings from these incomes are perforce reduced, the effect on the economic security of these people cannot be ignored.

But the major factor on which the success of this great adventure will hinge is the stimulation of private business investment, which now operates under the combined pressure of the hope of profit and the risk of loss. And the risk of loss must not be forgotten, though it is too often neglected by present-day reformers. The part played by the hope of large profits as a motive to business investment is already being substantially modified; but the prospect of loss, including loss of capital, still persists. A modest return will attract much investment today, if the risk of loss is not too great. But a mere reduction of the average rate of profit, leaving other things as they are, would probably increase the percentage of investments which suffer loss more than it would reduce the rate of earnings of the conspicuous, strong and profitable concerns. It is possible that one feature of a successful policy will need to be a reduction of the spread between high-cost and low-cost producers, in order to make possible a low average rate of profit without increasing the risk of loss. Only so can reduced rates of return be attractive to investors.

Some hold that the adventurous type of investment which pioneered ahead of assured demand and took command of our past spurts of prosperity is now largely a thing of the past. This is an ominous conclusion to accept, but there is much in present conditions to support it. Heavy business taxes will not help, since it is extremely difficult to construct such taxes without laying a discriminatory burden on the more venturesome forms of investment. This problem will need serious attention. So far as investment is of the more conservative type, which waits on fairly assured demand, it may be possible to stimulate it by actually reducing profits and correspondingly increasing wages, because this tends to increase the volume of consumer demand. In fact, this seems to be about the only method of stimulating investment contemplated by some present students. This is a desirable form of incentive to investment, as far as it works. But it will not take care of the whole situation, if private enterprise is to remain progressive. Among the most difficult of adjustments are those necessary to preserve a field for pioneering investment under conditions which seem certain to alter the traditional status of profits, if only through the increased bargaining power of labor.

No mention has been made of many important governmental activities in the field of international economic relations, as well as domestic matters such as education, personal rehabilitation, public health, soil conservation and numerous others. These I have taken for granted. I have also taken for granted that there will still be some unemployment, even of those not clearly unemployable, as well as dependence due to other causes, and that improved provision for these needs will be made. We may note that something of this sort would be necessary, even under a collectivist system, and that a drive for the fullest practicable operation of industry should not be judged to have failed because it does not eliminate everything that figures as unemployment in our statistics.

The ramifications of the problem are endless. For instance, as full employment is approached, this implies that employers will, and must, relax the standards of quality they have become accustomed to setting in the selection of employees. At least they cannot reject so large a percentage of applicants. This in turn implies that there will be a wider spread in efficiency between the best and the poorest workers employed. And this may imply the necessity for some modification of job requirements and adjustment of standard wage systems in the direction of greater differentiation. This, of course, may arouse opposition among labor unions. Thus wage workers, as well as high-salaried managers and receivers of profits, may have some unwelcome adjustments to make if this great common enterprise is to succeed.

CONCLUSION: WHAT IS NEEDED

In this chapter I have roughly sketched an economy in which the decisive factors governing the rate of operation are consciously influenced if not managed, this being the direction in which the forces of history appear to be driving us. Many of the single details in the program are not new; others are bound to come. The most distinctive novelty is the suggested attempt to gauge them quantitatively as units in an integrated and calculated program looking to adequate total spending. This means a large place for the administrative expert, with his batteries of statistics and his ingenious remedial devices. But he cannot do it alone, nor would it be entirely safe to let him try.

In fact, this enterprise probably cannot succeed unless it commands the active and loyal co-operation, not merely the passive tolerance, of all economic groups in the population. Pressure groups must learn intergroup teamwork; the grab bag must become a creative partnership; and this can happen only if the groups learn that the most important thing for each of them is to maintain a system of free collaboration and voluntary co-operation and to make it work.

There will be things involved which can best be done by private agencies; and the more active part they take in framing the whole policy the better. It is a too little recognized truth that labor unions and farm and industrial organizations already possess powers and exercise functions of a quasi-governmental character. If each can develop responsibility to the whole community commensurate with its power and position, and if understanding leadership can be developed, the future may not look too dark.

But if standards of responsibility remain at customary levels, one could easily paint the future in somber colors, except from the standpoint of those who would welcome a totalitarian outcome. It would be a picture, on the one side, of irresponsible grab-bag tactics on the part of private groups, pricing themselves partially out of the market and blaming others, or the "system," for failure to utilize our resources fully. On the other side, it would be a picture of bureaucratic vested interests, burdening industry with endlessly growing regulations, viewing with alarm a falling off of a WPA or a CCC enrollment and perhaps starting a recruiting campaign, or wishing to see that private enterprise does not make an unexpectedly vigorous recovery and thereby interfere with a public-works program already under way. This is, of course, a caricature of the perversions of bureaucracy; but it will be worth some vigilance to see that it never becomes a justified caricature.

In a social democratic working out of things, personal and group attitudes are all-important. Some wish for no change. They must be educated to the fact that there is something the matter, which is serious enough to be threatening, and that something had better be done about it if we wish to avert disaster. Some, including many labor groups, want the present system to continue, because for them it has, on the whole, made a pretty good grab bag. They should find a better reason. An economy which is only a grab bag is not going to survive the stresses of the coming generation.[3] Some seem to consider themselves neutral.

[3] Let us be more specific. If our economy had been exclusively dominated by private self-seeking, as some assume, it would probably have collapsed some time ago. If it is to survive in the future, it seems clear that private self-seeking must be less dominant, social consciousness and responsibility more dominant, than up to the present time.

They need to learn that the impact of changing economic eras, like the impact of total war, leaves few neutrals or noncombatants. Of those who are planning for the future combat with depression, too many are content to lay plans looking to keeping the economic system going a little while longer. If, with the time that still remains to us, this is all we can plan for, we shall deserve to have our system containing the potentialities of a social democracy keep going a little while longer.

The thing we must defend is not the present specific shape of so-called "private enterprise" but the essentials of a system in which free men have in the past, without surrender of real freedom, learned the art of combining their several efforts in a workable scheme of collaboration and may continue to learn and practice that difficult art under the more exacting conditions of the future. To this end we need people—and there are such—who realize both the need for change and the vital importance of maintaining continuity and an adequate measure of economic freedom and who will give equally active thought to both ends. Freedom will not be saved by lip service.

We need people who know why economic freedom is important and who also know what threatens it. We need leaders who know what the economic system as a whole is for and can bring that common purpose home to warring elements and make them realize that their part of the economic system cannot go on working for them unless the whole system is doing the thing for which it exists. We need such leaders, and they must have followers. All alike must stand ready to give up what the common good may demand and—equally necessary— they must have confidence in one another's readiness to do this. This sounds like a hard order for a people proverbially divided and inert on just such matters, and a people whom the crisis of this generation will find weary of crises, weary of governmental interferences, weary of being forced to pay attention to larger economic problems than those of their own shop. Yet the thing has to be done. For this generation there is to be no release from the stress of readjustment. Our best resource is to minimize the strain by a calm and matter-of-fact acceptance of this necessity.

We must be hardheaded. We must face ugly and discouraging facts and we must not let wishful thinking blind us to the defects of proposed remedies. We must set our standards of performance high, for timid standards will invite failure, but not so high as to be unattainable and so to court failure of a different sort. Some imperfections we must be prepared to put up with, or we shall nag the system to death in the attempt to rectify every abuse. But over major matters we must have the kind of settled purpose that goes on trying in the face of repeated failure.

The least we can do is to act as if our civilization and its most treasured values have a future, even if well aware that for that outcome there can be no absolute guaranty. But if the enterprise is to be successful, we shall need a more positive act of faith in the ultimate invincibility of personal freedom and social democracy. We have something to learn from those gallant leaders of liberty in the history of mankind whose faith survived adversity, reaching sources of strength which are more than personal, and in which lie the real hope of our perplexed and tortured age. We are forced to know what we are building, to an extent greater than has ever been necessary before, and our knowledge is alarmingly limited. But if all of us play our parts fully, we may still hope to build better than any one of us can now know.

ART, MAN AND MANUFACTURE

1 Culture originates in work, not in play; and man's activity consists in either a making or a doing. Both of these aspects of the active life depend for their correction upon the contemplative life. The making of things is governed by art, the doing of things by prudence. An absolute distinction of art from prudence is made for purposes of logical understanding.[1] But while we make this distinction we must not forget that the man is a whole man and cannot be justified as such merely by what he makes; the artist works "by art and willingly."[2] Even supposing that he avoids artistic sin, it is still essential to him as a man to have had a right will, and so to have avoided moral sin. We cannot absolve the artist from this moral responsibility by laying it upon the patron, or only if the artist be in some way compelled; for the artist is normally either his own patron, deciding what is to be made, or formally and freely consents to the will of the patron, which becomes his own as soon as the commission has been accepted, after which the artist is only concerned with the good of the work to be done. If any other motive affects him in his work, he has no longer any proper place in the social order. Manufacture is for use and not for profit. The artist is not a special kind of man, but every man who is not an artist in some field, every man without a vocation, is an idler. The kind of artist that a man should be, carpenter, painter, lawyer, farmer or priest, is determined by his own nature; in other words, by his nativity. The only man who has a right to abstain from all constructive activities is the monk, who has also surrendered all those uses that depend on things that can be made and is no longer a member of society. No man has a right to any social status who is not an artist.

[1] Cf. Plotinus, *Enneads*, IV. 3.7.
[2] *Per artem et ex voluntate* (St. Thomas Aquinas, *Sum. Theol.*, I. 45. 6; cf. 1. 14. 8c).

152

We are thus introduced at the outset to the problem of the use of art and the worth of the artist to a serious society. This use is in general the good of man, the good of society, and in particular the occasional good of an individual requirement. All these goods correspond to the desires of men; so that what is actually made in a given society is a key to the governing conception of the purpose of life in that society, which can be judged by its works in that sense, and better than in any other way. There can be no doubt about the purpose of art in a traditional society. When it has been decided that such and such a thing should be made, it is by art that it can be properly made. There can be no good use without art; that is, no good use if things are not properly made. The artist is producing a utility, something to be used. Mere pleasure is not a use from this point of view. Our aesthetic appreciation, essentially sentimental because it is just what the word "aesthetic" means, a kind of feeling rather than an understanding, has little or nothing to do with the *raison d'être* of things. To "enjoy" what does not correspond to any vital needs of our own and what we have not verified in our own life can only be described as an indulgence. It is luxurious to make mantelpiece ornaments of the artifacts of what we term uncivilized or superstitious people, whose culture we think of as much inferior to our own, and which our touch has destroyed. The attitude, however ignorant, of those who used to call these things "abominations" and "beastly devices of the heathen" was a much healthier one. It is the same if we read the scriptures of any tradition, or authors such as Dante and Ashvaghosha who tell us frankly that they wrote with other than "aesthetic" ends in view; or if we listen to sacrificial music for the ears' sake only. We have a right to be pleased by these things only through our understanding use of them.

In the philosophy that we are considering, only the contemplative and active lives are reckoned human. The life of pleasure, the end of which is pleasure, is subhuman; every animal "knows what it likes" and seeks for it. This is not an exclusion of pleasure from life as if pleasure were wrong in itself; it is an exclusion of the pursuit of pleasure thought of as a "diversion," and apart from "life." It is in life itself, in "proper operation," that pleasure arises naturally, and this very pleasure is said to "perfect the operation" itself.

It would be superfluous to say that from the traditional point of view there could hardly be found a stronger condemnation of the present social order than in the fact that the man at work is no longer doing what he likes best, but rather what he must, and in the general belief that a man can only be really happy when he "gets away" and is at play. For even if we mean by "happy" to enjoy the "higher things of life," it is a cruel error to pretend that this can be done at leisure if it has not been done at work. For "the man devoted to his own vocation finds perfection . . . That man whose prayer and praise of God are in the doing of his own work perfects himself." It is this way of life that our civilization denies to the vast majority of men, and in this respect that it is notably inferior to even the most primitive or savage societies with which it can be contrasted.

Manufacture, the practice of an art, is thus not only the production of utilities but in the highest possible sense the education of men. It can never be, unless for the sentimentalist who lives for pleasure, an "art for art's sake," that is to say, a production of "fine" or useless objects only that we may be delighted by "fine colors and sounds"; neither can we speak of our traditional art as a "decorative" art, for to think of decoration as its essence would be the same as to think of millinery as the essence of costume or of upholstery as the essence of furniture. The greater part of our boasted "love of art" is nothing but the enjoyment of comfortable feelings.

In our traditional view of art, in folk art, Christian and Oriental art, there is no essential distinction of a fine and useless art from a utilitarian craftsmanship. There is no distinction in principle of orator from carpenter, but only a distinction of things well and truly made from things not so made and of what is beautiful from what is ugly in terms of formality and informality. But, the reader may object, do not some things serve the uses of the spirit or intellect, and others those of the body; is not a symphony nobler than a bomb, an icon than a fireplace? Let us first of all beware of confusing art with ethics. "Noble" is an ethical value, and pertains to the *a priori* censorship of what ought or ought not to be made at all. The judgment of works of art from this point of view is not merely legitimate, but essential to a good life and the welfare of humanity. But it is not a judgment of the work of art as such. The bomb, for example, is only bad as a work of art if it fails to destroy and kill to the required extent. The distinction of artistic from moral sin which is so sharply drawn in Christian philosophy can be recognized again in Confucius, who speaks of a Succession Dance as being "at the same time perfect beauty and perfect goodness" and of the War Dance as being "perfect beauty but not perfect goodness." [3] It will be obvious that there can be no judgment of art itself, since it is not an act but a kind of knowledge or power by which things can be well made, whether for good or evil use. The art by which utilities are produced cannot be judged morally, because it is not a kind of willing but a kind of knowing.

Beauty in this philosophy is the attractive power of perfection.[4] There are perfections or beauties of different kinds of things or in different contexts, but we cannot arrange these beauties in a hierarchy, as we can the things themselves. We can no more say that a cathedral as such is "better" than a barn as such than we can say that a rose as such is "better" than a skunk cabbage as such; each is beautiful to the extent that it is what it purports to be, and in the same proportion good. To say that a perfect cathedral is a greater work of art than a perfect barn is either to assume that there can be degrees of perfection or to assume that the artist who made the barn was really trying to make a cathedral. We see that this is absurd; and yet it is just in this way that whoever believes that art "progresses" contrasts the most primitive with the most advanced (or decadent) styles of art, as though the primitive had been trying to do what we try to do, and had drawn like that while really trying to draw as we draw; and that is to impute artistic sin to the primitive. So far from this, the only test of excellence in a work of art is the measure of the artist's actual success in making what was intended.

One of the most important implications of this position is that beauty is objective, residing in the artifact and not in the spectator, who may or may not be qualified to recognize it. The work of art is good of its kind, or not good at all; its excellence is as independent of our reactions to its aesthetic surfaces as it is of our moral reaction to its thesis. Just as the artist conceives the form of the thing to be made only after he has consented to the patron's will, so we, if we are to judge as the artist could, must already have consented to the existence of the object before we can be free to compare its actual shape with its prototype in the artist. We must not condescend to "primitive" works by saying, "That was before they knew anything about anatomy, or

---

[3] *Analects*, III. 25.
[4] Plato, *Cratylus*, 416c; Dionysius Areopagiticus, *De div. nom.*, IV. 5; Ulrich of Strassburg, *De pulchro*; *Lankavatara Sutra*, 11. 118-119, etc.

perspective," or call their work "unnatural" because of its formality. We must have learned that these primitives did not feel our kind of interest in anatomy, nor intend to tell us what things are like; we must have learned that it is because they had something definite to say that their art is more abstract, more intellectual, and less than our own a matter of mere reminiscence or emotion. If the medieval artist's constructions corresponded to a certain way of thinking, it is evident that we cannot understand them except to the extent that we can identify ourselves with this way of thinking. The Middle Ages and the East are mysterious to us only because we know not what to think, but what we like to think. As humanists and individualists it flatters us to think that art is an expression of personal feelings and sentiments, preference and free choice, unfettered by the sciences of mathematics and cosmology. But medieval art was not like ours "free" to ignore truth. For medieval man, *Ars sine scientia nihil*; by "science" we mean, of course, the reference of all particulars to unifying principles, not the "laws" of statistical prediction.

The perfection of the object is something of which the critic cannot judge, its beauty something that he cannot feel, if he has not like the original artist made himself such as the thing itself should be; it is in this way that "criticism is reproduction" and "judgment the perfection of art." The "appreciation of art" must not be confused with a psychoanalysis of our likes and dislikes, dignified by the name of "aesthetic reactions." The study of art, if it is to have any cultural value in the new civilization, will demand two far more difficult operations than this: in the first place, an understanding and acceptance of the whole point of view from which the necessity for the work arose; in the second place, a bringing to life in ourselves of the form in which the artist conceived the work and by which he judged it. The wider the scope of his study in time and space the more must he cease to be a provincial, the more must he universalize himself, whatever may be his own temperament and training. He must assimilate whole cultures that seem strange to him, and must also be able to elevate his own levels of reference from those of observation to that of the vision of ideal forms. He must rather love than be curious about the subject of his study. It is just because so much is demanded that the study of "art" can have a cultural value, that is to say, may become a means of growth.

A need, or "indigence" as Plato calls it, is thus the first cause of the

production of a work of art. We spoke of spiritual and physical needs
and said that works of art could *not* be classified accordingly. If this is
difficult for us to admit, it is because we have forgotten what we are,
what "man" in this philosophy denotes, a spiritual as well as a psychophysical being. We are therefore well contented with a functional art,
good of its kind in so far as goodness does not interfere with profitable
salability, and can hardly understand how things to be used can also
have a meaning. It is true that what we have come to understand by
"man," namely, "the reasoning and mortal animal," [5] can live by "bread
alone," and that bread alone, make no mistake about it, is therefore a
good. To function is the very least that can be expected of any work of
art. "Bread alone" is the same thing as a "merely functional art." But
when it is said that man does not live by bread alone but "by every
word that proceedeth out of the mouth of God," [6] it is the whole man
that is meant. The "words of God" are precisely those ideas and principles which can be expressed whether verbally or visually by art; the
words or visual forms in which they are expressed are not merely sensible but also significant. To separate as we do the functional from the
significant art, applied from a so-called fine art, is to require of the vast
majority of men to live by the merely functional art, a "bread alone"
that is nothing but the "husks that the swine did eat." The insincerity
and inconsistency of the whole position is to be seen in the fact that we
do not expect from the "significant" art that it be significant *of* anything,
nor from the "fine" art anything but an "aesthetic" pleasure. If the
artist himself declares that the work is charged with meaning and exists for the sake of this meaning, we call it an irrelevance, but decide
that he may have been an artist in spite of it. In other words, if the
merely functional arts are the husks, the fine arts are the tinsel of life,
and art for us has no significance whatever.

Primitive man, despite the pressure of his struggle for existence, knew
nothing of such merely functional arts. The whole man is naturally a
metaphysician, and only later a philosopher and psychologist, a system-
atist. His reasoning is by analogy, or in other words, by means of an
"adequate symbolism." As a person rather than as an animal he knows
immortal through mortal things. [7] Primitive man made no real distinc-

---

[5] Boethus, *De consol.*, I. 6. 35.
[6] Matthew 4:4.
[7] *Aitareya Aranyaka*, II. 3.2: *Aitareya Brahmana*, VII. 10; *Katha Upanishad*, II. 10b.

tion of sacred from secular: his weapons, clothing, vehicles and house were all of them imitations of divine prototypes, and were to him even more what they meant than what they were in themselves; he made them this "more" by incantation and by rites.

The Indian actor prepares for his performance by prayer. The Indian architect is often spoken of as visiting heaven and there making notes on the prevailing forms of architecture, which he imitates here below. All traditional architecture, in fact, follows a cosmic pattern. Those who think of their house as only a "machine to live in" should judge their point of view by that of Neolithic man, who also lived in a house, but a house that embodied a cosmology. We are more than sufficiently provided with overheating systems. We should have found his house uncomfortable; but let us not forget that he identified the column of smoke that rose from his hearth to disappear from view through a hole in the roof with the Axis of the Universe, saw in this louver an image of the Heavenly Door, and in his hearth the Navel of the Earth, formulas that we at the present day are hardly capable of understanding; we, for whom "such knowledge as is not empirical is meaningless."

To have seen in his artifacts nothing but the things themselves, and in the myth a mere anecdote would have been a mortal sin, for this would have been the same as to see in oneself nothing but the "reasoning and mortal animal," to recognize only "this man," and never the "form of humanity." It is just in so far as we do now see only the things as they are in themselves, and only ourselves as we are in ourselves, that we have killed the metaphysical man and shut ourselves up in the dismal cave of functional and economic determinism. Does the reader begin to see now that works of art cannot be divided into the categories of the utilitarian and the spiritual, but pertain to both worlds, functional and significant, physical and metaphysical?

2 The artist has now accepted his commission and is expected to practice his art. It is by this art that he knows both what the thing should be like and how to impress this form upon the available material, so that it may be informed with what is actually alive in himself. His operation will be twofold, "free" and "servile," theoretical and operative, inventive and imitative. It is in terms of the freely invented formal cause that we can best explain

how the pattern of the thing to be made or arranged, this essay or this house, for example, is known. It is this cause by which the actual shape of the thing can best be understood; because "similitude is with respect to the form" of the thing to be made, and not with respect to the shape or appearance of some other and already existing thing; so that in saying "imitative" we are by no means saying "naturalistic." "Art imitates nature in her manner of operation," that is to say, God in his manner of creation, in which he does not repeat himself or exhibit deceptive illusions in which the species of things are confused.

How is the form of the thing to be made evoked? This is the kernel of our doctrine, and the answer can be made in a great many different ways. The art of God is the Son "through whom all things are made." In the same way the art in the human artist is his child through which some one thing is to be made. The intuition-expression of an imitable form is an intellectual conception born of the artist's wisdom. The image arises naturally in his spirit, not by way of an aimless inspiration, but in purposeful and vital operation, "by a word *conceived* in intellect." [8] It is this filial image, and not a retinal reflection or the memory of a retinal reflection that he imitates in the material, just as at the creation of the world "God's will beheld that beauteous world and imitated it," that is to say, impressed on primary matter a "world picture" already "painted by the spirit on the canvas of the spirit." All things are to be seen in this eternal mirror better than in any other way; for there the artist's models are all alive and more alive than those which are posed when we are taught in schools of art to draw "from life." If shapes of natural origin often enter into the artist's compositions, this does not mean that they pertain to his art, but that they are the material in which the form is clothed; just as the poet uses sounds, which are not his thesis, but only his means. The artist's spirals are the forms of life, and not only of this or that life. The superficial resemblances of art to "nature" are accidental; and when they are deliberately sought, the art is already in its anecdotage. It is not by the looks of existing things, but, as Augustine says, by their ideas, that we know what we propose to make should be like. He who does not see more vividly and clearly than this perishing mortal eye can see does not see creatively at all. [9]

[8] *Per verbum in intellectu conceptum*, St. Thomas Aquinas, *Sum. Theol.*, 1.45 6c.
[9] William Blake.

"The city can never otherwise be happy unless it is drawn by those painters who follow a divine original." [10]

What do we mean by "invention"? The entertainment of ideas; the intuition of things as they are on higher than empirical levels of reference. We must digress to explain that in using the terms "intuition" and "expression" as the equivalents of "conception" or "generation" we are not thinking either of Bergson or of Croce. By "intuition" we mean with Augustine an intellection extending beyond the range of dialectic to that of the ternal reasons [11]—a contemplation, therefore, rather than a thinking. By "expression" we mean with Bonaventure a begotten rather than a calculated likeness.

It may be asked, How can the artist's primary act of imagination be spoken of as "free," if in fact he is working to some formula, specification or iconographic prescription, or even drawing from nature? If in fact a man is blindly copying a shape defined in words or already visibly existing, he is not a free agent, but only performing a servile operation. This is the case in quantitative production; here the craftsman's work, however skillful, can be called mechanical rather than artistic, and it is only in this sense that the phrase "mere craftsmanship" acquires a meaning. It would be the same with the performance of any rite, to the extent that performance becomes a habit, unenlivened by any recollection. The mechanical product may still be a work of art; but the art was not the workman's, nor the workman an artist, but a hireling; and this is one of the many ways in which an "industry without art is brutality."

The artist's theoretical or imaginative act is said to be "free" because it is *not* assumed or admitted that he is blindly copying any model extrinsic to himself, but expressing himself, even in adhering to a prescription or responding to requirements that may remain essentially the same for millennia. It is true that to be properly expressed a thing must proceed from within, moved by its form; and yet it is not true that in practicing an art that has "fixed ends and ascertained means of operation" [12] the artist's freedom is denied; it is only the academician and the hireling whose work is under constraint. It is true that if the

[10] Plato, *Republic*.
[11] Gilson, *Introduction à l'Etude de Saint Augustin*, 1931, p. 121, note 2.
[12] St. Thomas Aquinas, *Sum. Theol.*, II-II. 47.4 ad. 2.

artist has not conformed *himself* to the pattern of the thing to be made he has not really known it and cannot work originally. But if he has thus conformed himself, he will be in fact expressing *himself* in bringing it forth.[13] Not indeed expressing his "personality," himself as "this man" So-and-so, but himself *sub specie aeternitatis*, and apart from individual idiosyncrasy. The idea of the thing to be made is brought to life in him, and it will be from this supraindividual life of the artist himself that the vitality of the finished work will be derived. "It is not the tongue, but our very life that sings the new song." In this way too the human operation reflects the manner of operation *in divinis*: "All things that were made were life in Him." [14]

"Through the mouth of Hermes the divine Eros began to speak." [15] We must not conclude from the form of the words that the artist is a passive instrument, like a stenographer. "He" is much rather actively and consciously making use of "himself" as an instrument. Body and mind are not the man, but only his instrument and vehicle. The man is passive only when he identifies himself with the psychophysical ego, letting it take him where it will; but is active when he directs it. Inspiration and aspiration are not exclusive alternatives, but one and the same; because the spirit to which both words refer cannot work in the man except to the extent that *he* is "in the spirit." It is only when the form of the thing to be made has been known that the artist returns to "himself," performing the servile operation with good will, a will directed solely to the good of the thing to be made. The man incapable of contemplation cannot be an artist, but only a skillful workman. It is demanded of the artist to be both a contemplative and a good workman.

What is implied by contemplation is to raise our level of reference from the empirical to the ideal, from observation to vision, from any auditory sensation to audition: the imager (or worshiper, for no distinction can be made here) "taking ideal form under the action of the vision, while remaining only potentially 'himself.'" [16] "I am one," says Dante, accounting for his *dolce stil nuovo*, "who when Love inspires me take note, and go setting it forth in such wise as He dictates within

[13] Since in this case "Die Künste sint Meister in dem Meister" (Eckhart, Pfeiffer, p. 390).
[14] John 1:3.
[15] Hermetica, *Asclepius*, prologue.
[16] Plotinus, *Enneads*, IV. 4.2.

me." "Lo, make all things in accordance with the pattern that was shown thee on the Mount." [17] "It is in imitation of angelic works of art that any work of art is wrought here." The "crafts such as building and carpentry take their principles from that realm and from the thinking there." [18] "Thou madest," as Augustine says, "that *ingenium* whereby the artificer may take his art, and may see within what he has to do without." [19] It is the light of this Spirit that becomes "the light of a mechanical art." Augustine's *ingenium* corresponds to Greek *daimon*, but not to what we mean today by "genius." No man, considered as So-and-so, can *be* a genius: but all men *have* a genius, to be served or disobeyed at their own peril. There can be no property in ideas, because these are gifts of the Spirit, and not to be confused with talents. Ideas are never made, but can only be "invented," that is, "found," and entertained. No matter how many times they may already have been "applied" by others, whoever conforms himself to an idea and so makes it his own will be working originally, but not so if he is expressing only his own ideals or opinions.

To "think for oneself" is always to think of oneself. What is called "free thought" is therefore the natural expression of a humanistic philosophy. We are at the mercy of our thoughts and corresponding desires. Free thought is a passion; it is much rather the thoughts than ourselves that are free. We cannot too much emphasize that contemplation is not a passion but an act; and that where modern psychology sees in "inspiration" the uprush of an instinctive and *sub*conscious will, the orthodox philosophy sees an elevation of the artist's being to *super*conscious and *supra*individual levels. Where the psychologist invokes a demon, the metaphysician invokes a daemon: what is for the one the "libido" is for the other "the divine Eros." [20]

There is also a sense in which the man as an individual "expresses himself," whether he will or no. This is inevitable, only because nothing can be known or done except in accordance with the mode of the knower. So the man himself, as he is in himself, appears in style and handling, and can be recognized accordingly. The uses and significance of works of art may remain the same for millennia, and yet we can

[17] Exodus 25:40.
[18] Plotinus, *Enneads,* V. 9.11. The builder and carpenter are then doing the will of God "on earth *as* it is done in heaven."
[19] Confessions, XI. 5.
[20] Plato, *Timaeus,* 90 A.

often date and place a work at first glance. Human idiosyncrasy is thus the explanation of style and of stylistic sequences. Styles are the basis of our histories of art, which are written like other histories to flatter our human vanity. But the artist whom we have in view is innocent of history and unaware of the existence of stylistic sequences. Styles are the accident and by no means the essence of art; the free man is not trying to express himself, but that which is to be expressed. Our conception of art as essentially the expression of a personality, our whole view of genius, our impertinent curiosities about the artist's private life, all these things are the products of a perverted individualism and prevent our understanding of the nature of art. The modern mania for attribution is the expression of Renaissance conceit and nineteenth century humanism; it has nothing to do with the nature of art, and becomes a pathetic fallacy when applied to it.

In all respects the traditional artist devotes himself to the good of the work to be done. The operation is a rite, the celebrant neither intentionally nor even consciously expressing himself. It is by no accident of time, but in accordance with a governing concept of the meaning of life, of which the goal is implied in St. Paul's *Vivo autem jam non ego,* that works of traditional art, whether Christian, Oriental or folk art, are hardly ever signed. The artist is anonymous, or if a name has survived, we know little or nothing of the man. This is true as much for literary as for plastic artifacts. In traditional arts it is never Who said? but only What was said? that concerns us; for "all that is true, by whomsoever it has been said, has its origin in the Spirit." [21]

So the first sane questions that can be asked about a work of art are What was it for? and What does it mean? We have seen already that whatever, and however humble, the functional purpose of the work of art may have been, it had always a spiritual meaning, by no means an arbitrary meaning, but one which the function itself expresses adequately by analogy. Function and meaning cannot be forced apart; the meaning of the work of art is its intrinsic form as much as the soul is the form of the body. Meaning is even historically prior to utilitarian application. Forms such as that of the dome, arch and circle have not been "evolved," but only applied; the circle can no more have been suggested by the wheel than a myth by a mimetic rite. The ontology of useful inventions parallels that of the world; in both "creations" the

[21] Cf. I Corinthians 2:13.

Sun is the single form of many different things. That this is actually so in the case of human production by art will be realized by everyone who is sufficiently familiar with the solar significance of almost every known type of circular or annular artifact or part of an artifact. The meaning is literally the "spirit" of the performance. Iconography, in other words, is art: that art by which the actual forms of things are determined; and the final problem of research in the field of art is to understand the iconographic form of whatever composition it may be that we are studying. It is only when we have understood the *raison d'être* of iconography that we can be said to have gone back to first principles; and that is what we mean by the "Reduction of Art to Theology." [22] The student understands the logic of the composition; the illiterate only its aesthetic value.[23]

The anonymity of the artist belongs to a type of culture dominated by the longing to be liberated from oneself. All the force of this philosophy is directed against the delusion "I am the doer." "I" am not in fact the doer, but the instrument; human individuality is not an end but only a means. The supreme achievement of individual consciousness is to lose or find (both words mean the same) itself in what is both its first beginning and its last end. All that is required of the instrument is efficiency and obedience; it is not for the subject to aspire to the throne; the constitution of man is not a democracy, but the hierarchy of body, soul and spirit. Is it for the Christian to consider any work "his own" when even Christ has said that "I do nothing of myself"? Or for the Hindu, when Krishna has said, "The Comprehensor cannot form the concept 'I am the doer'"? Or the Buddhist, for whom it has been said that "To wish that it may be made known that 'I was the author' is the thought of a man not yet adult"? [24]

There is another aspect of the question that has to do with the patron rather than the artist; this too must be understood if we are not to mistake the intentions of traditional art. It will have been observed that in traditional arts the effigy of an individual, for whatever purpose it may have been made, is rarely a likeness in the sense that we conceive a likeness, but much rather the representation of a type. The man is represented by his function rather than by his appearance; the effigy is

[22] The title of a work by St. Bonaventure.
[23] Quintilian, IX. 4.
[24] *Dhammapada*, 74.

of the king, the soldier, the merchant or the smith, rather than of So-and-so. The ultimate reasons for this have nothing to do with any technical inabilities or lack of the power of observation in the artist, but are hard to explain to ourselves whose preoccupations are so different and whose faith in the eternal values of "personality" is so naïve; hard to explain to ourselves, who shrink from the saying that a man must "hate" himself, "if he would be my disciple." [25] The whole position is bound up with a traditional view that also finds expression in the doctrine of the hereditary transmission of character and function, because of which the man can die in peace knowing that his work will be carried on by another representative. As So-and-so, the man is re-born in his descendants, each of whom occupies in turn what was much rather an office than a person. For in what we call personality tradition sees only a temporal function "which you hold in lease." The very person of the king, surviving death, may be manifested in some way in some other ensemble of possibilities than these; but the royal personality descends from generation to generation, by hereditary and ritual delegation; and so we say, "The king is dead, long live the king." It is the same if the man has been a merchant or craftsman; if the son to whom his personality has been transmitted is not also, for example, a blacksmith, the blacksmith of a given community, the family line is at an end; and if personal functions are not in this way transmitted from generation to generation, the social order itself has come to an end, and chaos supervenes.

We find accordingly that if an ancestral image or tomb effigy is to be set up for reasons bound up with what is rather loosely called "ancestor worship," this image has two peculiarities: (1) it is identified as the image of the deceased by the insignia and costume of his vocation and the inscription of his name; (2) for the rest, it is an individually indeterminate type, or what is called an "ideal" likeness. In this way both selves of the man are represented; the one which is to be inherited, and that which corresponds to an intrinsic and regenerated form that he should have built up for himself in the course of life itself, considered as a sacrificial operation terminating at death. The whole purpose of life has been that this man should realize himself in this other and essential form, in which alone the form of divinity can be thought of as adequately reflected. As St. Augustine expresses it, "*This* likeness

25 Luke 14:26.

begins now to be formed again in us." [26] It is not surprising that even in life a man would rather be represented thus, not as he is but as he ought to be, impassibly superior to the accidents of temporal manifestation. It is characteristic of ancestral images in many parts of the East that they cannot be recognized, except by their legends, as the portraits of individuals; there is nothing else to distinguish them from the form of the divinity to whom the spirit has been returned when the man "gave up the ghost." Almost in the same way an angelic serenity and the absence of human imperfection, and of the signs of age, are characteristic of the Christian effigy before the thirteenth century when the study of death masks came back into fashion and modern portraiture was born in the charnel house. The traditional image is of the man as he would be at the Resurrection, in an ageless body of glory, not as he was accidentally: "I would go down unto Annihilation and Eternal Death, lest the Last Judgment come and find me Unannihilate, and I be seiz'd and giv'n into the hands of my own Selfhood."

The same holds good for the heroes of epic and romance. For modern criticism these are "unreal types" and there is no "psychological analysis." We ought to have realized that if this is not a humanistic art this may have been its essential virtue. We ought to have known that this was a typal art by right of long inheritance; the romance is still essentially an epic, the epic essentially a myth; and that it is just because the hero exhibits universal qualities, without individual peculiarity or limitations, that he can be a pattern imitable by every man alike in accordance with his own possibilities whatever these may be. In the last analysis the hero is always God, whose only idiosyncrasy is being, and to whom it would be absurd to attribute individual characteristics. It is only when the artist, whatever his subject may be, is chiefly concerned to exhibit himself, and when we descend to the level of the psychological novel, that the study and analysis of individuality acquire an importance. Then only does portraiture in our sense take the place of what was once an iconographic portrayal.

All these things apply so much the more if we are to consider the deliberate portrayal of a divinity the fundamental thesis of all traditional arts. An adequate knowledge of theology and cosmology is then indispensable to an understanding of the history of art, in so far as the actual shapes and structures of works of art are determined by

[26] *De spiritu et littera*, 37.

their real content. Christian art, for example, begins with the representation of Deity by abstract symbols, which may be geometrical, vege-
table or theriomorphic and are devoid of any sentimental appeal whatever. An anthropomorphic symbol follows, but this is still a form and
not a figuration; not made as though to function biologically or as if to
illustrate a textbook on anatomy or on dramatic expression. Still later,
the form is sentimentalized: the features of the crucified are made to
exhibit human suffering, the type is completely humanized; and where
we began with the shape of humanity as an analogical representation
of the idea of God, we end with the portrait of the artist's mistress posing
as the Madonna and the representation of an all-too-human baby; the
Christ is no longer a man-God, but the sort of man of whom we can ap-
prove. With what extraordinary prescience St. Thomas Aquinas commends the use of the lower rather than the nobler forms of existence
as divine symbols, "especially for those who can think of nothing nobler
than bodies"!

The course of art reflects the course of thought. The artist, asserting
a specious liberty, expresses himself; our age commends the man who
thinks for himself, and therefore of himself. We can see in the hero
only an imperfectly remembered historical figure, around which there
have gathered mythical and miraculous accretions; the hero's manhood
interests us more than his divinity, and this applies as much to our
conception of Christ or Krishna or Buddha as it does to our conceptions of Cuchulainn or Sigurd or Gilgamesh. We treat the mythical
elements of the story, which are its essence, as its accidents and substitute anecdote for meaning. The secularization of art and the rationalization of religion are inseparably connected, however unaware of it we
may be. It follows that for any man who can still believe in the eternal
birth of any avatar ("Before Abraham was, I am") the content of
works of art cannot be a matter of indifference; the artistic humaniza-
tion of the Son or of the Mother of God is as much a denial of Christian
truth as any form of verbal rationalism or other heretical position. The
vulgarity of humanism from which the *humanitas* has been eliminated
appears naked and unashamed in all euhemerism.

It is by no accident that it should have been discovered only comparatively recently that art is essentially an "aesthetic" activity. No
real distinction can be drawn between aesthetic and materialistic;
aisthesis being sensation, and matter that which can be sensed. So we

regard the lack of interest in anatomy as a defect of art, the absence of psychological analysis as evidence of undeveloped character; we deprecate the representation of the Bambino as a little man rather than as a child, and think of the frontality of the imagery as due to an inability to realize the three-dimensional mass of existing things; in place of the abstract light that corresponds to the gnomic aorists of the legend itself we demand the cast shadows that belong to momentary effects. We speak of a want of scientific perspective, forgetting that perspective in art is a kind of visual syntax and only a means to an end. We forget that, while our perspective serves the purposes of representation in which we are primarily interested, there are other perspectives that are more intelligible and better adapted to the communicative purposes of the traditional arts.

In deprecating the secularization of art we are not confusing religion with art, but seeking to understand the content of art at different times with a view to unbiased judgment. In speaking of the decadence of art, it is really the decadence of man, from intellectual to sentimental interests, that we mean. For the artist's skill may remain the same throughout: he is able to do what he intends. It is the mental image to which he works that changes. That "art has fixed ends" is no longer true as soon as we know what we like instead of liking what we know. Our point is that without an understanding of the change the integrity of even a supposedly objective historical study is destroyed; we judge the traditional works not by their actual accomplishment, but by our own intentions, and so inevitably come to believe in a progress of art as we do in the progress of man.

Ignorant of the traditional philosophy and of its formulas we often think of the artist as having been trying to do just what he may have been consciously avoiding. For example, if Damascene says that Christ from the moment of his conception possessed a "rational and intellectual soul," if, as St. Thomas Aquinas says, "his body was perfectly formed and assumed in the first instant," if the Buddha is said to have spoken in the womb and to have taken seven strides at birth, from one end to the other of the universe, could the artist have intended to represent either of the newborn children as a puling infant? If we are disturbed by what we call the "vacancy" of a Buddha's expression, ought we not to bear in mind that he is thought of as the Eye in the World, the

impassible spectator of things as they really are, and that it would have
been impertinent to give him features molded by human curiosity or
passion? If it was an artistic canon that veins and bones should not be
made apparent, can we blame the Indian artist as an artist for not displaying such a knowledge of anatomy as might have evoked *our*
admiration? If we know from authoritative literary sources that the
lotus on which the Buddha sits or stands is not a botanical specimen,
but the universal ground of existence inflorescent in the waters of its
indefinite possibilities, how inappropriate it would have been to represent him in the solid flesh precariously balanced on the surface of a
real and fragile flower! The same considerations will apply to all our
reading of mythology and fairy tale, and to all our judgments of primitive, savage or folk art. The anthropologist whose interest is in a culture is a better historian of such arts than is the critic whose only interest is in the aesthetic surfaces of the artifacts themselves.

In the traditional philosophy, as we cannot too often repeat, "art has
to do with cognition"; [27] beauty is the attractive power of a perfect expression. This we can only judge and only really enjoy as an "intelligible good, which is the good of reason," if we have really known what
it was that was to be expressed. If sophistry be "ornament more than is
appropriate to the thesis of the work," [28] can we judge of what is or is
not sophistry if we ourselves remain indifferent to this content? Evi-
dently not. One might as well attempt the study of Christian or Buddhist
art without a knowledge of the corresponding philosophies as attempt
the study of a mathematical papyrus without the knowledge of mathematics.

3   It will be evident that in a civilization in which any concept of order survives, what is believed to be the truth
must have an immediate bearing on activity, which otherwise would be irrational and insignificant. And as regards the productive activity, since it is by *art*, art in the artist, that things are made,
and since "art is the right reason, or principle, of manufacture," what
we understand by "art" will be the ultimate criterion in all manufacture "for good use" and the satisfaction of needs—unless we propose

[27] *Sum. Theol.*, I. 5.4. ad 1.
[28] St. Augustine, *De doc. christ.*, II. 31.

to tolerate a manufacture for other ends than that of good use, and of things for which there is no need, but for which a "want" can be induced by suggestive advertisement.

The common theory of art outlined above provides us, therefore, not merely with the necessary basis for the understanding of works of art belonging to past times or other peoples but with a criterion of truth and value in the civilization which is emerging that can be applied to our own productions and methods of production. It is not, like the contemporary aesthetics, a speaking *in der Luft herein*, but enunciates rational principles that can be applied to all practical ends. Manufacture can be considered either from the point of view of the consumer or from that of the maker; although it is in fact considered almost exclusively from the standpoint of the salesman who, as such, neither makes nor uses, and whose only "trade" is to buy labor cheap and to sell products dear. It would appear to be axiomatic that manufacture should be for the good of the consumer, and that the consumer may not buy his goods at the price of the maker's degradation. For, if neither of these conditions is fulfilled, how can manufacture be excused or justified in any rational or moral community?

It may be better to consider first the maker, since it is upon his procedure that the nature of the product depends, while the consumer can only use what the maker produces. If "industry without art is brutality," then the industrial worker for wages is a "brute." How so? By virtue of the fact that the working classes under the existing conditions of production for profit have "nothing to offer and sell but their physical strength and skill"—which is the definition of a prostitute, or anybody "kept." No wonder if the workman's body "having lost, in his own eyes, well-nigh all its importance as an instrument of skilled production, interests him almost exclusively as a source of pleasure and discomfort." [29] Actually, in a factory or other institution for production in quantity, the percentage of skilled workers may fall as low as two per cent of the total.

I specified above the "worker for wages," meaning the hired and fired man, because, as has often been pointed out, the normal workman is not a merchant of himself or his product, but only sells the latter in order to obtain the means of going on with the work with which he is in love and for which he is responsible to himself and to his neighbor.

[29] Znaniecki.

The division of the artist from the artisan, of fine from applied art, corresponds exactly to the current opposition of liberal to technical education, and of learning to manual skill, as if these were incompatibles. In fact, in the industrialized democracies, whether totalitarian as in Russia or capitalistic as in America, there has developed a new class distinction which divides those who can afford to be gentlemen artists from those who can live only by an artless industry and are expected to enjoy the "higher things of life" (if at all) only in their hours of "leisure"; or, to speak more accurately, "idleness," since leisure properly means nothing but freedom to do one's own *work* unhindered by extraneous compulsions. Here and now in America the man who is earning his living by doing what he would rather be doing than anything else in the world, the free man, is an exception.

This system of production is in complete agreement with the prevailing contemporary philosophy, from which "values" are excluded; the philosophy, in other words, that denies the possibility of making rational choices in the field of the pursuit and avoidance of things desirable or undesirable. This denial of free will is reflected in the complacent denial of responsibility and choice to workmen who are free only to vote, but *must* make what a supposed economic necessity, really the salesman's ambition to own a yacht, demands from him. This is what we mean by saying that the industrial system (as contrasted with a vocational order of society) reduces the producer to a subhuman level of subsistence. But what exactly do we mean by subhuman or animal? No disparagement of animals as such, but the recognition of a difference between animals *and animal men,* on the one hand, and men, on the other; the former are moved by "hunger and thirst," the latter also recognize "immaterial values" and *act* accordingly; the animal "behaves," the man makes rational choices. This distinction is denied in theory by a "mechanistic" philosophy, and in practice in the labor market, where hands are hired to go through certain motions, often under pressure exerted by "efficiency experts," much as a horse is employed to pull a cart and so earns its keep; and like the horse, the hired and fired man is not in the proper sense of the word an agent, but only a passive reagent to external stimuli.

So, as Eric Gill has so often pointed out, "a civilization denying free will naturally and inevitably produces slaves, not artists; and in such a civilization few men are artists, and those few are simply lap-dogs of

the rich and a great fuss is made about them . . . The factory system
. . . is the system naturally growing out of a philosophy which denies
free will, and which, as a natural consequence, has degraded man
to the level of a mere tool." [30] All this is only what Ruskin meant when
he said that in our factories everything is made, *excepting only men*.

Turn to the consumer. Where it was still true that the artist was not
a special kind of man, but every man a special kind of artist—and it is
a necessary part of the definition of an "artist" that he is naturally inclined by justice to make his work as perfect as possible—all the consumer's goods and chattels were really works of art, "made by art"
—*et aptus et pulcher,* like St. Augustine's writing style. Gautier held that
"tout ce qui est utile est laide, car c'est l'expression de quelque besoin, et
ceux d'hommes sont ignobles et dégoutantes"; but Socrates declared,
"the same house which is both beautiful and useful is a lesson in the
art of building houses as they ought to be." But Socrates belonged to
the school of those who hold that the science of society, our "sociology,"
is more than a matter of statistical record; it is one of knowing what
ought to be and of how to make it be. But now as always the consumer
lives in the same world with the producer, whether or not he too produces; and the consumer as such can only obtain for his use, under
present conditions, what the factory produces. Even the millionaire
cannot acquire goods of "museum quality," except as "antiques." By
and large, the consumer cannot afford the work of such "artists" as there
are, nor do these produce the "utilities" that he requires. It is often,
indeed, claimed for the "artist" that his "fine" work is useless as well
as meaningless. In a country as poor as this, the man who can afford
to buy custom, or handmade, goods is the exception.

Qualitatively, the consumer's standard of living is determined for
him by the salesman, and it hardly occurs to him to question a situation to which he has become inured. Like the workman, the consumer
is really incapacitated from making any rational choices; his life is not
his own; *caveat emptor* has lost its meaning for us, the consumer no
longer knowing what he needs, but only what he can be persuaded to
want—and that is, of course, what the salesman has in his pack. Salability, a matter of price as distinct from worth, is the criterion of production, and the art of persuasion, literally "sweetening," has been

[30] Eric Gill, *It All Goes Together*, p. 12.

developed to such a pitch that men can be persuaded by skillful advertisement to want any gadget whether they need it or not. The consumer
is as much standardized as the product, and "the standardized product
of our mills and factories is a disgrace. Nor is this merely a localized
condition; gadgets can be so easily produced in factories in quantities
greater than can be sold locally that persuasion—rationalized and justified by the contention or conviction that the creation of new wants
is a civilizing process—has to be exported in order to capture foreign
markets which are flooded, in their turn, with the standardized products
of industrialism, for which those who once worked as vocational artists
in their own environment now serve as producers of *raw* materials. All
this is possible, of course, because the strangers, whose own traditions
have been broken down by the kinds of education that their conquerors
have imposed upon them, can as readily as the native American be
persuaded that the quantitative standard of living will be for their good;
and there remain few, or few at least in power, who can say with the
pasha of Marrakech that "we do not want the incredible American
way of life," or with Gandhi defend the pattern of a social order composed of free individuals, where there would be no need for the institutions that concentrate power into the hands of oligarchies or of that
kind of technocratic control of nature which really means nothing
but the control of the majority by a minority possessed of the most
efficient means of coercion by violence.

That all these things are the causes of wars, and wars the causes of
making the rich still richer and the poor still poorer, is beside the present
point; which is, that it might well be asked of themselves by conscien-
tious men, who can still distinguish worth from price, value from cost,
Why should India or China "be helped along the path that leads to
the degradation of work, to the enslavement of the human person, to
soil erosion and to the atomic bomb"? I cite the question as actually
propounded by a learned English Christian, Walter Shewring. The
answer we know, and it is, in the words of an Englishman, Sir George
Watt, whose Christianity may be questioned, that "however much
. . . individuals may suffer, progression in line with the manufacturing enterprise of civilization must be allowed free course." In that
"must" we recognize again the contemporary fatalism, which denies
to the modern man the freedom to make rational or moral decisions

for himself or in relation to his neighbor, and as the result of which modern democratic man is content to live in all the squalor that surrounds him.

So it appears that the theory of beauty and the concept of art that men accept are more than matters of academic interest to be considered "at leisure"; they are matters of literally *vital* significance and relevance for the proper evaluation of the new civilization. There is more than chance involved in the fact that an aesthetic (sentimental) interpretation of art, reversing the older concept of art as that kind of rational knowledge which has to do with the making of things (*ars circum factibilia*), has become only within the past two hundred years so universally accepted that few are aware that any other theory was ever entertained. What is involved is no mere matter of the misinterpretation of ancient arts, no mere matter of the pathetic fallacy of attributing to the "primitives" and others our own aestheticism, though that is by no means a negligible example of current confusions. More than that, the aesthetic interpretation is the only appropriate resource by means of which the aesthetic man can justify his treatment of himself merely as an animal "behaviorist" or blind himself to the poverty of the environment that he regards with so much pride.

It follows that for his re-education, or "renewal in knowledge," these two things, the vocal teaching of the history of art in schools and colleges and the silent teaching of the museums (homes of the Muses, daughters of Memory), are of far more serious import than we had supposed. From the one it could be learned that until recently "art" had meant something more than a heightened form of the nervous sensibility that we share with the other animals, from the amoeba on; and from the other, that the divorce of beauty from utility and of art from industry involves a needless human sacrifice and can only be explained in terms of the current system of production for profit conditioned by the advertiser's almighty censorship. Above all, this is the silent teaching of history: that there have been times and places when and where manufacture could provide for the needs of the soul and body simultaneously. That it is not so now, that there are reasons why it is no longer so, and that it could and will be so again, yes, shall be so again, mankind will experience when the freedom of the Common Man, the Man in these too-common men, has been recovered.

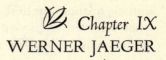
THE FUTURE OF TRADITION

Our time is one of profound change which affects our society and all its institutions, our habits of thought, and in this sense, our tradition. It is therefore not unnatural to ask the question, What is going to endure of the cultural heritage which we have received from former ages and which has been the foundation of our intellectual and moral civilization up to the present day? We call this heritage our humanistic tradition. For centuries, or rather millennia, mankind has seen in it a realm of unchanging and timeless values on which man could fix his gaze whenever the language of change and decline which history speaks seemed to become too overwhelming for the human heart. In the time of transition from the Greek city-state to the universal civilization of the Hellenistic age a Greek poet wrote: "Our culture no one can take from us." Similarly, at the time when the ancient Graeco-Roman civilization of the fourth century A.D. was giving way to the new Christian world and its ideas, one of the outstanding representatives of the classical tradition, the rhetor Libanius, wrote to his old friend, the leader of the Christian church in Asia Minor, Basil of Caesarea: "Hold on to the literature with the less polished form and the better contents—as you say [he means the Christian literature, and especially the Bible] who would mind your doing so? But the roots of that culture which always remains mine and which used to be yours will last in you nevertheless; and they will last as long as you live, and time will never destroy them, even if you do not water them." Is this heritage going to share, in our own age, the fate of so many other elements of our social structure, of which it has formed an indispensable part for centuries, or do we possess an element of permanence in that kind of tradition, and if so, how are we to be sure what part of it will be of lasting value?

In the eighteenth century the leading spirits were completely sure in their relationship to the past of what was definitely antiquated and what deserved to survive the radical criticism of that period of "enlightenment." They felt that they could find the criterion of lasting and not-lasting elements in their own triumphant civilization and in the rational postulates on which it was founded. But the new creative humanism that followed this stage of modern historical development only one generation later took as point of departure the common experience which animated all its greatest artists, poets and philosophers: the experience that it was quite impossible to measure the greatness and fertility of the spiritual creations of the past by the dogmatic standards of eighteenth-century civilization without narrowing down to an unbearable degree the concept of human nature and the ideals of culture, the boundaries of poetic imagination, and the sources of philosophical insight as they were defined by the achievements of former ages and particularly of ancient Greece. This experience must warn us against any attempt to arrive at a dogmatic differentiation of lasting and not-lasting elements in our humanistic tradition. The attitude of the humanist with regard to tradition must always be undogmatic and free. A spiritual tradition is not a set of doctrines which we may accept or reject for certain reasons. We must approach it as a whole if we want to understand why it has endured so long and why we are what we are. And the same attitude is necessary when we want to determine its value for the future. Our question is, therefore, What does our humanistic tradition stand for as a whole? In order to determine its character we must go back to its principles, as they appear in its historical origin.

In calling our tradition "humanistic" we do not deny the value of other great traditions or bestow on our own a merely vague and pretentious title, for humanism is a distinctive mark of our tradition in a very concrete historical sense. The tradition that we call humanistic is centered about the ideal of *humanitas*. The humanists of the Italian Renaissance understood by *humanitas* that pattern of life which they found expressed in Greek and Roman literature as a whole and which they tried to revive. They took the word "humanitas" from their master Cicero, who, according to the Latin grammarian Aulus Gellius, used this term to define the Greek ideal of *paideia,* or culture, as we call it. This use of *humanitas* implies a meaning different from the more common one "philanthropy," Gellius tells us, and thus humanism is different from humanitarianism. Cicero's philhellenism did not stop with his appreciation of Greek authors or individual works of Greek literature, or with the adoption of any special ideas that appealed to him in Greek philosophy; rather, he represented in each of his dialogues the symphony of Greek philosophy in all its schools, and not from the point of view of a Platonist or an Epicurean or a Stoic. He wanted to make the Romans see Greek philosophy and Greek life as a whole, as the Greek ideal of *paideia* had taught him to do. *Paideia* comprised everything, poetry and music, law and custom, philosophy and science, in a unified and balanced pattern of culture. This ideal pattern was supposed to reveal the true nature of man and the task for which he was born—the task of educating and shaping his own self into a true man. In calling this Greek *paideia*-tradition *humanitas,* Romans such as Cicero and Varro proclaimed its lasting truth and denied that it was solely an affair of the Greeks and a transitory historical phenomenon. They thought it worth imitating and thereby expanded and developed it. Thus they became the first humanists. After the Middle Ages the humanists of the Renaissance were the first again to see ancient civilization in this light, that is, as a whole. Their concept of *humanitas* was taken from Cicero's cultural ideal, but it now stood for both Greek and Latin literature and included the Christian. It meant the essence of the entire tradition and the ideal which the humanists adopted as their own cultural aim. The national civilizations of the modern world which developed out of the culture of the Renaissance tried to realize this ideal in a national literature of their own and in the medium of their own languages: this entire system of cultures we call the Humanities. This name makes clear what they all have in common in spite of their national differences, that is, the classical ideal of human culture as the supreme goal of man's earthly life.

Our humanistic tradition, if understood in this sense, is the intellectual universe in which the Western mind moves and has its being. It constitutes the historicity of our existence. It gives the three millennia of our historical past their unity and meaning as a whole. We are what we are because the Greeks were what they were, and the same is true with regard to all the other historical stages that have preceded us. Our civilization has manifested itself in a wide variety of individual forms, literary and intellectual. In our modern somewhat abstract perspective this rich heritage may appear to some as merely an overwhelming wealth of contradictory possibilities between which we have to choose or which we may reject altogether. But the idea of tradition implies some kind of fundamental truth which ought not to be lost. We have, of course, to admit the reality of change. In revolutionary times the word "tradition" has been applied loosely to all sorts of prejudices and conventions of an established but antiquated social order. But the original meaning of tradition is something quite different from this. Genuine spiritual tradition is not a dead weight, a heritage whose passive acceptance may more easily oppress than free our minds. Rather, its very concept implies the passing on of mankind's most precious possessions, the knowledge of the fundamental experiences of man's life which have taken their classical shape in the works of the greatest sons of the human race. Such works can never die. Their symbol is the flame of the burning torch which one champion passes on to the next in the race for the highest prize of human life. They teach us, to speak with Dante,

come l'uom' s'eterna.

If the historical life of man, with its rhythm of coming-to-be and passing-away of ever new individual phenomena, resembles the eternal flux of Heraclitus, then tradition is like the *Logos* in Heraclitus' philosophy, the eternal *Word* that permeates the whole process, the divine fire that works in each of us, even if we are not aware of it. There stands behind our Western tradition, just as behind the great traditions of the East, a common metaphysical faith which transcends all schisms and conflicts within it. This faith is based on a number of ideas in which the spirit of Western civilization has found its classical expression and without which it could not exist—ideas such as the progressive technical domination of man over nature, symbolized in the spark of Promethean fire. On the other hand, there are the spiritual foundations of our moral and social order: the infinite value of the human personality, or "soul," as the ancient Greek and Christian tradition calls it, the concepts of the good, of truth, of beauty, of reason, law and freedom, and a social order built on these basic postulates of ancient Greek culture. To them Christianity has added its call for charity, brotherly love, which has given those ancient ideals a new meaning. It is these elements that constitute the lasting essence of our humanistic tradition. Our modern age has insisted more than any former century on the need for ever-further expansion of these ideas and their application to all the members of human society, in a gradual progress from an original stage in which culture was the excellence of a small élite to a civilization in which all may participate. But what has made this process possible is the universal humanistic power of the ideals underlying this tradition from the beginning.

The lasting nature of our cultural tradition is revealed by history in the continuous process by which a form of culture, originally related to a definite social pattern, proves its ability to adapt itself to ever-changing conditions. To illustrate this we may turn to ancient Greece, for she is one of the most striking examples of the permanence of such a cultural form, and she is the fountainhead of our humanistic tradition. The history of Greek cultural ideals offers the spectacle of the constancy of certain basic forms and ideas throughout a process of continuous social change and intellectual development. The original form maintains itself by *transformation*. Only the greatest and most powerful creations of the Greek genius have survived every change in their original form. Such are Homer and the three tragic poets, and of all the hundreds of philosophers only Plato and Aristotle, with a few of their followers. In this sense tradition is a process of selection according to the highest criteria established by itself. This is the place of what we call the *classical*. The "classical" is not the arbitrary fiction of a retrospective class of learned people but the natural product of a mature civilization which has reached the highest level of self-expression by way of poetic, artistic and philosophical creation. It is not easy to say what gives this self-expression the rank of the classical, but it is undoubtedly a particular kind of perfection which is easily and almost instantly recognized by all as soon as it appears and is ratified by the impartial judgment of succeeding ages. The final criterion is the test of time, according to the late ancient critics who have left us their reflections on this phenomenon, such as the author of *On the Sublime*. They had experienced this fact in the Greek literature of earlier centuries. The perfection of form and the heights of human wisdom that were attained in the works of the classical age were never surpassed later by the modernists of the Hellenistic centuries. Hence in its later phases the Greek spirit was bound to reassert the unique value of the classical and to return to it. Greek literature gradually became either a worship of its own classical heritage, constantly varied in sportive and increasingly aesthetic fashion by its imitators, or a scholarship devoted to the preservation of the treasures of the past.

But neither form of tradition would have had the power to perpetuate that great heritage far beyond the existence of the Greek nation had not another process of a truly creative character, parallel with this conservative classicism, kept its spirit alive. This process is what we may call the *eternal renaissance,* if we may so use the name of one historical period to refer to a general phenomenon of our cultural history. What is characteristic of the so-called Italian Renaissance is the coincidence of a revival of classical culture with a revival of the human mind itself and its creative energies in every field of activity. But this coincidence has not come about only once in history; it has occurred again and again since the days when Rome first met with the genius of Hellas and took from this deep spiritual experience the inspiration for her own literature and culture. The same thing that happened then to a great European nation happened later to a great Asiatic religion when Christianity found its most complete and universal expression in the forms of classical Greek and Roman philosophy and culture. It thereby gave birth to something new: the Christian world-civilization from which we derive. The new flourishing of Greek and Latin literature in the fourth century A.D. was the effect of this classical-Christian renaissance. Two of the greatest philosophies of Western civilization are the products of this synthesis of the Christian faith and ancient Greek culture: those of St. Augustine and St. Thomas. In these forms Platonism and Aristotelianism lived on through the ages in unbroken continuity, even after Greek literature was forgotten in the West. As Whitehead has wittily remarked, the entire history of philosophy is nothing but the footnotes to the text of ancient Greek thought.

It is not my intention to trace the workings of the principle of renaissance through the entire history of Western civilization. Tradition appears in it not as a dogmatic authority which imposes itself on later generations like a rigid law from without. There is a natural shift of emphasis from age to age corresponding to the changing needs of the times absorbing the tradition. History is not all progress, and the spirit in which every age approaches the heritage tradition offers it is as different as the situation and capacity of man at various periods of his life. For the primitive centuries of the early Middle Ages, ancient tradition was an inexhaustible source of encyclopedic information; but a more cultivated age soon returned to the attitude of late ancient classicism: it looked upon the masterpieces of ancient literature as timeless models of form to be imitated. The scholastic philosophy of the Middle Ages received its logical training in the school of Aristotle and found in Ptolemy and Galen's works the key to the riddle of the universe. In the modern age we have learned to turn upon the works of the past the light of their own times, that is, to approach them historically. This implies the danger of relativism and historism; but history itself teaches us to trace the continuous influence of every great personality and work of our humanistic tradition through all ages and to see the eternity of those personalities and works as a historical fact rather than as an abstract norm, as it was understood by the humanists of former centuries. History shows, as we have tried to illustrate by examples, that this influence has been strongest in the periods which are the culminating points of the creative power of the human race. In those periods of renaissance the binding and liberating effects of tradition are in complete balance, and they are no longer felt as "tradition."

Will there be another renaissance in the new civilization? Our historical experience alone cannot answer this question. Whether our humanistic tradition will be alive in the future will depend on the creative power of our own civilization and on its sense of true greatness. History tells us of ages during which the light was very dim and nearly extinguished, barbarous centuries of migration and brute force, when freedom was to be found only in some lonely oasis, in the life of a hermit in the wilderness like St. Jerome, or in the shelter of one of those famous monasteries which have been seminaries of culture for centuries. The historian is not a prophet. But a few questions seem to suggest themselves in our historical situation.

There is a strong idealistic trend in the emergent civilization toward one world. Certainly we cannot attain this goal if we begin by giving up the strongest unifying force in our intellectual life, the classical tradition which has implanted in us the ideals of humanity and of universal brotherhood, and substitute for it science and industry. These ideals are the homogeneous basis which Western man needs in order to reach a true understanding with the great religious traditions of the East; and at the same time they are the common ground of the nations of our own hellenocentric world, which equally includes East and West. If we are praying that this one world of the future may be a better world, the improvement certainly cannot begin by throwing away the noblest part of our cultural heritage and by the unilateral cultivation of another part of it which, if deprived of the standards of our humanistic tradition, may lead us to destruction. For all progress, if it is only an improvement of technical means and methods of science without the knowledge of a higher wisdom to which those means and methods must be directed, will only hasten man's ruin. What we need is a new synthesis of our culture which neglects no essential element of man's nature but restores to it a wholesome balance. It was the aim of the philosophy of Plato and Aristotle to bring this about, and the problem we are discussing is in reality their basic problem. They were born in a period of history which had lost this balance. Power politics had claimed the first place in life and had ruined the culturally leading states; freedom of the individual had been carried to an extreme in the intellectual as well as the economic sphere, and national egotism was the rule that dictated the conduct of states. When we read the works of the classical philosophers today we recognize at last that our history has moved in a full circle. It is this experience and not any special dogma that gives the philosophical thought of the greatest Greeks its new actuality. Without being a prophet one may predict that in the age to come those philosophers will be more at the center of man's intellectual life than at any time in modern history.

It is hard to imagine the coming age as a revival of classical art, as was the case in the Renaissance. The function of any humanistic revival that may be ahead of us will not be primarily aesthetic but critical in the broadest sense, a critique of culture as a whole. The line of development of modern humanism leads from Winckelmann's classicism, the imitation of a timeless ideal of beauty, to the critique of culture which we have witnessed during the past half century. This critique of culture may take the form of a new and intensified understanding of the cultural ideals of the past in their relation to us or the form of pure philosophy. This twofold aspect of our humanism reflects the process that has been going on for centuries in our civilization, the great dispute between tradition and reason. Philosophy, the meaning, the purpose of existence, if it wants to reassert itself, must reassert reason. But from Greek philosophy we can learn that even the purest and most radical rationality of approach does not exclude conservatism, which maintains the inherited organic form of our spiritual existence. The new form must include the older one and preserve it on a higher level. If it is true that the history of Western civilization is the history of human freedom, the emergent civilization must build for the future a healthy human society which will give that old ideal of freedom a new and deeper, more responsible meaning.

ETHICAL PRINCIPLES OF THE NEW CIVILIZATION

We are living in an age pervaded by strident overtones of insecurity and apprehension. We sense the necessity of adapting both our modes of thought and the pattern of our institutions to requirements imposed upon us by the unprecedented circumstances that confront us. The belief that we have arrived at the end of an era is widespread. There is a sense of urgency and of crisis, of the necessity of decision and of fresh ventures in the total enterprise of human living.

The successful harnessing of atomic energy, achieved but yesterday, serves but as a vivid symbol of the problematic situation in which we now find ourselves. It has accentuated and made vividly concrete the nature of the paradox and dilemma that have issued from the major forces responsible for the development of our modern Western civilization. Had the nuclear physicists at Los Alamos met with failure instead of success, the underlying problems would still be with us, fraught with only a little less dramatic appeal and urgency. The plain, untutored man now realizes, if but vaguely and dimly, how supremely pressing and practical are the problems and issues that lie at the heart of ethics and moral philosophy. These matters have ceased overnight to wear the appearance of something bookish and academic.

For if it be true, as it apparently is, that something on the order of a hundred bombs suitably placed would destroy all life upon this planet, it is also true that, short of this, any use of atomic weapons for war and destruction will cause mankind to revert to a condition of life which Hobbes depicted as the natural state of man, "short, brutish and nasty." But it would be infinitely worse than this, because some memory of his past promise, achievement and failure will linger on to make

184

more bitter the fate that will have befallen him. In any future war neither victor nor vanquished, if such there be, will be in a position to carry forward the torch of civilization in a manner comparable with the way in which the birth of a new civilization has, in the past, followed upon the defeat or collapse of an older or alien civilization.

The perils that evoke this pervasive sense of fear and insecurity do not originate in the massive and relentless sweep of the forces of physical nature over which puny man has no control. It is not as if a new Ice Age or the running down of the sun's energy threatened the continuity and development of human life. Man is and will ever remain helpless in the face of cosmic circumstances over which he exercises no control and which pertain to an order of things in the making of which he has had no share. It is well that man should be reminded that he is, so far as the life of his body is concerned, a veritable child of nature. Save for some tiny sector of what lies near at hand, knowledge is not power and is not the instrument of practical mastery and control. The vast sweep of cosmic energy does not wait upon man's bidding. If, however, mankind is overtaken by the tensions and conflicts resident within the pattern of his own living, his own civilization and institutions, he will have been overcome not by the titanic forces of an alien physical world, but by the demonic energies of his own nature, by his own pride, folly and ignorance, and by his failure to understand and to master himself and his own life.

It is because of this that the central and crucial matter at stake is primarily an affair of morals and of ethics. In the understanding of man's life, of the human situation, ethics plays a role analogous to that performed by mathematics in acquiring an intellectual mastery of physical nature. Mathematical analysis yields the clue to a knowledge of the physical world. The more comprehensive and exact does our physical knowledge become, the more indispensable do differential equations and statistical probabilities become. Man's life and experience throughout, the activities and structures that are characteristic of the human situation, are pervaded by a concern for values and meanings. Man's understanding of himself and his career is contingent upon his coming to terms with these values and meanings. This is the task and the province of ethics and of moral philosophy. Its primary and major business is not to inform men as to what, specifically and concretely, they are to do. Ethics prescribes no direct answer to the question, *Quid faciendum est?* In this sense, it is not "practical." Its intent is insight and illumination, an insight which cannot stop short of comprehending the true nature of man and the relation in which he stands to whatever realities surround and encompass him. Viewed in this perspective, the unprecedented circumstances of our situation today take on an aspect somewhat less intransigent and forbidding than they might otherwise possess. They lose none of their urgency and pathos. But they need to be seen upon the vaster background provided by the essential ingredients and characteristics of the human situation as such. There is a constancy and deeper permanence in the position in which man ever finds himself. The basic problems posed for his living and his apprehension do not shift and fluctuate nearly so much as do the transient occasions and circumstances of a day. Our absorption in the exigencies of the moment should not cause us to lose sight of this wider and more stable background of our immediate and more practical concerns. There may be principles inherent in the very nature of the total and perennial human situation, analogous to those mathematical principles whose discovery has proved so fruitful to our understanding of physical nature.

The dominant, outstanding achievement of modern man, signalized and symbolized by the atomic bomb, is his mastery of physical energies. His technology is the fruit of his science. This has won for him power both over nature and, as in war and the threat of war, over his fellow men. What is now everywhere recognized is that the possession of instruments of practical mastery lies within a wider context. That wider context is a matter of morals, in a sense of "moral" more profound and significant than is customarily attached to that term. It is now brought home to the awareness and imagination of men everywhere that the possession of power does not dictate or prescribe the purposes for which that power may be used. Something is required beyond the knowledge, skill and intelligence displayed in any of the instruments devised by human wit and cunning. This something more is the subject matter of moral inquiry and effort. Is this something more, so sorely needed, to be sought for through an extension to the human situation of essentially the same methods and procedures that have won for us our mastery of physical nature? This question is basic and fundamental. Upon its answer hinges the direction to be taken by our efforts and our plans. Here is the source of the great divide along the entire front of reflective thinking and of the considered appraisal of the nature of the task now confronting us.

To say that man's mastery of nature has vastly outdistanced his mastery of his own life and society has become a commonplace. It is frequently urged that man's understanding of his own life, of his own nature and needs, has advanced little further than had the understanding of nature at the time, say, of Thales or even Aristotle. Statements to this effect commonly carry an implication. They imply that the major if not the sole source of our ever-increasing confusions and perplexities lies in our failure to utilize the methods and habits of thought which have proved to be so startlingly fruitful in winning a mastery of nature, for achieving a comparable mastery of the human world, of human relationships and society. If only the social scientists and psychologists could have at their disposal a few billion dollars they could uncover the hidden forces operative within history, society and human nature. Men would then be in possession of the key to their own destiny through such an advance of scientific knowledge deployed upon the human situation. The root of our difficulties is thought to lie in our acceptance of cleavages, divisions and dualities inherited from an outmoded past. We are bidden to envisage the whole of man's life as continuous with the processes and transactions of one inclusive world which we have learned to call "nature." Here within this one world, endlessly varied and changing, is to be found the locus of all that pertains to the life of man, the sources and objects of all his interests and loyalties. With a thousand variants and crosscurrents, the tides of naturalism have swept over the scene that is characteristically modern, fashioned by all the formative forces of our technical and secular civilization. So much is this the case that any questioning of the premises of this naturalistic drift is taken to be but a nostalgic symptom, bred of an unwillingness to accept wholeheartedly the accredited findings of modern science, and a wistful longing to reinstate beliefs and institutions discarded by the progressive march of events. A morality and an ethics, pertinent to our world, must be based upon the findings of anthropology and sociology, of history, and above all, of a scientific psychology. Any other basis of human morality will but echo the deep-seated divisions and dualities that have vitiated man's life throughout most of his history.

What, then, calls for inquiry, so far as our present thinking and beliefs are concerned, is the question as to whether there is anything significant and valid attaching to those modes of thought which envisage the human situation in terms of some basic, problematic type of duality, inherent in man's own nature and being. If such there be, it does not follow that any of the historic forms that have given expression to this recognition of duality, and which have by now receded into the past, can or should be revived. It would, however, mean that a naturalistic ethics which would eliminate every trace of such dualities and tensions in man's life will not be adequate for an understanding or mastery of the full round of human energies. To see human life solely within the context of nature as known by the sciences, physical, biological, social and psychological, will not comprise the whole story about man nor will it yield the total insight needed for the guidance of men's actions. The persuasion that finds utterance in some such manner as this is, at bottom, sound. It calls for incessant clarification, both to fathom its own meaning and to guard against the confusion and vagaries that so readily attend it.

That we are suffering from the divorce between morals and intelligence is not to be gainsaid. Man's quest for knowledge, his intellectual life as exhibited in his sciences and philosophies, lies within a wider context. It has social and moral implications. Of these we need to become aware and to take them into our reckoning. Likewise, the practical interests that determine the direction of men's efforts, the ways in which life and society are organized (which is morality as a going concern), stand in need of a clarification and a justification which only intelligence and knowledge of some kind can provide. Otherwise, the practical activities in which men engage are at the mercy of passion and prejudice, bigotry and fanaticism. But it is not through any development of the premises and the logic of naturalism that the breach between morals and intelligence, between the direction of the will and the illumination yielded by intelligence and knowledge, is to be healed. There is far more to hope for if we seize upon the insight that has found expression in the recognition of some of those very dualities and tensions which naturalism and a so-called humanism bid us discard as otiose and perverse.

Intelligence is not unambiguous. And when it is asked of us that we infuse morality with intelligence and acquire an apprehension of the moral implications of intellectual pursuits, we need to know with what accent intelligence is weighted and with what it is linked. There are procedures and habits of thought responsible for the great successive technological inventions which men have made, and the ways of dealing with things which make these achievements possible that are modes of man's intelligence. His technical intelligence has won for him whatever mastery he has gained over his world and his life. Looking at the picture in the large and with particular concern for the historical career of Western man, what stares us in the face is the invasion by technical intelligence of territory once subsumed under a quite different type of sovereignty. Custom and tradition, magic and superstition, religion and morals for long ages claimed jurisdiction over large provinces of man's life and experience. The word "morals" itself indicates its kinship with socially inherited and traditionally binding ways of behavior dictated not by intelligent skills and techniques but solely by custom and tradition. Some rudimentary degree of technical skill based upon an observation of nature's rhythms, some reliance upon and utilization of inductive inference fetched from empirical matter of fact, must always have been present. The successful carrying on of any practical art depends upon such techniques. The getting of food and the fashioning of implements are contingent upon due attention to empirical and prosaic data. But in primitive cultures these practical arts were embedded in a matrix of rites and taboos, of customs and mores belonging to a totally different dimension, lacking any intrinsic continuity with habits of thought engendered by technical efficiency and skill. The principles of magic, religion and morals, of law and custom, were sanctioned not by empirical, matter-of-fact evidence, but by superempirical and supernatural agencies. Thus, the division in man's experience between the domain to which the procedures of technical intelligence are applicable and the territory belonging to morals went hand in hand with all the other great dualities that have left so deep a mark upon all our inherited ideas. Over against nature was some supernature, over against human needs and satisfactions stood divine laws and imperatives, and within man himself these dualities found an echo in the idea of an invisible soul separate from his palpable body. The spread and expansion of intelligence over the whole of man's experience appear to demand the excision of all such fundamental dualities. A sense of freedom and emancipation and the deployment of human effort and interest within the dimensions of a single, undivided world wait upon closing the gap

between all these ancient dualities and the strain and disquietude that
they engender. Naturalism and humanism bid us relinquish every trace
of these far-flung, pervasive tensions as we prepare ourselves for a final
desperate venture, that of constructing a universal human order embracing under one sovereignty the warring interests of diverse nations
and races.

The hope that man's technical intelligence may spread to every province of human action and the belief that it should do so, thereby an-
nulling the chasm between morals and intelligence, between life and
knowledge, are nourished by various roots. There is, first of all, the
actual success that has attended the development of technologies in
engineering and agriculture, in medicine and public health. All these
advances are the fruit of patient experiment, guided and illumined
by intuitions and hypotheses suggested by the observation and analysis
of factual data. Possibilities of controlled activity are disclosed by the
nature of the material with which one is dealing, the disposition and
grain of its component parts, and the laws that are descriptive of their
relations and behavior. What a field there is for the display of technical
competence and intelligence in constructing the administrative machinery of a modern city or state or business concern and in keeping it
running smoothly and efficiently! The skill and training of the expert,
of the technically intelligent man, is called for throughout. The good
craftsman, artisan or worker in any field is the one who possesses the
technical skill and knowledge requisite for his task. Let no one define
too narrowly the limits of technical intelligence or restrict the areas
to which it is applicable. Do the virtue and the excellence properly
denominated "moral" belong to a dimension fundamentally disparate
from that which characterizes the goodness of a skilled artisan? Does
not the success of the art of living, in all its reaches, depend upon the
skill and intelligence by which action is guided?

Those who answer this question in the affirmative appear to speak
in the authentic idiom of Socrates and of his successors. The legacy
that Greek thought bequeathed to European civilization is a belief in
both the possibility and the necessity of extending the domain of intelligence over all the areas comprised within the fabric of man's life and
experience. The entire gamut of man's purposes and actions, including
morals and politics, needs guidance and illumination such as can be
fetched only from insight and knowledge. Nevertheless, Socrates' in-

sistence upon the indispensable role to be played by intelligence in the life of action, his assimilation of the skill required in the art of living to the skill of the craftsman, was accompanied and overlaid by another set of requirements. At the human level, intelligence implies more than technical skill, however far it may be developed and refined. A knowledge of the values and ends that are served by skills and techniques, a knowledge of the Good, also is required. Only when this is operative within human action does the life of reason become a possibility. To canalize the ideas and ideals implicit within the life of reason into the channel marked out by the range and application of technical skill and scientific knowledge, however broad that channel may become, is to forfeit an insight of which we stand today in more desperate need than ever before.

The significant legacy of the Greek thinkers cannot be restricted to the impetus they gave to the development of science and to the use of technical intelligence in the art of living. The ideas they set in motion were rooted in the belief that man's life is bipolar, that the energies native to man are not to be organized around one single center. There is, in human life, a duality. Man's life is no simple prolongation of the energies and processes of nature. There looms into view a dimension of being, discrepant with anything which, to use our language, can be disclosed within nature by physics, biology, sociology, or a "scientific" psychology. This dimension of being is accessible to man's reason, it bears upon his purposes and interests, it haunts his imagination and disturbs the rhythms and harmonies of his "natural" existence. It is not strange that man when he faces this duality, with all the burdens and tensions it imposes upon him, should shrink back from them and endeavor to conceive his own nature and destiny in a manner which will, at the least cost, resolve these tensions and complexities and, in this too easy manner, endow his life with unity and single-mindedness. The major drift of naturalism, and the kind of humanism with which it has become allied, lies in just this direction. It fits in with the logic of this development, to assimilate everything significant which the Greek thinkers intended to denote by the term "reason" to the procedures of practical skill and technical intelligence. The remainder is relegated to linguistic tautologies useless both for the organization of practical interests and for the acquisition of knowledge. Hume is the authentic spokesman for the modern retreat from reason.

The duality inherent in the human situation as such is clearly evident in the life of action at the human level, in all that belongs to morality. The problem of human living and of the organization of man's life is complicated by the presence of a kind of requirement different from any to be found in animal life, or in human life in so far as it is a mode of animal life. All life is the seat of demands which the living organism makes upon its world. The problem posed for all life is the problem of getting what it wants and needs from the resources proffered by its environment. How can I get what I want and what I require? is the perennial question that life asks. The direction of all effort, in this perspective supplied by life, is determined from within, by the nature of the demands made by life. These demands vary endlessly. Yet they cluster about some few basic and dominant drives and interests which are definitive of the very nature of life. Now, all these centrifugal demands, things wanted by life, are, at the level of man's experience and action, cut across by demands of a completely different sort. There are demands whose vectorial direction, so to speak, is opposite to the direction taken on by all vital demands. There are demands not made *by* man and by the current of his interests and desires, but laid *upon* him. It is not enough to enumerate the many things that men want which are of no concern to any other animal. What requires recognition is the presence not only of all such multifarious and diverse interests and desires, but also demands made upon the total congeries of interests which make up his life. There is that to which man owes allegiance, beyond all the vitalities and interests of which his life is compacted. Man is somehow linked to an order and dimension of being other than that which satisfies the requirements made by all his vital demands. The duality thereby introduced into man's experience is disconcerting. It is accompanied by hazards. The problems that enmesh us would be enormously simplified if this duality could be obliterated and forgotten and if man could cease to be troubled by the haunting notion that the meaning of his own life is fetched from beyond any of the demands that stem solely from himself.

The problematic duality of means and ends is here in question. When the practical and moral question is put in the form, How can men get what they want? all of the weight falls upon means. All that is needful comes within the span of technology and technical intelligence. For the ethics of hedonism, as for any naturalistic ethics, all practical problems are technical problems. For hedonism, there is no doubt about the status of pleasure or satisfaction as the one inclusive and supreme end. The only matter in doubt is the question as to how to get it, and that is wholly an affair of means, calling for the exercise of skill, prudence and technical intelligence. This is *animal* intelligence, which becomes more and more in evidence in the upper reaches of the scale of animal life. How much of the marvelous cunning and contrivances exhibited by insects, birds and beavers is due to the initiative and experience of the individual organism and how much to the massive wisdom of nature which the organism but inherits and transmits, may be in doubt. We do know that man is able deliberately to utilize his experience and observation, contriving tools and instrumentalities, thereby extending seemingly without limit his dominion over nature. One continuous thread of technological intelligence runs through all the episodes in the evolution of animal and human behavior. Trial and error, failure and success, defeat and triumph, attend the long series of experiments which life has made to sustain and to further itself. But with man something new comes into view, distinguishable from the order of animal intelligence, and even more to be distinguished from blind feeling and passion, from habit and sheer animal faith.

It is animal life that is marked by a preoccupation with means. The ends which are served, the end of life itself, are nature's ends, not those of the living organism. The individual animal does not freely and knowingly choose and espouse the ends to which his cunning and ingenuity, his instinctive proclivities and his intelligence contribute. The ends are provided for him, leaving the whole of his activity to be engrossed in the contriving and manipulating of instrumentalities. It is as if Nature did not thus far dare to entrust to any of her creatures an understanding of why they live and suffer, are born and die. Nor has Nature been willing to leave to animal life the decision as to whether the game is worth playing or not. The zest of life, whatever it cost in pain and suffering, privation and defeat, is Nature's hint that nothing whatever is to count when measured against her necessity that life shall carry on. She endows her creatures with skills and techniques which she bids them use to exploit every possible resource in the service of life and the satisfaction of its needs.

With man, this preoccupation with means, with technology and animal intelligence, is countered by a new and disturbing force which shatters the complacency and equilibrium of nature's vitalities. Man is never wholly content to accept the desires, wants and interests that define his life energies with the same tacit confidence and obedience implicit in animal life. There supervenes upon his struggle to get what he wants a moving force belonging to a different order. To speak of this as just another desire is wide of the mark. For it is a desire not for some specific thing capable of satisfying a specific want. It is the "desire" that the object of his desire and effort, whatever it may be, shall be itself *desirable*, worth pursuing because of its intrinsic worth and goodness. The full scope of human energy is never enlisted unless there exists the belief that the object of one's devotion and loyalty is such as rightfully to lay claim upon us. The belief that the course he is following and the ends he is seeking are objectively valid, that he ought to direct his effort toward them whether or not he happens to desire or prefer them, the necessity of this belief is an ineluctable part of our human situation. This belief ought not to exist if the sole concern of the human animal, like all other animals, was in getting what he wanted, in satisfying the demands he makes upon his world.

Impressive examples of this belief are found in conflicts which arise in man's life, as, for instance, in war. No nation is willing to go to war in the absence of the persuasion that its cause is just and right. In fighting for its own interests, its own life and survival, it must be persuaded that it is also fighting for ends and values which are objectively valid. The fact that men involve themselves and others in deception and duplicity, their proneness to conceal their own interests and lusts for power under the cloak of objectively valid ends, is not in question nor is it here to the point. The momentous and startling thing is the actual presence in man's life of this necessity. It places human conflicts in a class by themselves, different from anything to be found elsewhere in the struggle of life with life. Were the contestants in a dogfight to make articulate the grounds of their combat, each would say only, "You have that which I want and which I propose to get if I can." There would be no reference to any objective criterion of rightness or justice. No taint of duplicity and self-deception would encumber the transparent honesty of such a pronouncement. Why not ask of men in their conflicts and warfare that they be just as honest and sincere? This is exactly what is intended by all variants of the ethical theory according to which the pronouncement "This is good and right" is a verbal disguise for the wholly factual statement "This is what I or we happen to want." Naturalistic theories of ethics are weighted with a sense of the essential continuity of human life and all other life, seeing in the growth of man's technical intelligence, continuous with animal sagacity, the chief mark of his own stature. These perspectives of the human situation reject any suggestion that there is that about man, his reason or spirit, which links him to an order and dimension of being other than that comprised within the contingencies of nature. They view as wholly illusory any hint that man lives his life at the turbulent crossroads of the demands made *by* his vital interests and the claims laid *upon* all his vital energies stemming from an objective realm of meaning and value.

Man thus has the "desire," rooted in his human nature, that the final object of his desires be truly desirable and capable of being known as such. He can never be content, as all other forms of life presumably are, to pursue ends solely because they are dictated by the momentum of his vital impulses and interests. The ambiguity of the term "desirable," upon which Mill foundered, brings out the point in question. A sound is audible if it can be heard, and the test of its audibility is the fact that someone does hear it. Is the criterion of the desirability of anything, in like manner, the fact that there happens to exist somewhere the desire for that thing? To answer in the affirmative is a betrayal of language. This is not what men intend to say when they assert that something is desirable. They mean to utter the belief that, whether or not there happens to exist any desire for the desirable thing, it *is* desirable and men ought to desire it because it is good and intrinsically worthy of their effort. The belief may well be mistaken, but the utterance is a judgment about something there, objective and discoverable, and independent of the caprices and contingencies of men's *de facto* likes and dislikes. This is the most significant characteristic of man, that he does give utterance to persuasions of this order, and that only such ends as are believed to be bathed in the light of a transparent objectivity can enlist the full measure of his devotion. Nor is it the part of wisdom to suppose that such persuasions are bred in his mind solely because man is, unwittingly, a dupe of language. The view that the verbal form of judgments of value has led him to misconceive the objectivity of values on the analogy of the objectivity of fact entirely misreads the situation. The hidden wisdom that language incorporates may not be so readily discounted. Nor is it safe to judge the meaning and validity of discourse in terms of prior restrictions upon what words must mean, derived from some particular theory. Were an animal, say a tiger, pursuing his prey in the jungle, to justify the goal of his endeavor by uttering a judgment of objective value, we would refuse to take the tiger at his word. We would have no difficulty in penetrating beneath his linguistic stratagem and in exposing the vital interest it might seek to conceal. The tiger has no need of language because the horizon of his world does not stretch beyond the domain of nature's matter of fact. All his energies are enlisted in the service of his vital wants and drives. The longing that the goal of his efforts, the object of his desire, shall be good, reasonable and desirable is not to be counted among his native or acquired drives.

Both man's search for knowledge and his moral life spring from this concern for objectivity. There is no enterprise, no domain of action characteristically human, that is immune from this flair for objectivity and its unceasing quest. It is just this which lends a moral quality to skilled craftsmanship of every kind. The skillful artisan is he who knows the nature of the material with which he is working, and who is guided by that knowledge. He is continually sensitive and responsive to the ever-changing demands made upon him by the objective situation there and then confronting him. He has developed powers of discrimination and sensitivity of eye and hand which equip him to handle and to treat things for what they are. It is this which makes his activity intelligent. The generic concern for objectivity is never in abeyance in any of the skills, excellencies and virtues that men prize. Discrimination and sensitivity in the presence of significant values and a responsiveness to the demands they make upon the will is the earmark of moral intelligence. But the range of such moral sensitivity and objectivity far transcends the limited and partial scope defined by any centrifugal vital interest.

The paradoxical nature of the "interests," of the concerns that come within the orbit of man's reason, is indicated by the adjective "disinterested," which we apply to them. How paradoxical is a disinterested interest! To be disinterested might seem to be synonymous with indifference, a lack of concern for anything that stirs to action and enlists the emotions and the will. To demonstrate the psychological impossibility of disinterested action has been the purport of familiar and recurrent themes from the Sophists through Hobbes, Bentham and Freud. Yet nothing is more evident in the moral experience of the race than the supreme worth that falls within the orbit of disinterestedness. No moral excellence, no virtue, is untouched by this quality. It is a quality of action, and of the will and character that action expresses. For this reason, if for no other, the moral sense has never been willing to lodge the ethical quality of actions solely in their consequences. Disinterestedness cannot be ascribed to consequences. It attaches only to motives. To be disinterested is to acknowledge the valid claim that objective, significant structures make upon us, to be responded to with the minimum of bias and partisan interest on our side.

Objectivity of judgment, disinterestedness, are ideals which belong implicitly to the life of reason and to all the activities and interests specifically characteristic of the human spirit. These ideals define the goal and the principle both of man's quest for knowledge and of his restless struggle to build a moral and social order commensurate with the requirements laid upon him by his membership in an ideal order. The entire situation is problematic, hazardous and paradoxical because man still remains, as the child of Nature, subject to her vicissitudes and contingencies. In the grand strategy of Nature, mind and spirit appear to have come upon the scene harnessed to the needs of life and tied down to the fortunes of an animal body. Life is the master; intelligence and mind are its servants. And both life and mind give every appearance of being inextricably interwoven with the processes of nature, caught up in a nexus of interacting events—physical, biological and social, comprising one single world. To conceive of any dimension of being which transcends the space-time world of Nature's happenings and structures and to admit the possibility that human thought and action can be determined by intrusions from another order of existence run counter to the accumulated insight of centuries of intellectual achievement. Man is no less enmeshed in the flux of Nature, tied down to some local, partial and contingent fragment of things, than is any other form of life. How, then, can it be asked of the mind that it be disinterested and aspire to any measure of objectivity in its judgments and its perspective? To achieve this, the mind would have to emancipate itself from the circumstances to which it owes its birth and transcend the limitations of its own partiality and bias. But this is just the miracle that does happen if there be anything won by the mind fit to be called knowledge. For knowledge is the achievement of a spectator who stands outside of the scene he observes, reports and interprets. Only a spectator can meet the requirements of objectivity and disinterestedness. This is the intent of man's pursuit of knowledge and his quest for truth. Let it be admitted that the ideal is not capable of complete fulfillment and realization. But it is difficult to see how man could even be troubled by the thought of such an ideal if the horizon of his view were wholly bounded by the contingent forces and events that play upon him and by the vital drives that impel him from within his own nature. If, now, one disbelieves in any possibility of the mind's freeing itself from the concatenation of the contingent happenings of Nature, if one declines, as does naturalism, to acknowledge an order of being other than that of Nature's events, there is but one course to follow. The idea of knowledge and of truth will need to be transformed so drastically as to be virtually relinquished. Instead of being insight into the objective nature of things, discovery of structure, form and relations, knowledge becomes assimilated to action and practice, to power and mastery. These are the prerogatives of life and of the thrust of vital energies. Held within their orbit, there is no escape from the interplay and conflict of particular, partial interests.

And what of the quest for those ends and values which give meaning to the human life of purpose and of action, the effort to achieve justice and peace, to effect an ordering of man's life transcending the array of conflicting, partial interests, the dream of a kingdom of brotherhood and good will? The resolute will to embark on such a moral venture is no less dependent upon objectivity of judgment and disinterestedness than is the search for knowledge and truth. An open society, unmarred by any closure against strange and alien races and nations, free from the dominance of some one class in possession of economic and political power, requires the operation of motives and forces which are tangential to all the partiality and bias of vital interests. Men will not devote themselves to the realization of these ideals unless they believe in their compelling validity and unless they also hold to the persuasion that it is possible to transcend the limitations arising from their own partialities and local, particular interests. Faith in the mind's capacity to overcome the prejudice and bias inherent in all vital impulse and action, to cease being wholly at the mercy of factual circumstance, to embark upon the task of achieving objectivity, this is the nerve both of man's pursuit of knowledge and of his concern with morality. The possession of this capacity is the distinguishing characteristic of the human spirit. It is this which introduces into man's experience a duality, leaving an indelible stamp upon all his effort and purposings, upon all that is of concern to him in both his practice and his theory.

Three centuries and more of intellectual scientific development have left as their deposit in the prevailing "common sense" of our age a profound distrust in the possibility of any objectivity of judgment, of detachment from the exigencies of life, from the circumstances that play upon the shaping of our convictions and our loyalties. We know so much about the turgid sources of our preferences, ideals and valuations, about the irrational roots of the human psyche in the dark depths of the blind unconscious stirrings of animal impulse. We trace the formation and the contour of physical and mathematical theories to the state of the industrial arts, the dominant technology, the requirements of commerce and of war. All organized and systematic knowledge, which we know as science, is viewed as an instrument, an organ of society, or of some vigorous segment of society, expressing and furthering its power and mastery. The mind and all that pertains to it is thus embedded within the one order of Nature's events, with no possibility of detachment and emancipation from the sovereignty exercised by her structures and processes. This is the essential theme of the now dominant philosophies of naturalism. The strange thing is that the very results of scientific development which are held to discredit any belief in the autonomy of the human spirit, or in the notion that the mind is not resolvable into biological or social behavior—these very fruits of science are themselves dependent upon the mind's capacity to survey nature, society, history and even itself as a disinterested spectator. To affirm, as does naturalism, that the mind participates in no other order than that of Nature's events even when expanded to include the happenings of all historical and social development is to destroy the roots that nourish man's intellectual and moral life. Philosophy has an indispensable and urgent function to perform. Upon it lies the burden of showing that there are purposes and loyalties which are sanctioned not by what men happen to want and to like because contingent circumstances have so conditioned them, but by objectively

valid and significant values and ideals in the service of which man ceases
to be servile and becomes free.

The hazards and perils that attend all experience at the level of
human life and that belong to our human situation as such are inescapable. They pervade both man's basic theoretical beliefs and his
philosophies, and also the organization of his purposes around some
focus which will lend coherence and meaning to the life of action.
These hazards are twofold. Men are prone to credit their theoretical
beliefs with a greater measure of objectivity and truth than they are
entitled to in view of their actual entanglement in biological and
social contingencies. They accord to the world as perceived by the
senses a finality and objectivity, unmindful or forgetful of the manifold ways in which the mechanisms of body and brain condition all
our sensory perceptions. Also, in the world of action and practice men
are prone to accept as final and absolute some contingent and partial
interest and power, some historically conditioned institution, some
particular nation or state, race or class. Along this path lie fanaticism
and pride, blindness and myopia, an unwillingness to acknowledge
the relativities and contingencies inherent in everything temporal and
historical. On the other hand, the evils that result from endowing any
frail, limited and partial structure with an absolute and final sovereignty tempt men to reject as meaningless and fatuous any notion that
there may be valid claims made upon their devotion and allegiance by
something other than their own *de facto* wants and desires. To avoid
the risks and hazards of self-deception and "rationalization" men are
bidden to renounce all reference to objective standards and principles
which lie beyond the relativities of all historical situations.

A belief in the possibility of transcending the limitations imposed
upon men's actions by the contingent factualities of history, of all self-
and group interests, is an indispensable prerequisite to any hope of
constructing an order of life commensurate with the situation now
confronting men. Such a belief prescribes, by itself, no specific plan
of action. It supplies no blueprints for the political and social structures of which we stand in need if humanity itself is not to perish.
All such prescription, tentative and experimental, is an affair of technical intelligence, of devising and administering means and instrumentalities. Ingenuity and inventiveness of the highest order are here
called for. But unless these be sustained by the temper of good will,

nourished by man's belief in the possibility of transcending the limitations of his own bias and partiality, the structures devised by human wit will not avail to ward off disaster.

It is a twilight zone in which our human lot is cast. On one side lie the requirements of the near at hand, the here and now, of the necessities that spring from the precarious contingencies of life and history. On the other side is the requirement for man that he shall arrange his life in view of his participation in an order of being not identifiable with anything located within the flux of nature's events. This belief, however it may have found expression in an endless variety of symbol and even myth, is not an illusion. It alone can supply the living nerve of the supreme venture men are now called upon to make, of encompassing the whole of humanity within a single moral order binding upon the interests and caprices of each constituent group, and capable of eliciting the loyalty of men everywhere.

THE FUTURE OF FREE SOCIETY

One of the main facts in modern civilization, a fact about the economic order, a fact so abundantly recognized as to be a commonplace, is that it has become inextricably entangled with the political order, and beyond that with social relations and moral ideals. Economics has not only gone into politics; it has in fact pre-empted the center of the political stage, and its problems have become the outstanding and crucial issues in our democracy and in the world. To say this is not necessarily to subscribe to any form of "economic interpretation" as one's philosophy of history and general view of man and conduct; such a course the writer at least considers one of the leading intellectual confusions in later nineteenth century thinking. It is surely a fallacy to interpret the past and attempt to forecast the future in terms of any single "independent variable," whose course one essays to map and carry forward in the manner of predicting the path of a comet or the trajectory of a missile; and the notion that the independent variable can be identified with the economic as a distinct department of life is a further oversimplification and a superficial view of social-historical reality. What the merging of economics and politics actually means is simply that the future of civilization in these two aspects must be considered in close connection, and that in both regards it is a matter of social choice and action.

What has been said above is only a beginning of a statement of the problem, the first step in a rational attack upon it. We must go on to recognize that in the nature of the problem itself nothing properly to be called a "solution" is to be expected, or is even theoretically possible. An objective discussion of the future, with respect to human beings—in their distinctively human and social character, in contrast with the physical and biological—must begin by disclaiming all intention and thought of actual, concrete prediction, and may usefully devote a short first section to the special character of the problem of forecasting events in this field. The least exposure to social science reveals not only that there is no crystal ball in which any reliance is to be placed; we know also that there is no science of history that is more than very remotely analogous to the celestial mechanics by which an astronomer can predict eclipses forward and backward over thousands of years and timed out to several decimal places.

As a preliminary, we may be reminded by the problem of weather forecasting that even in the field of purely physical and macroscopic events the results of science still leave much to be desired in the way of concrete foreknowledge. But where human action is in any way involved, science affords no possibility of actual prediction. It predicts only hypothetically: "if" the man, or men, in the case behaves in some assumed way, "then" the physical consequences will be such and such. The science of medicine can tell a good deal about the effects of taking a given dose of arsenic or opium, as other sciences can do for other acts, if they are performed. But the question as to whether any person —and especially the questioner!—will perform the initial act in the sequence is largely unanswerable. Difficulty of analysis is really aggravated by the fact that *afterward* more or less plausible reasons can be found that make the result seem inevitable. And in many cases where the individual instance is unpredictable, observation of a class of cases makes it possible to predict statistically with some accuracy and so to state a "probability" for the individual case. But application of this "insurance principle" to human conduct is narrowly limited by the "moral hazard." In general, even probable prediction is possible only in connection with given, familiar departures from an established and known routine, and not with real, historical change. Behavior involving such a change is experimental and it is an *a priori* impossibility to predict the result of any experiment; for, to the extent that prediction is possible, the act is not an experiment (from the standpoint of the predictor); it is either a means to a foreseen and intended result or there is no point in performing it at all. In the physics laboratory itself, the investigator can tell what will—or would—follow from his manipulating a familiar piece of apparatus in a familiar way. But he will usually be unable to predict what he will actually be doing with the apparatus for even a short time, and an outsider, however versed in the science, would be quite helpless in the face of the task.

We note, too, that prediction of one's own behavior is in a minor degree based on scientific thinking or procedure. It is usually not in substance prediction at all, so much as making a choice or commitment, which is likely to have the character of a promise and to create an obligation of some sort. Thinking about one's own conduct, deciding and planning, commonly runs in terms of two stages of choice, election of ends and selection of the means and manipulations adapted to their achievement. This is really but a beginning of the actual complexity, since all concrete ends become means as fast as their achievement is in prospect and an end is rarely fully defined until it is achieved; but for present purposes the analysis need not be pursued further. The importance of the means-end view here is its role in prediction. When the behavior of others is in question, we think in terms of motives, in this twofold form; they are imputed on the basis of whatever knowledge we have of the personality or character—knowledge which is highly intuitive—and not directly in terms of previously observed physical behavior. The place of motives in conduct is somewhat analogous to that of "forces" in a physical process. These also are metaphysical and logically superfluous; yet they seem to have an inevitable place in our thinking. And in conduct there is this vital difference and further complication: the notion of gravitation, for example, cannot interfere with our observation and use of the facts of the motions it is thought of as producing, since it is known only from these motions and measured by them; but we have knowledge of human motives from other and subtle sources besides observed gross behavior—intercommunication and inference from one's own consciousness—and we "know" at least as certainly as we know physical facts from sense observation that conduct is affected by "error" and so fails in all degrees to correspond with the motives of the person acting. Error, which is contrary to the nature of causal sequence, enters in different ways into both the recognized stages of choice, i.e., choice of ends and of means.

This way of thinking is particularly important in considering "economic" behavior. The term has no meaning whatever in connection with the behavior—if we should call it that—of inert objects in nature. Prediction of economic behavior rests on knowledge of three sets of factors: the ends pursued and the means available, and the procedures or techniques open to use. All three, in so far as they are data at all, are not merely or primarily physical facts, but are "cultural" phenomena (in the anthropological meaning of the term). They are historical products and can be understood only through a study of the history of the particular culture in question; thus the problem of prediction is primarily one of historical causality rather than that exemplified in the repetitive events dealt with by the laboratory sciences.

Again, the problem with which we are concerned here is that of predicting the future history of a culture by persons who are a part of it, members of the social group which "carries" it. This fact suggests another important limitation. An anthropologist can make predictions of considerable value with respect to a society which he observes entirely from the outside, especially a "primitive" society, which is the only sort the scientific student ever really views from without. But this is because of two facts: first, primitive societies are subject to comparatively little change; second, and more important, they never know what the anthropologist writes about them. If his predictions should be reported to the societies concerned, and any attention paid to them, they would suggest numerous reasons for behaving otherwise and so invalidating the result. (It is a general condition of scientific knowledge that the observing and reporting do not change the facts themselves; modern relativity theory shows that the assumption is not rigorously valid even for seeing or photographing physical events, but the discrepancy is negligible in comparison with other sources of error.) The fact that is essential here is that predictions of the future of one's own society not merely do change the course of events itself but are made primarily for that purpose. They have the function of disclosing opportunity for action, hence that of invitation, admonition or warning.

Thus the relation between knowledge and its application in action is entirely different in the social field from that of the physical world, and this relation always vitally affects the process of knowing itself. In such fields as astronomy and meteorology, we strive to predict in order to adapt our own behavior accordingly. In the fields of the laboratory sciences we hope to change the behavior of the subject matter itself, by contrived manipulation or intelligent "control," into channels more suited than what would happen naturally to our comfort or convenience or some interest or other. The social problem, or social aspect of human problems, is very different from that of man's relation to inert nature. In the first place, all control of men by other men is contrary to the ethical ideals of free society, and is regularly applied only to criminals and defectives, in connection with the literal enforcement of laws which they have no part in making. In the second place, in ordinary peaceable social relations efforts at control or "influence" are mutual. But mutual control is a manifest impossibility; any degree of success by one party must rest on a greater failure of the other. In such contests the heart of the matter is "strategy," literally a form of deception, including concealment of intent and of contemplated moves. If such efforts are carried far, if they are not closely limited by "rules of the game" respected by or enforced upon all, one of two results will follow: society may become a shambles, the famous war of all against all, or some particular individual may establish his arbitrary will as law and make himself dictator. Even in this case, in the most extreme example which it is realistic to imagine, the technique must be largely one of deception, persuasion or coercion, concepts which have no meaning in the control of passive nature by intelligent and purposive man.

For the purpose in view here, in contemplation of the future of free society, the problem of social knowledge and action is not one of prediction-and-control at all, but of intelligent consensus in choice of policy embodied in law governing the conduct of all. It centers in legislation, not in law enforcement; if much of the latter is called for, society cannot be democratic and free. As already suggested, the problem of predicting the future is that of deciding, through reaching an agreement, on what kind of society we want to be and to become. As a social problem, the question centers in the form of organization rather than in what, concretely, is to be done, by individual members of the organization or by the organization itself as a unit. Assuming that the supreme desideratum is freedom, our task is to make the political decisions that will give us the advantages of the large-scale economic organization necessary to utilize modern technology, with the minimum of control of anyone by anyone else. We wish to be able to predict that, as far as it is reasonably possible, each person shall choose his own type of life and achieve it in his own way. This means that the content must and should be unpredictable, even in theory, beyond the general fact of "improvement" with reference to the three factors in economic action—refinement of wants and increase of resources and of efficiency in the technique by which they are employed. The function of law in free society cannot be that of enjoining, or even in any large measure prohibiting, concrete acts; it must be that of laying down general rules, of the nature of traffic rules, in sharp contrast with prescribing when, where or how men shall travel. The requisite for living intelligently and at the same time enjoying liberty is for each to have reasonably confident expectations as to how others will behave, so as to act rationally in his relations with them. In addition to making and enforcing such general laws, every independent society has to act as a unit in meeting various internal needs and in its relations to other societies. A free society is one in which both sets of decisions are reached through open discussion and with the closest possible approach to unanimity; they must reflect an intelligent consensus of the whole membership, not merely the special interest of any majority. It is from this point of view that the future of economic life in Western civilization is to be considered; and the consequences of action upon the nature of the political and social structure are more important than the results for economic life itself, in any distinctive meaning of economics.

*   *   *   *

Such knowledge of the future as is possible and as we can consistently desire—conditional and meager as it is—must, as a matter of course, be derived from the careful study of the present and of the past through which it came to be. At the beginning of any such study, the first fact which should strike the attention is the historical uniqueness of modern Western civilization and the profoundly revolutionary character of the few centuries of change by which it came into being. The best name for it is liberalism, or individualism as a more objective synonym; its essential and distinctive feature is freedom of the individual to build his own life and find his own place in society. Rather an incident, though indispensable, is political democracy, government by representatives held responsible to the whole people; what is really fundamental is freedom of thought and expression, criticism and inquiry, from which freedom of associated action and other freedoms follow as a matter of course. Even the political order of democracy, in anything like an inclusive sense, is unheard of elsewhere, at least in connection with groups of substantial size and advanced civilization. Greek democracy, from which we take the word, was no exception, since it rested on slavery and involved only a limited citizen class among the free population; it also existed in tiny units and was intolerant of religious or intellectual nonconformity. Freedom is peculiar to a small region of Western Europe and lands colonized from that area, and to a period of a century or two, though as a matter of course "beginnings" can be found much further back in time.

The growth of liberalism marks an essential inversion of the values by which all other civilizations have maintained peace and order and been able to survive; for the moral foundations have always rested on the bedrock of conformity to tradition and obedience to established authority. If we look at human society in a comprehensive sense, we find that at the earliest stage of which we have any knowledge, it has been ruled almost exclusively by custom and tradition. In so far as the individual is conditioned in infancy to conform with established behavior patterns, he will indeed feel no coercion, but he clearly is not free. Custom is a different kind of mechanism from that of instinct, which controls animal societies, but is still a mechanism, though biologically superior in that it admits of adaptive change more readily than the chances of genetic mutation. However, men have apparently never been machines, in the sense in which the individual unit in an insect society may be so characterized. Men seem never to conform either unconsciously or altogether gladly. Savages are kept in order, made to conform and submit, by the fear of "spirits" or supernatural powers of one kind or another, though authorities are also present to act decisively, with the aid of the mob, in case of serious infractions.

Primitive society is necessarily a phenomenon of quite small groups. The achievement of a tolerably high civilization seems to have been an accompaniment of unification on a much larger scale under conquerors (variously associated with "prophetic" leaders) who became rulers and claimed the "divine right" to make and change law contrary to custom, and to act without regard to any law but their own wills, and who secured the support of religion for their position. In short, and using the modern word, these early kingdoms and empires were "authoritarian." At the same time, they were based on a more or less elaborate and rigid caste or hereditary-class structure of society, from the monarch down to the serf and slave. To a degree hardly greater than in the majority of savage or barbarian societies was the ordinary man free to choose or make his own way of life, to better the position in which he found himself through birth; and he was far more subject to arbitrary spoliation and personal maltreatment by his "betters." The rise of such civilizations and their decay or destruction through diverse causes fill the pages of history, re-enacted with infinite variation, in different settings. In some cases, small city-states have lived for a time under a "democracy" of a political and cultural élite, as in the familiar case of Greece. While the resemblance to modern great-nation democracy is less important than the differences, some of the same problems of organization were met and discussed and we can learn much from the record if we interpret it carefully.

Following the ossification of classical civilization under imperial Rome, and its "decline and fall," Western, and particularly Northern, Europe became the seat of virtually primitive, customary, small-unit civilization. Its usages and class structures were religiously sanctioned by Christianity in the form in which this cult, of Asiatic origin, had become established and organized in the centuries of decadence. In the course of time, the "Dark Age" was superseded by what we call the medieval civilization of the twelfth to the fifteenth centuries. This developed under the stimulus of various contacts with the Byzantine survival of classical culture and the Moslem inheritance and transformation, enriched with elements from India and China. The advance from postclassical to modern conditions may be viewed in terms of two general stages of transformation. The first followed the broad pattern already suggested. Occupying the later Middle Ages and the period of the Renaissance, this epoch was marked by the growth of power in the hands of kings and the final establishment of absolute monarchy, by "divine right." An important incident of this process was the religious "Reformation," which disrupted credal and ecclesiastical unity and domination and established national churches under the new states. (This last is only less true of countries which remained nominally Catholic than of those which became nominally Protestant.) However, any adequate account would have to stress other factors, especially the role of commerce and then of industry, under a new technology. The latter developed in connection with a scientific movement very different in spirit from anything known to classical antiquity (or anywhere else in history). It was through a tacit alliance with the rising business classes that the kings were able to establish their authority over the higher nobility and clergy. And there was, of course, the great "revival of learning," the aesthetic, literary and speculative awakening that was both cause and effect of the rediscovery, in Western Europe, of ancient Greek works. Also beginning far back, the silent disappearance of slavery and serfdom suggests some obscure underlying social force working in the direction of individualism. A conspicuous and highly important manifestation was the constant appearance of more or less heretical prophets and movements, and the proliferation of sects in connection with the Reformation. For the main thing from which Europe had to be liberated, if it was to be modernized, was "orthodoxy," in the aggravated form of the idea of a single true religion and rightful authoritarian church for all the world.

It was the second stage of change that was literally unprecedented historically, in its character and results. It consisted on the political side in the democratization of government, breaking of the power of absolute monarchs in favor of parliaments, and progressively establishing the latter on the basis of wider and wider representation and more effective responsibility through election by an extending suffrage. In terms of social causality, the more fundamental change was the achievement of intellectual liberty. This came rather anomalously as a by-product of religious toleration, which in turn was a result of weariness of war between churches and sects, but historically it was the vital issue at stake in the religious struggles. Granted intellectual freedom, liberty in action and responsibility of rulers to the governed follow inevitably. After the failure of the Reformation on the Continent to achieve any substantial freedom of conscience and of the mind, a new and somewhat more effective impulse toward liberalism was provided by a kind of second Reformation in England, the Puritan revolution of the middle of the seventeenth century. This was exactly contemporary with the settlement of Westphalia (1648), which fastened on Continental Europe the twofold doctrine of sovereignty, the supremacy of the state over the lives of its subjects and that of the hereditary divine-right monarch within the state.

The events of this time marked a great turning point in European history, in fundamental ideals and ideas of man and the world, as well as in political and religious forms. Thinking in terms of the individual gradually replaced thinking in terms of the state, as this had replaced or was replacing the church as the basic social entity. Reason, both abstract and empirical and utilitarian, replaced dogmatic faith, and the political-economic interest or "game" replaced struggle over religion and church, as men turned from yearning for salvation in a future life and from the monastic formula of poverty, chastity and obedience as the way to secure it, to the pursuit of material and cultural, intellectual and aesthetic well-being, for themselves and for society, in this world. The doctrine of original sin gave way to buoyant optimism, confidence in human nature, and a general demand for the human rights of freedom and equality. The transition period was one of economic and political rivalry and struggle for "power and pelf" between states; but the more important fact was the rise of activism, the spirit of progress through criticism and investigation, with equal emphasis on humanitarianism, all in place of traditionalism and dogmatism, submission and repression.

The growing spirit of the Enlightenment, or Age of Reason, was solidified in England after the second revolution (of 1688) by the work of Newton and Locke, while it was being transplanted by Dissenters and adventurers to the British colonies in North America. Presently it was also carried to France by such able writers as Montesquieu and Voltaire. In both regions the individualistic and rationalistic attitude was intensified; in France as a doctrine to be used against church and state authoritarianism, in America by the conditions of frontier life. In the later eighteenth century an equally potent force working in the same direction appeared in England in the great wave of technological advance called the Industrial Revolution. The American and French political revolutions of the same period are usually taken as the gateway into the nineteenth century. State control over economic as well as religious and cultural life rapidly disintegrated in favor of individual liberty and free association in all fields of endeavor. ("Laissez faire" is really a synonym for "freedom" and only by historical accident came to refer specifically to governmental noninterference in economic affairs.) Individualism naturally implies cosmopolitanism, and for a few generations it seemed that state and nationality were really losing importance, that the ideal of mankind as a universal society or brotherhood, with freedom of action and of movement over the earth under a minimum of coercive government, was actually on the way to ascendancy. Originally, the primary meaning of political freedom was the negative one of a sweeping reduction in the functions and powers of the state. Democratic institutions were designed to be a safeguard against official infringement of individual rights. The state was to be restricted to defense, the police functions of suppressing violence and fraud, and such "public works" as could be recognized by all or a vast majority to be for the general good, but which for any reason it would not be profitable for an individual or voluntary group to provide for payment by those directly benefited.

*   *   *   *

The age of liberalism thus ushered in was destined for a short and remarkable history. The main facts are familiar, and can be briefly called to mind. On the one hand, the world region of Western civilization experienced progress so unexampled that the advance in a single century has been seriously compared with that of all previous history, at least since the beginning of written records. This progress was by no means merely "material"—a term of doubtful meaning and most commonly used as an epithet; it affected as well pure science and philosophy, and humanitarianism, and especially the diffusion of education and cultural participation among the masses of the people, along with comfort and security of life. Much of this was not only provided gratis at public expense (from the taxes of the well-to-do) but was made compulsory, as was true also of the basic health services. It came to be a trite observation that the poor had enjoyments and privileges that a few generations before were luxuries or even inaccessible to kings, or were entirely unknown. The great scourges of pestilence and of war seemed on the way to disappearance.

Yet all this amazing improvement did not lead to contentment among the masses, but rather the opposite; the attitude of outrage and revolt spread rapidly. Spokesmen who were more and more listened to and politically followed told "the workers" that they had been liberated from the despotism of state, nobility and church only to be handed over to equal exploitation under a different form of slavery in the wage system, for the benefit of property owners, the "capitalist class." Propaganda for the "socialization" through the state of property, and the management of production and exchange was rife in England itself early in the nineteenth century; and before the middle of it, Marx and Engels published their famous "Manifesto" calling the world proletariat to unite for violent revolution, assuring them of a world to gain and nothing to lose but their chains. Meanwhile, some of the conditions associated with the new industrialism seemed to the privileged and ruling classes themselves so intolerable that political measures were taken to deal with them—the "factory acts" and similar measures.

By the 1870's, when the political and economic theory of individualism received its classical formulation at the hands of Herbert Spencer and the subjective-value economists, it began to be apparent that the moral tide of individualism and cosmopolitanism was ebbing, giving way to a revival of statism, imperialism and increasing international rivalry. It is surely evident that antagonism between states would naturally grow with increased recourse to governmental action to meet internal evils and problems. But the opposite view has been held by the propagandists for socialism; they have plausibly painted their movement as alone promising the conditions necessary for "real" democracy and especially for internationalism, through aligning the exploited against the exploiting class the world over. The first nationalistic, or "world," war, of 1914-1918, seemed to furnish visible demonstration of the error in this view. Class loyalty and international spirit were no match for the combination of patriotism and the sheer power of established governments, notably in Germany and France where the whole movement was most advanced. This same war, however, led to the anomalous triumph of Marxist proletarian dictatorship in industrially and politically backward Russia, to be followed by the surrender of parliamentary regimes to anti-Marxist nationalistic minority parties in Italy, Germany and elsewhere. But the world-revolutionary aims and pretensions of the Bolsheviks rapidly evaporated to disclose in even intensified form the nationalistic expansionism as well as the autocracy of the old Czarist Russia. Conflict between the Russian and German nationalist dictatorships and fear of both by the democracies was the main real basis of World War II, though historical accidents and political blunders made it begin with Germany in opposition to the Western European democracies, with Russia neutral, and end with Russia and the democracies in alliance. Unpleasant as the fact is from the liberal standpoint, it can hardly be disputed that the democracies survived only because of the ineptitude of the German leaders in attacking Russia and of the Japanese leaders in attacking the United States.

*   *   *   *

The next step in forming a judgment as to where we may go from here, economically speaking, or how conditions and our own acts will operate to determine our future will be to call to mind the main features of the economic order of liberal society. This must be thought of first largely in terms of ideals rather than reality, as the system under which people thought they were in a way to live, say, in Britain and the United States in the later nineteenth century. Keeping in mind that intellectual and cultural freedom (a by-product of the struggle for religious toleration) was prior to economic, both logically and in time, we observe that the economic order implied by the same ideal of free action and association is an organization through production and exchange in the open market. (By exchange we shall mean purchase and sale against money as an intermediary; at a later point it will be necessary to mention complications due to business speculation in which money plays a somewhat independent role.) The political and social turmoil of our times, including international wars, is chiefly due to revolt, or threatened revolt, against the "evils" of this economic system. The evils chiefly denounced are inequality, injustice and oppression, and liability to crisis and depression, with unemployment of workers and equipment, and consequent suffering. It should go without saying that in the scope of this chapter we can give only a schematic and considerably idealized or "theoretical" description.

At the beginning of such a discussion, it ought to be emphasized that the more general "principles" of economics apply to individual and social behavior in a way so abstract that they are essentially timeless. We are unable to imagine human beings who do not use means (including their own members and faculties and external things) to realize ends and make choices among ends and ways of using means, with a view to efficiency, a synonym for economy. The concept of economic behavior involves these three factors—ends, means, techniques. Without summarizing an elementary treatise on economics we can only assert that the first principles do apply in so far as behavior is actually effective or economical, regardless of the concrete content, i.e., what ends are pursued or what resources or technology are employed. Similarly, we cannot imagine human beings who do not live in societies, or societies without some division of labor and co-operation, some doing things for one another, in the interest of greater efficiency (along with other interests), hence the substance of exchange, whatever may be the form. In fact, no human beings are known who do not carry on considerable trade, in regular markets, though in primitive society this occurs much more between tribes than between members of the same tribe, and prices are largely fixed by custom. Again, the first principles of economy through specialization mediated by exchange, at the most general and abstract level, are independent of what is exchanged or the form of market organization. In short, certain choices have to be made in human social life and the meaning of making them economically does not depend on who makes them or the concrete alternatives. Since it would be mere stultification to predict the concrete content of economic life any distance in the future, and since the most general principles are changeless, our discussion can relate only to certain intermediate features of the liberal economic order as it has grown up, under men's quest of the good life through economy in the use of means, or as a result of conflict or historical accident.

The "modern economic order" is regularly called an "exchange economy," but the expression does not properly apply. The system is not one in which individuals—or families, the real primary units in any society—typically produce and exchange (sell and buy) products. Modern technology, in connection with which the economy grew up, calls for a further stage of specialization. Individuals are specialized not merely to the production of a single product but to the performance of some particular operation in production, among a vast number of operations, and hence of individuals, required to turn out a particular product. The physical equipment and even the direction, all furnished by independent individuals, are similarly specialized. A further requirement is that production is carried on by a highly organized technical unit called the enterprise, not by individuals working separately with their own tools and equipment. (In reality an enterprise usually produces a number of partial products, made from other partial products of earlier stages, so that a practically unlimited number of enterprises as well as individuals are concerned with any actual product as it reaches the ultimate consumer.) Predicting hypothetically, we can say that if scientific technology is to be used, it must be used in such organized units. Enterprises must exist; hence they must be organized internally in some way; and there must be some social mechanism for co-ordinating the activities of different enterprises so as to supply the consumer units of society with the various products in requisite volume. Thus arise the two primary problems of economic organization, narrowly defined.

As the liberal economy has grown up in the course of history, the second stage of organization, the social co-ordination of enterprises, is worked out chiefly through the "competitive" marketing of products, much as would be true for individuals in a more primitive, or "handicraft," economy—and as was more or less true of the European economy in the later Middle Ages. Production is finally directed by consumers' demand expressed in purchases. For practical reasons, the internal organization cannot be effected in this way. The close co-ordination of activities that is necessary has been achieved through the enterprise organized as a unit purchasing the services of the human beings (labor of all grades) and other agents, and all work under centralized direction. This unitary organization might conceivably have been an inclusive partnership or democratic producer's co-operative, embracing all participants in production, with any constitution on which they could agree. But it has happened otherwise. At first the common form was that called individual entrepreneurship. Some enterprising person, usually with substantial resources of his own, would lease property or borrow "capital," create or hire whatever special equipment he required, and hire the appropriate kinds of labor or personal services, all in the open market, at stipulated rates of payment (rent, interest and wages); he would then proceed to make and market his product. (It is to be noted that in free society labor can only be hired while property can be either rented or bought with borrowed money, according to the convenience of the parties.) The "entrepreneur" would expect to sell his product for more than the outlays incurred in producing it, leaving a "profit" for his own contribution and compensation for running the risk of loss, which might actually result. It will be seen that in contrast with a handicraft, or "exchange," economy this system involves a second set of markets, for dealing in productive services of all kinds, in addition to the general market, or system of markets, for consumers' goods.

In the course of time, enterprises grew in size and complexity of operations. Partnerships of varying extent and terms of association tended to replace individual entrepreneurs and in turn gave place to the stock company or corporation. In form, the corporation is a co-operative association, with a constitution (embodied in its charter) similar in form to the political democracy. Its government is representative; but the membership includes only a part of those who supply property or its services—roughly the owners of voting common stock. The personnel of the organization participate only if they also individually own stock, and participation is not equal—one-man-one-vote—but in proportion to the stock owned, the capital ventured. Actual management is in the hands of salaried functionaries selected by the directors who represent the stockholders, making the officials agents of the proprietors.

The complaints, frictions and conflicts that now constitute the main problems of political life center in the working of the economic order at both stages. Advocates of radical change clamor for internal democratization of the enterprise, which is alleged to underpay and tyrannize over the "workers," and perhaps a part of the investors also, in favor of "insiders," and to be inefficient in serving the interests of consumers. And they also clamor for a central authority representing society as a whole, a "planning board" or the like, to control all enterprises, all production and distribution, in the interest of everybody. This over-all organization would clearly be identical with the state. According to the socialists, it would be democratic, but according to communists and fascists it would be a dictatorship with custody over the general interest and deriving its inspiration and authority from the working class, in the one case, from the nationality, or "folk," in the other. Living as we do in a society still committed to the democratic ideal, the only political questions we shall need to consider have to do with the compatibility of freedom with centralized political control of economic life, and the more directly economic consequences of substituting such control for market competition.

It should be kept in mind that the conflict situation is in a general way a three-cornered affair at the top, but with many subdivisions and ramifications. Politically significant reaction against the market economy developed first in organizations of wage earners, where "unions" were more or less direct descendants of the medieval guilds. Employers' associations of a formal sort appeared in opposition to labor unions as an agency for combating them. Not far behind, in America, were organizations of the "farmer" interest, directed against "business" as alleged controller of the prices of agricultural products and in less degree of the prices of things bought by farmers. But sometimes it is held merely that the market is chaotic or anarchic and requires interference to make it "orderly." Both farmer and worker organizations strive especially to raise the prices of the things the groups have to sell—wages in the second case—and strive more and more to enlist the aid of the government in this endeavor. The claim of the wage earners is that employers naturally have greatly superior "bargaining power" and in addition are informally if not formally organized to keep wages low. The problem of the merits of these and other regulatory measures and of socialism and other policies will be touched upon in our concluding section.

*   *   *   *

To shed light on the possibilities of improving the economic organization through political action, we must consider some of the conditions under which it operates, particularly the use of technology based on advanced scientific knowledge. It must be evident that utilization of such technology calls for wide and intensive specialization, which in turn entails interdependence and consequent limitations on individual freedom. The necessity of fitting into a pattern and keeping up a scheduled performance is the price that must be paid for the vast increase in productive efficiency. The enlarged income extends the economic power of the individual, the range of choice open to him, both as consumer and as producer, hence his effective freedom. But this power or freedom is enjoyed subject to harmonizing one's behavior with the will of others; and it seems to be human nature to be more conscious of the restrictive conditions than of the advantages, and so to "feel" coerced. This will clearly be true in some way and degree whatever the form of the organization, and some compromise must ultimately be struck between efficiency and literal freedom. An analytical view of the problem might consider first a situation in which scientific procedure is employed by an individual specialist, apart from any organized technical unit. An example would be medical practice, where the patient is under the power of the doctor; but this is balanced by his freedom to choose his doctor and to change at will. What is essential is that the ordinary person is confronted with problems which he knows can be solved in the best way only by the application of knowledge and technique he does not possess and for which he must turn to the appropriate specialist and submit to control of his conduct by the latter.

If production in most lines is to be efficient, operations must be closely co-ordinated under the guidance of competent administrators as well as technical experts. There must be production units, each organized and governed as a unit. This might conceivably be achieved by "democratic" methods, either of the direct, town-meeting, or the representative type. However, partly because of the risk of absolute loss of property investment, but chiefly because of considerations of efficiency, it has worked out that enterprises are managed by agents of entrepreneur groups who take the risks of failure or success along with responsibility for the major decisions, and for the selection of the agents who make those of a more detailed character. It must be recognized in any case that the theoretical possibilities for democratic control are limited; any large amount of freedom in momentary behavior is simply incompatible with effective group action. As an action group increases in size, the influence of the individual member in controlling it soon becomes psychologically insignificant and the costs in time and effort of securing agreement become prohibitive, while frictions and tensions threaten disorganization. Finally, at the utmost, the minority on any issue must yield to the majority, or numerous minorities to a plurality, leaving actual control in the hands of a fraction. In practice, after extensive trial by enthusiastic advocates, in the form of producer co-operatives, even indirect democratic control of large productive enterprise has proved a failure and unable to survive. Large groups of workers are found to be incapable of agreeing upon policies or agents to determine policy, and chaos results, or they make wrong decisions and run into bankruptcy. At least workers do not generally wish to have this form of control with the costs and risks it turns out to involve; they prefer to exert organized pressure on management. Otherwise enterprises would actually have this form, for there has been no legal or arbitrary prevention of any organization satisfactory to the parties concerned. Organizations of "labor" might hire capital, instead of the reverse, and undoubtedly would do so if they could manage production as effectively.

But this does not in the least mean that the workers as employees have no voice in the control of production, or the detailed conditions of their work, or that they have to organize and negotiate and bring pressure in order to secure influence. Their main channel of action is through their purchases as consumers. Buying the goods most wanted at the cheapest price is the primary force in an enterprise economy for directing production into the right channels and compelling adoption of the most efficient methods. But enterprises also compete in the labor market, and freedom of choice of employers by workers must be compared with various ways of bringing overt pressure, as a method of exercising effective and desirable control.

*   *   *   *

We turn to the second line of radical change proposed, the centralization of control of production under the authority of the state—socialism or collectivism, or "planned economy." We must observe that this amounts to making the nation one vast producer co-operative association, and the failure of this system on a small scale points to the same result on the enormously larger scale, where the difficulties would be increased at least in proportion. General reasoning and recent history, notably in Russia, seem to join in proving that a collectivist economy, in order to secure the necessary minimum of efficiency, will have to give the directorate absolute power. It would apparently have to be in a position to make decisions without debate, and furthermore to be immune from political attack and so from all criticism. Hence some group or clique would have to seize permanent tenure and prohibit all opposition, even if in the abstract they, like Cromwell, abhorred irresponsible power; and the notion that persons of this disposition would be the ones to get into the position of authority in a power regime is surely so improbable as to be dismissed from thought.

Even if the forms and the substance of democracy could be maintained in a collectivist economy on a national scale, the amount of benefit which could reasonably be expected is enormously magnified by the advocates. Assuming, again, that modern scientific technology is to be employed, the general pattern of production and distribution would have to be about the same as under the existing market economy. Markets with competitive prices of goods and services would have to be maintained as the main framework of the organization, if only to bring the administrative problem within the scope of human capacity. The socialistic states that have been established, specifically Russia, have recognized this fact, and indeed socialists have rarely proposed anything else, and this is clearly the only form of economic constitution that allows individual freedom of choice to consumers and producers, along with large-scale productive organization. On the other hand, all liberal states have included a considerable amount of public enterprise, and the amount has strongly tended to grow. The difference between economic individualism and state collectivism is at best a matter of degree; no one seriously proposes going all the way in either direction, and the more one studies the problem the smaller the difference will seem.

There is room for a wide divergence in type of socialization policy, as well as its extent. Socialists seem to have in mind a combination of public ownership of the "more important" productive wealth with political appointment of the managers of enterprise. There is little necessary connection between these two features; either enterprise or property ownership could be socialized without socializing the other. Of course seizure of property, judged by the moral standards of historical liberalism, is "confiscation" and immoral; but again, there is no line between confiscation and legitimate taxation, especially if the change in system should be carried out gradually and with the burden equitably distributed, as is the policy of the Labor party government in Britain. However, the complete and permanent socialization of wealth would deprive people of the right to accumulate, to save and invest, which has been a fundamental economic liberty. Perhaps more important, it would reduce and seriously complicate the opportunity of parents to make provision for their children, a serious inroad upon the nature and functions of the family as an institution, and a corresponding aggrandizement of the state. And, as we have suggested before, this would intensify rivalries between states, since inequality among countries is about as conspicuous as among individuals. To work at all, socialism would probably have to be world-wide in scope, with a corresponding intensification of the problem of management under centralized control.

The reference to taxation suggests that levies upon income and inheritance have already carried this to a point which would have been regarded as outright and indefensible confiscation a generation or two ago. And the use of the proceeds for providing public services—especially free education—involves a fairly extensive redistribution and equalization. In theory this might be carried as far and as fast as it is found feasible to solve the political and administrative problems, and most of the objectives of socialism might be achieved in this way; the difficulties are serious but rather less so than those involved in socialization. However, there is a large economic area in which progressive-minded economists will probably agree that socialization is called for. That is the field of "natural monopolies," in which technical conditions make effective competition impossible. The best example is the "municipal public utilities"—street railways or buses, telephone, water, gas and electric systems, with the cross-country railways and communication systems really in the same class. There is good reason to believe that the policy of "regulation" of prices and service can never be reasonably successful. In fact, it may not be too much to say that all price control and concrete regulation are bad; they involve a plurality and pyramiding of authorities which can hardly make for efficiency, and they must be largely restricted to negative measures.

*   *   *   *

To come to our final word, it is apparent that a hard scrutiny of the future of civilization will reveal that there is no purely economic element in the problem. The role of economics as a science, or discipline, is, however, not to be underestimated and must be recognized as having a twofold character. It formulates certain abstract principles of economy in individual behavior; these are summed up in the doctrine of "marginalism" and are of no direct value for the guidance of either private conduct or social policy and action. They are for use in the second and main function, which is to explain the mechanism of economic organization through the free market. The fundamental principle here is that each individual makes the transactions most advantageous to himself subject to the one formal ethical restriction that all transactions are by free mutual assent, that each shall respect the equal rights of others by avoiding force and fraud and all collusive and restrictive action. It is assumed that in so far as people do not conform voluntarily to this ideal, there will be laws and a state to see that they do so, and to make rules for their more concrete guidance and interpret and enforce them in doubtful cases; further, the state must unquestionably perform whatever useful social functions clearly will not be properly taken care of by voluntary arrangements between the individuals directly affected. Even this limited role of the state presents serious problems, but the major issues arise in connection with social and human needs and demands which go beyond the narrow bounds of free and effective economic co-operation.

Problems are "economic" when they set the political order the task of making the individualistic economic order conform more closely to the individualistic pattern as worked out in economic theory. The problems of the mechanics of organization that cause most concern are monopoly and the business cycle. If the markets for goods and services are to remain even approximately free, social action is necessary to counteract the tendency for those on either side, sellers or buyers (but more usually the former) to act collusively, or to form groups of such size as to have substantial "bargaining power," which is true only of monopolies. This problem becomes acute where productive efficiency calls for units relatively large in relation to the output demanded in any market area. It becomes impossible of solution in many cases, under special conditions, such as the municipal public utilities and other "natural monopolies" already referred to.

While the problem of monopoly is serious enough, it is both exaggerated and misunderstood in the public mind; it is not nearly so important for the future of free society as the tendency of the market economy to cyclical oscillation between boom and depression. The latter, of course, entails serious unemployment of labor and other resources and widespread suffering, as everyone recalls from the late twenties and prewar thirties. The primary cause is undoubtedly speculation in the future value of money. An expectation of rising prices is a powerful stimulus to investment in heavy, durable productive equipment (since sale of the product at a higher price level than that at which the fixed costs are incurred will add to profit) while the opposite expectation will discourage investment. This expansion and contraction of investment spreads to the market for consumption goods through its effect on the demand for these. With respect to this problem it is possible only to say briefly (1) that it does not rest on any conflict of interest, since the rich lose their wealth when the poor are unemployed; (2) no constitutional problem is involved, since the regulation of money (like that of other units of measurement) has been an unquestioned function of government from the time when the modern state came into existence; and (3) to the extent that a socialistic economy used money and allowed freedom in its expenditure it would encounter the same problem. In other words, the control of depressions is a problem for economic science and political administration, not one of radical social change.

But there is a problem, or set of problems, of a quite different sort, involving the very foundations of social structure. It arises not because "competition does not work" but out of the nature of the market organization and economic freedom itself. As regards inequality and injustice

—the major accusations brought against the modern economic order—elementary economic analysis shows at once that the difficulty lies not in the organization for co-operation but in the conditions under which it operates, specifically the grossly unequal "economic capacity" with which individuals come to the market. The most serious aspect of the matter is that such inequality is a natural result of freedom and is intensified by the functioning of the private family, the basic institution of society and one surrounded with social and mental inertia reinforced by moral and religious sanctity. The elementary fact is that where economic and social analysis (properly for its task) takes individuals as data and discusses the problem of organization, the ultimate facts are palpably to the contrary. Co-operation is a relation between given individuals; but the real significance of this is that any thoroughgoing and intelligent attack on the social problem must go further back. It must consider what makes the co-operating individual what he is, and in particular the forces that give him his endowment with economic resources and so determine his earning power. Now, this is in part, but is not merely or primarily, a matter of the individual's moral qualities or humanly unalterable natural endowments; to a much greater degree it depends on his social inheritance through the family, of property, education, and stimulation and "contacts." The common disposition is to stress inheritance of property almost exclusively, but the other factors are undoubtedly quite as important on the whole. Practically all productive capacity has been produced in the course of history, human qualities as well as implements and materials; it is obvious that a human being in the raw state of nature would be a liability and not an asset. People have anything but an equal start in life, and the possession of a superior advantage of any kind places one in a position to secure more economic power and increase the difference in his favor. There is no difference in principle between property in physical things and technical or professional training or "personality." The cumulative tendency is as clear in the case of knowledge as in that of capital in the usual sense of the word; or, knowledge is really a form of capital, and in all cases the institution of the family enables this tendency toward cumulative increase in economic inequality (to him that hath shall be given) to go on beyond the individual lifetime, from generation to generation.

There can be no doubt that an extreme degree of inequality destroys freedom for the weaker party, giving to the superior power over the inferior as well as greater power over the nonhuman world. The problem set for a society which cherishes the ideals of freedom and equality is not merely difficult but clearly admits of no definitive solution. The notion of organized co-operation without some inequality of status and of power and its perquisites seems to be a utopian dream, not in harmony with the nature of man or the world. It is not realized even in the small units with select membership; and with reference to the world as a whole, it is clearly fantastic. Men are not equal in the limited aspects we can assume as "given"; and far more important, they are not data for the most part but institutional products, and the culture process in any social area shows a strong tendency toward differentiation and gradation. We must also face the fact that an approach to equality of individuals—really meaning families and other groups— within any "country" accentuates the inequality between countries. All civilized life is artificial; freedom is nothing if it is not freedom to "get ahead," to mount in the human cultural scale; and the effort on which progress depends must always tend to accentuate the inequality that exists at any time, in all those factors of ability or capacity which are developed by training or use, as well as inequality of external possessions. Organizing ability and power of persuasion are probably more important forms of power than is mere ownership of wealth. The "luck" factor also is highly important, and its operation may be expected to cause many shifts of rank order in the contest (a contest whether or not rivalry enters as a motive) but is more likely to increase than to reduce the over-all spread.

Inequality, amounting to power relations, between individuals and between families and states and every sort of community or group that acts as a unit and strives to improve itself and its position, seems to be inexorably a part of the price of freedom. Thus freedom tends to run into its own negation. We can hardly imagine a social order in which no person or group would be prevented from bettering himself or itself without carrying all others along to the same degree. This seems to be the ideal of communism, though it is doubtful whether any person of intelligence and critical judgment ever seriously believed in literal equalitarianism including himself, as a possibility (and its moral desirability is open to serious question). History has shown often enough—and now on a national scale in Russia—what anyone of good sense must have expected. The effort to establish communism means, or immediately runs into, a kind of specious equality among the subjects of a dictatorship by men infinitely superior in status. The inequality and one-sided power relations are polarized and fixed at once in a form far more extreme than has occurred in "capitalism" at its worst; and the self-contradiction of freedom and equality through communism is correspondingly more aggravated than the result of seeking the objective by way of free mutuality and exchange. What this observation ought to suggest, however, is that literal freedom of trade and enterprise, subject only to suppression of force and fraud and monopoly, has never existed either, nor been seriously advocated. All human social systems, perhaps all that can even be imagined, are combinations in varying proportions of all the theoretical types. It is between such mixtures, possible in infinite variety, that the issues lie.

*   *   *   *

We might develop at length the unpleasant theme of the inherent limitations on the achievement of ideal justice, which is not to be closely approached in this world in any relation of life, to say nothing of doing it through the coercions of law and politics. (People stand only a limited chance of getting the friends—or mates!—they deserve, much less the chance of having the merited children and hardly any of the parents—a fatality which goes far to determine their position and course of life, economically and in other respects.) But it will be better to bring this chapter to a close on a note of emphasis on the vast opportunities that are open for beneficial action. Room for further improvement is suggested by the progress already made in qualifying the individual's pursuit of his own chosen ends, conditioned only by mutual individual advantage for the direct parties to transactions, in the interest of wider social well-being and humane progress. As we have indicated at various points, this action has proceeded along many lines. Among the first, in order of obvious necessity, is the effort to control the tendency to business expansion and contraction, i.e., to stabilize the economy at a level of approximately full employment of its resources. But this effort and the voluminous discussion of the problem have not yet produced agreement on an effective and feasible policy. Another line of action well established and obviously called for is "antitrust," the breaking up and prevention of monopolies. Still another is progressive taxation of incomes and inheritances, with use of the proceeds to relieve the poor of the burden of maintaining the ordinary functions of government and to provide these through public agencies with such services as recreation and health, and especially education for the young. Nor should we forget the role of private benevolence, which transfers large sums from the rich or relatively well-to-do to the support of many necessary public institutions, charitable in the narrow sense, or especially, educational in a very broad sense.

All these policies can, and must, be pushed much further if free society is to achieve its moral goals or even save itself by solving the problems that threaten its existence. None of them looks to social revolution, such as would be involved in the outright prohibition of private accumulation of wealth, its investment and transmission by inheritance or testation, even if the forms of political democracy should be maintained, and the possibility of this is open to serious question. Complete socialism, or "planning," if it proved feasible—on the world-unit scale that would be necessary to accomplish its objectives—would call for centralized control which would at best deprive the citizen of essential economic liberties and give him in exchange one vote among hundreds of millions in the ultimate decisions of policy or selection of the policy maker. And a matter of at least equal importance is the opportunity afforded to the ordinary citizen to make a career on the basis of merit, in contrast with family, group or personal "favoritism" or a cramping traditionalism. The main argument against all schemes for socialization or planning is the danger that in seeking to preserve freedom and equality they will practically kill both outright. In any case, they propose to replace business controlled by market competition with politics ostensibly controlled by political competition and mass voting.

It would seem that in view of the impossibility of political prediction, and the vastly greater probability of harm than good from random or unintelligent action, we must at least give up radical measures and resign ourselves to "gradualism." This does not mean that "public ownership and operation" of industries should not be extended in comparison with present conditions in the United States. The general objections to socialization do not apply as long as there is an area of free individual bargaining broad enough in scope to set standards of value and of performance for public enterprise, and to give the individual effective freedom of choice as to which system he will work under. Something tantamount to socialization is indicated for such "fluid" natural resources as oil and gas, where the effects of competition are palpably wasteful and vicious. For other undeveloped resources and for those already in use, it is purely a practical question of what system of administration will work best, or of some social value to which private interest is indifferent or hostile. In many cases the desired result can be secured by general measures of regulation or a suitable tax policy. The regulation that is to be condemned on principle is price fixing. This is restrictive and has all the vices of monopoly, and can hardly be enforced in a free society in time of peace. Neither wage fixing nor the case of agricultural products is any exception, and our policies in these fields have resulted in the most serious monopolies we have. If social policy elects to place a "floor under wages," the way is to provide an alternative at the level desired, not to prohibit employment by law where it is to the advantage of both parties. Enforcement of safety measures and compensation for occupational hazards is a different case, for what is involved here is simply making a product or industry bear the costs it would have to bear if market competition were intelligent and effective.

We cannot get away from the fundamental principles of free enterprise, that the normal individual is usually a better judge of his interest than some "bureaucrat" is likely to be, and the more important one that freedom is itself a good and the condition of moral self-development, which is the supreme value for liberal ethics. From these it follows that men should be allowed to make their own terms of association, by mutual agreement, where no special reason to the contrary can be shown. There is no defensible basic standard other than the terms set by freedom of each to close with that other who makes the most satisfactory offer—and this is the whole meaning of the market and what is unfortunately termed "competition." In many cases this principle will work badly, and it must be supplemented or corrected by whatever form of social action is most effective and appropriate, according to the free consensus of society as a whole. Public opinion, of course, is not infallible, either; but it is the only court of final appeal, for men who do not believe in the superrational and supernatural designation of some particular individual or organization as a final authority to settle all matters that are in question at the human level. Many compromises are inevitable. Free enterprise can, within limits (never completely), allow each person to follow his own tastes in consumption and his preferences as to vocation. But it is "impossible *a priori*" to give everyone the forms of association, the social and legal order, that he would individually prefer, as long as there is any disagreement; these must be the same for all if there is to be any society, and agreement on something is more important than what is ordinarily at stake in a conflict of views. The highest possibility is simply the compromise that involves the minimum of residual conflict and sacrifice; this is what is aimed at by the machinery of representative democracy, *provided* that dictation by a majority to a minority also is minimized. It goes without saying that a majority may be as odious a tyrant as a minority party or an individual autocrat. For this vital provision the only hope is moral restraint and political intelligence.

Justice includes not only equality in exchange but reasonable provision for the strong or the fortunate to share the burdens of the weak or unfortunate. This can best be done, with the least compromise of freedom and individual responsibility, through an equitable system of taxation and assistance of those who prove unable to maintain suitable standards for themselves and bear an equal share of the common burden. In any case, beyond all question of idealism or sentiment, a free society must safeguard the physical, mental and moral health and adequate training of its youth, who will be society itself in the impending future.

Above all, we must not forget that "efficiency" and a high standard of living are only half the case for freedom, and rather the less important half. Freedom is a value on its own account. Free government must within limits be balanced against good government, even if there were fair assurance that some form of aristocratic control would be better. And in the economic organization, the open opportunity to choose one's way of life and develop one's capacities—including external as well as internal possessions, since no clear separation is possible between means and ends—is finally more important than the use of capacity to produce the highest possible level of consumption. It is difficult to explain the tendency in nineteenth century political discussion to stress almost exclusively the less important instrumental side of freedom, to the neglect of its intrinsic moral significance. Our institutions have been wiser than our talk, for the laws of free society do prohibit the contracting away of freedom for any tangible benefit conditioned upon a servile status. And the social values of free association are likewise fully as important as the gain in efficiency that comes through co-operation.

*   *   *   *

In conclusion, then, the significance of the principles for the emergent civilization is political and as much negative as positive. If the distinctive values of modern civilization are to be preserved, the masses who make up the electorate must have a general understanding of these principles in their dual aspect, the role of means and ends in the good life for the individual and the nature and role of organization for the more effective use of means in the life of society. The latter has its "economic" aspect in the narrow sense of co-operation through voluntary association, in which markets and prices inevitably become the main structural feature as co-operation becomes rational and systematic, and its "political" aspect, meaning over-all control by society acting as a unit. The political side of economic relations, so defined, has again two divisions: the making of general rules or laws to govern free association and the provision of services directly through some public organ or agency.

As a matter of fact, the discontents of modern man center largely in the economic aspect of social organization, though as we have seen this is only in part justified. Consequently it is imperative for peace and order and the preservation of civilization itself, and even of life, that men understand much better than they do at present the relations between these different aspects of life in general and of society. And in particular, they must better understand what government can and cannot do if it is to be free. And it must be kept free or it will both stifle moral development and do what the rulers personally desire, which is not likely to be the general welfare as judged by the people for themselves, even if people wanted to be made well-off by being treated as domesticated pets. Free government, by its nature, cannot, finally, do things for its citizens; it is itself a co-operative organization, which enables them to do things for each other. It can only decide the terms of mutual and unilateral relations, the rules for living and working together.

THE NEW EVOLUTION

In this analysis of the new responsibility of science for the future of man and society, I am comforted by the reflection that some of the most abstract ethical problems have in recent times become intensely and increasingly practical. Fifty years ago Thomas H. Huxley could, it seems, consider what he called the ethical process as based on general principles which were both immutable and rationally self-evident. Since his time his conception of absolute and unquestioned ethical standards has steadily become less tenable, to be replaced by an ever more thoroughgoing ethical relativism. But this process did not only manifest itself in the intellectual sphere. It emerged into the domain of brutal and gigantic fact. Fascism, notably in its National Socialist guise, developed its own ethical principles, in which millions of our fellow men firmly believed; and these were almost diametrically opposed to anything which Huxley considered as self-evident. We lived under the grim material necessity of defeating the totalitarian system, ethics and all, but no less under the spiritual and intellectual necessity not merely of feeling or believing but of *knowing* that totalitarian ethics is not just different from the ethics of social democracy, but is wrong and false; or at least less right and less true.

Nazi Germany, nevertheless, demonstrated what strength a society can draw from its ethical beliefs, however distorted. Meanwhile for the world the fateful responsibilities of a society based on peace loom daily larger. Split them up as you will, into their economic and political compartments, into devices for technical and administrative improvement, they must add up to make a better world. No jesting Pilate can escape the implications of that word "better." To know that the new world at which we aim is better than the old is to have some assurance of the adequacy of our own ethical beliefs to meet the new situation.

Yet this is precisely what we lack. There has been a collapse of our traditional values, so that we live in a bewildering atmosphere of ethical relativity. Thus there is the immediate duty of contributing anything one can to the urgent business of clarifying our general ethical principles: the relation between ethics and evolution, between man and science, may not be so abstract after all.

This is a daunting task, and a bewildering one. Yet a biologist may, I hope, make his contribution to the science of culture by showing how some of the knowledge slowly amassed by thousands of his fellow scientists may be used as the outline of a map of these difficult and dangerous verges, and so help to bring them within the assured domain of human safety and order.

A map is not reality; it does not even attempt to reproduce or evoke reality, only to give a convenient representation of certain of its physical features. And a small-scale outline map must concentrate on major features, leaving the details to be filled in later. I am perfectly aware of the immense complexity of our moral lives, each of which, and every separate ethical problem within each life, is unique. But they are irrelevant to this business of map drawing. Nor, in a brief chapter, has an author space for documentation or for technical discussion of the steps in his argument. If I make what appear to be sweeping pronouncements on biological or psychological matters, it is because I conceive it my business here merely to present the broad outlines of a map.

For Thomas H. Huxley there was a fundamental contradiction between the ethical process and the cosmic process. By the former, he meant the universalist ethics of the Victorian enlightenment, bred by nineteenth century humanitarianism out of traditional Christian ethics, and in him personally tinged by a noble but stern puritanism and an almost fanatical devotion to scientific truth and its pursuit. And the latter he restricted almost entirely to biological evolution and to the selective struggle for existence on which it depends. "The ethical progress of society," he stated, "consists, not in imitating the cosmic process, still less in running away from it, but in combating it."

Today that contradiction can, I believe, be resolved—on the one hand, by extending the concept of evolution both backward into the inorganic and forward into the human domain and, on the other, by considering ethics not as a body of fixed principles, but as a product of evolution, and itself evolving. In both cases, the intellectual tool which has given us new insight is that of developmental analysis—the scientific study of change, of becoming, of the production of novelty, whether of life from not-life, of a baby from an ovum and a man from a baby, of ants and swallows and tigers out of ancestral protozoa, of civilized societies out of barbarism and barbarism out of the dim beginnings of social life.

Ethics is not an entity. It is the name we assign to the results of the working of a particular psychological mechanism. This ethical mechanism is an agency for securing that certain of our actions and thoughts shall be consciously felt and judged to have the qualities of rightness or wrongness. It gives us what is popularly called our moral sense. This sense of rightness or wrongness is charged with the driving force of strong emotions, so that the ethical mechanism, once established, helps to determine both our actions and those potential actions which are included under the head of sentiments, beliefs or principles. On the other hand, it provides no guarantee that the feelings it engenders are correct, or its judgments objectively valid.

Our ethics can be classified, like our backbone, among our supporting mechanisms. The backbone, together with the rest of the bony skeleton, the cartilages, tendons and all the connective tissues, serves as a supporting physical framework. Our ethical mechanism, together with our conditioned reflexes, skills, habits, likes and dislikes, serves as a supporting psychological framework. Its peculiarity is that it charges all that passes through its mill with the special emotive qualities of rightness or wrongness.

We cannot make a map of the strange world of ethics until we study the embryology and later development of the ethical mechanism. The development of the mind has this in common with that of the body, that we have no recollection at all of its earlier stages, and that even later the most important changes take place below the surface, to be unraveled only by painstaking scientific investigation. Mental embryology today is still a young science, no further advanced than physical embryology perhaps a century ago. The map we can derive from it is still crude and full of blanks, mistakes and distortions, like the maps of the world produced by the early explorers.

The ovum has no ethics, any more than it has a backbone. Ethics, like the backbone, comes out of nonexistence into existence *de novo* in each individual development. Somewhat as the physical stiffening of the backbone is later built round an embryological forerunner in the shape of the notochord, so the normal infant develops a forerunner for the moral stiffening of adult ethics. The Freudians call it the primitive superego. I will venture to coin a more noncommittal term—the proto-ethical mechanism.

This spiritual notochord appears to be formed early in the infant's second year of postnatal life. It arises as the result of a special kind of conflict among the chaos of unregulated impulses with which the infant is originally endowed.

As the baby begins to draw a distinction between itself and outer reality, it is the mother [1] who comes to represent the external world and to mediate its impacts on the child. But she dawns upon its growing consciousness under two opposite aspects. She is the child's chief object of love and its fountainhead of satisfaction, security and peace. But she is also authority, the chief source of power mysteriously set over the child and arbitrarily thwarting some of the impulses along whose paths its new life quests outward.

The frustration of infantile impulse generates anger, hate and de-structive wishes—what the psychologists generally style aggression—directed against the thwarting authority. But the hated authority is also the loved mother. The infant is thus faced with the primal conflict. Two irreconcilable sets of impulses are directed toward the same object, and that object is the center of its surrounding universe.

The conflict is normally won by love. The anger and the aggression, the accompanying magic fantasies of death-wishes and the like, become branded and tinged with the quality of guilt—in other words, wrongness —and more or less completely banished. They emerge occasionally into action in the form of rages and tempers, but for the most part they are either suppressed into the background of consciousness or wholly re-pressed into the unconscious. If repressed, part of the charge of guilt (to borrow a metaphor from electricity) accompanies them into the unconscious; and in the unconscious they continue to exist, refused conscious recognition but constantly demanding an outlet in some dis-guised form.

The proto-ethical mechanism may be considered as a special adapta-tion to the peculiar conditions of human infancy. During this period,

---

[1] And/or any efficient mother-substitute, such as a nurse who takes over the care of the baby, or a large part of it.

owing largely to the plastic and decompartmentalized nature of the human mind, the infant is faced with all kinds of conflicts to which other animal species are not subject, but is unable to solve them rationally for lack of a requisite basis of experience. How, then, shall action be secured?

The same general type of problem has had to be solved by life on many occasions, and has been met by the evolution of nervous machinery whereby one of the conflicting impulses is inhibited when the other comes into action. This occurs on the muscular level: when the flexors of our arm are thrown into action and contracted, the antagonistic extensors are automatically thrown out of action and relaxed. It occurs on the reflex level: the throwing into activity of one reflex inhibits other reflexes, especially those which demand the use of the same muscles. It seems also to occur on the instinctual level: the student of animal behavior is constantly struck by the way in which instincts which compete, if one may use the phrase, for the possession of the animal's activity, alternate in an all-or-nothing way. And finally, in man, the same all-or-nothing mechanism seems to operate on the highest level of thought and behavior, whether by suppression or repression. In repression particularly, the mechanism is somewhat different from what is found in lower forms: instead of an alternating all-or-nothing activity of two rival tendencies, there is a permanent inhibition of one of the competitors.[2] In conscious suppression, the same type of adaptive inhibitory mechanism must be at work, but does not operate with the same degree of automaticity and completeness.

From the biological point of view, the proto-ethical mechanism is in part an adaptation for securing action instead of indecision in the face of conflict. But it is something more—it is an adaptation for weighting the scales between the conflicting impulses, by attaching a load of guilt to one of them, and thus securing the complete or partial ascendancy of the other. It is not merely an adaptation for securing action instead of indecision, but also one for securing one kind of action rather than another.

Almost certainly there is always some true repression involved in

[2] However, in cases of dual or multiple personality, there is an alternation of complete repression between two conflicting partial systems. Complete alternation of conflicting moods is exemplified in manic-depressives and in conscious suppression there is frequently an occasional complete emergence of what is normally suppressed.

the formation of the proto-ethical mechanism; but the amount will vary immensely from one child to another, both according to inherited temperament and, still more, to its relations with its mother.

The discoveries of modern psychology concerning the proto-ethical mechanism and its function have finally put out of court all purely intuitive theories of ethics. All that the child inherits is a capacity for building up what we have called a proto-ethical mechanism; and even that will not take place in all circumstances. Its "intuitions" as to what constitutes right or wrong are derived from its environment, largely mediated through its mother.

Our modern knowledge also helps us to understand the absolute, categorical and otherworldly quality of moral obligation, on which moral philosophers lay such stress. It is due in the first instance to the compulsive all-or-nothing mechanism by which the primitive superego operates. It is due also to the fact that, as Waddington points out, the external world first intrudes itself into the baby's magic solipsism in the form of the parents' demands for control over primitive impulses, so that infantile ethics embodies the shock of the child's discovery of a world outside itself and unamenable to its wishes.

This quality of absoluteness is later reinforced by the natural human desire for certitude, as well as by certain peculiarities of our language mechanism, which I shall discuss later. Thus the absoluteness of moral obligation turns out on analysis to be no true absolute, but a result of ontological qualities, the nature of our infantile mental machinery, combined with later rationalization and wish fulfillment.

And there may be other complications. The impulses whose thwarting generated the guilty hate may themselves become colored with guilt, or be repressed. Or, if the impulses of love alone are too weak to ensure obedience, the repressed aggression may be turned against the original offending impulse and employed as it were as a policeman or jailer. These and other variations on the main theme must be studied in textbooks and case histories. But the central fact remains that out of this primal conflict there grows the beginning of ethics. Primitive love conquers primitive hate by saddling it with the burden of primal guilt; and with this the polarity of right and wrong becomes attached to our thoughts and actions.

None of us normally remembers this first stage in our moral development. Part of it may sometimes be recovered by special psychological procedures; but in the main the proto-ethical mechanism is an intellectual construction, deduced on scientific grounds, like the atom or the gene.

That this is so is particularly evidenced by recent studies of so-called "moral defectives"—children who lack any normally operative moral sense. In the majority this is due not to any hereditary defect of mental make-up, but to the absence in the infant's life of a mother or effective mother-substitute during the crucial period from about one to three years old. Without a mother, no strong love focused on a personal object; without such love, no conflict of irreconcilable impulses; without such conflict, no guilt; and without such guilt, no effective moral sense.

Neither is the moral sense a mere affair of conditioned reflexes. It develops only when the child's mind is able to grasp the mother as a separate person, not merely as a set of stimuli or sensory cues setting off or conditioning this or that reaction. During its first twelve months the child acquires many habits and may be conditioned in various ways; for instance, in regard to cleanliness. But unless this conditioning is brought into relation with the dynamic structure of focused impulse which develops in the second year, it will wear out or break down.

Once the moral sense is developed, the developing human being can continue to tilt the balance of action and thought by means of the ethical forces now at its disposal—the moral load of guilt or felt wrongness, the moral wings of felt rightness. These can be attached to any conflict, but always in relation to some person or thing for whom we feel love or respect, either alone or blended into awe or other ambivalent feeling—parents, teachers, public opinion, God, one's own self-respect, a country or a cause.

But our central problem remains to haunt us as insistently as ever. How can we be sure that the objects or aims to which our moral sense affixes the labels of felt rightness and wrongness are in fact right or wrong? What objective or ontological standards have we for the validity of our moral sense? We must leave this problem until we have been brought back to it by another route; for the moment we must continue our brief outline of individual ethical development.

After the embryonic mental structure has been thus laid down, the main development of the mind has still to unfold itself. It must undertake what Walter Lippmann has called the passage to maturity. The infant, endowed by nature with unlimited desires, must grow up in a world where they can be satisfied only to a limited extent. His earliest thought, unbacked by experience and unfortified by reason, is a form of magic operating almost wholly by nonrational fantasy; it must be adjusted to external reality, and must learn to incorporate experience with the aid of reason. He is beset by conflicts, both external and internal, which must in some measure be resolved before he can think clearly or act decisively.

His primitive and absolutist ethics, based on nonrational and unconscious mental processes, inevitably tends to an undue restriction of his human activities by locking up conflicting psychological "energies" in the repressive mechanism of the unconscious. To arrive at a constructive and truly humanistic ethics, he needs to liberate these forces from their unconscious grappling.

But mental development differs from physical in being far less standardized. It can be varied to an enormous extent at any stage, including the earliest; and early variations exert a lasting effect, so that adult character is to a large extent determined by the form given to the mind in infancy, through processes which we have irrevocably forgotten.

There is one kind of variation in our mental development that particularly concerns us—the degree to which our ethical mechanism is itself unrealistic, to use the neutral term psychologists prefer, though *untrue* or *irrational* might often be more descriptive. It is unrealistic when unjust or merely stupid treatment of the child superimposes on the normal and healthy, guilt evoked by hate for those whom we must at all costs love, an excess load which does not correspond with any reality, and so is too great to be discharged in the simple happy business of living. This may lead to an unbearable and quite irrational sense of unworthiness and even self-hatred—"Hell under the skull bones, Death under the breast-bones," as Walt Whitman wrote.

This excess load of unrealistic guilt leads on to further distortions, as when authority is injected into the growing mind as an overharsh superego, or reprojected outward in the form of a jealous and vengeful God; or when, unable to bear the condemnation of his superego, the persecution maniac projects this into society, thus removing his own feeling of guilt while at the same time being able to accuse the world of cruelty or oppression.

Again, our ethics will be unrealistic if, after dividing our impulses into sheep and goats, we then with the aid of a form of magic thinking transform the goats into scapegoats, by projecting into others the evil we cannot bear to acknowledge in ourselves. Most Nazis genuinely believed that Jews were a major source of evil; they could do so because they projected the beastliness in their own souls into them. The terrible feature of such projection is that it can turn one's vices into virtues: thus, granted the Nazi believed the Jews were evil, it was his moral duty to indulge his repressed aggression in cruelty and violence toward them. It is an ethical mechanism, but a grossly unrealistic one.

Thus conscience itself, and also our beliefs concerning it, can become distorted or unrealistic. I will give three quotations in illustration. A modern theologian writes that "conscience is a special exercise or activity of the faculty of reason . . . conscience is the mind of man when it is passing moral or ethical judgments." This is unrealistic in leaving out all the irrational and compulsive elements in conscience, and in failing to consider its developmental origin.

Mark Twain's Huckleberry Finn at least faces the facts—"It don't make no difference whether you do right or wrong, a person's conscience ain't got no sense and just goes for him anyway. If I had a yaller dog that didn't know more than a person's conscience does, I'd pizon him. It takes up more room than all the rest of a person's insides, and yet ain't no good nohow. Tom Sawyer says the same." We may hazard the guess that Huck Finn was burdened with a moderate excess of unrealistic guilt.

Finally Jonathan Swift—"Is not conscience a pair of breeches, which, though a cover for lewdness as well as nastiness, is easily slipt down for the service of both." The gloomiest dean of all was only too well aware of the gross distortions to which our ethical mechanism may be subjected, though he doubtless never realized the extent of his own deformation.

This is not to deny the importance of conscience. Conscience develops directly out of the proto-ethical mechanism, which as we have seen is a necessary adaptation in our early years for securing action backed by a sense of rightness. And in so far as the proto-ethical mechanism is itself undistorted and its feeling of rightness reflects, albeit in embryonic form, a morality that is objectively right, it can then be developed by reason and aspiration into a conscience which will be an indispensable moral guide. What psychologists and sociologists demonstrate is that conscience can set up no claims to absolute authority. They can point out further that such claims are peculiarly dangerous, since those who make them are likely to be victims of a distorted and hyperactive conscience, charged with aggression which seeks an outlet in attacking in others all those tendencies of which it itself bears the unconscious guilty burden.

However, in favorable circumstances human beings *are* able to develop without these overdoses of untruth and unreality in their moral system. It is perfectly realistic to feel some guilt about hating one's beloved mother. But the load need not be too heavy and can be dissipated in acts of obedience, love and co-operation. True repression into the unconscious may be so small in extent as not at all dangerously to disturb later development. The unrealistic mists of magic fantasy-thinking can be in large measure dispersed. Reason and reasonableness can be brought in to aid the development of the mind; the internal judgments of ethics can be checked against the external facts of experience; conflicts can achieve some sort of resolution in the realistic business of earning a living and bringing up a family; and the individual, if not grossly frustrated or oppressed, can adjust himself without too much unreality and illusion to the ethical standards of his society.

It is thus a fact that human beings can, in certain circumstances, achieve an internal ethical realism. And it is, I think, self-evident that it must be *better* to be realistic in one's ethics than unrealistic. Thus here we find one element in their external validation.

However, ethics can be looked at from the angle of society as well as from that of the individual; and once we consider social ethics, we perceive that there is an external realism as well as an internal. A man may be well and realistically adjusted to the ethical standards of his society, but they may themselves be unrealistic. When this is so, the primary reason is lack of knowledge. In many primitive societies every death or disaster is ascribed to witchcraft or some other form of magic. For a tribal African the ethical duty of smelling out and killing or punishing a guilty witch is realistic: for us, with the knowledge at our disposal, it is wholly unrealistic.

Similarly it has become ethically unrealistic for us to make expiation in face of volcanic eruptions or other natural catastrophes, to treat disease as a divine punishment or the insane as possessed by evil spirits, or to propitiate God by human sacrifice. We are beginning to think it ethically unrealistic for any human group to regard itself as a Chosen People or in any way inherently superior to others, or to believe that we alone are in receipt of the Divine Will as regards our morality. Sometime in the future we can be sure that much that today is ethically quite realistic will prove wholly unrealistic—for instance, if I am to hazard a personal guess, in the fields of our sexual morality and our current attitude toward the Deity.

It will not, of course, become unrealistic until the entire social scene has become transformed—its state of knowledge, its intellectual and moral climate, its social and economic structure, the very quality of the human beings living in it. But we are apt to forget that this has been happening to man for hundreds of thousands of years. Human societies and the effective, not ontological, nature of the human beings composing them have radically changed: evolution has been at work and has produced a series of new results.

This at once implies a relativity of ethics. Individual ethics develop, social ethics evolve. And the evolution of ethical systems and standards shows a broad correlation with that of the societies in which they flourish. I shall not attempt to document this thesis, on which there is a whole library of learned works available, but shall confine myself to a few generalizations, which I am quite aware are oversweeping.

First, however, I must clear a stumbling block out of the way. Much recent anthropological work seems at first sight not to confirm this concept of ethical relativity, but to point rather toward an ethical chaos. Thus a recent study on thirteen primitive societies from all over the world in most instances failed to find any correlation between the degree of competitiveness or co-operation enjoined by the ethical system in vogue, and the mode of life imposed upon the society by nature. The same lack of social correlation has been shown to apply elsewhere to other ethical qualities, such as those on the scale from peaceable to aggressive. In other words, the distinctive characteristics of an ethical system may have no detectable significance for the particular group in which it is found.

On further analysis, however, this disconcerting fact is found to apply only as between societies on the same general level of social evolution, and indeed to be confined in the main to primitive groups which are small and fairly well isolated culturally. It is doubtless analogous to the similar fact seen in biological evolution, that small and well-isolated populations develop nonadaptive variations. In both cases the circumstances permit chance to exert an abnormally large effect—in fixing random hereditary variations in the one case, random cultural variations in the other.

But as between societies at different cultural levels, or between advanced societies on quite different lines of cultural and economic development, chaotic ethical variability becomes negligible and ethical relatedness the rule.

Broadly speaking, and allowing for much overlapping and blurring, one can distinguish certain main stages in the evolution of our ethics. In savage pre-agricultural communities, ethics grades over into the prescriptions of totem and taboo; it is largely concerned with propitiation and group solidarity, and its form is conditioned by magic. In post-agricultural barbarism, and especially in the early phases of civilization, the ethics of class domination and of group rivalry comes to the front; the form of ethics begins to be affected by theology, and particular moral codes are laid down as the will of God.

The most important ethical change during the historical period was the appearance of universalist ethics, which seems to have been initiated toward the middle of the first millennium B.C. In some cases this accompanied the emergence of the idea of a single Deity from the rivalry of hostile tribal gods; while elsewhere, as in Greece, it was associated with the rise of free intellectual inquiry and involved the recognition of some standard beyond and above that of polytheist divinities.

By universalist ethics I mean, of course, the conception that ethical principles apply to all humanity, irrespective of race, language, creed or station. In the earlier ethics of small closed groups, a different treatment of those outside the group is usually implied and often expressly enjoined.

Even within a universalist framework, many social adjustments of ethical outlook and emphasis have occurred. One of the most striking examples of such ethical relativity was the change in moral beliefs and attitude associated with the emergence of modern capitalism, which has been fully analyzed by Weber and Tawney. The removal of the ethical ban on lending money at interest; the emphasis on the moral value of thrift and of individual independence and initiative—these and many other changes in ethical judgment were at one and the same time products of the economic revolution and agencies accelerating its accomplishment. The net result was to clothe individualist capitalism with the respectability and the driving force of morality.

Another example was the investment of nineteenth century laissez faire with an ethical halo, in the doctrine that the freest play of individualist competition would automatically secure the most rapid and extensive progress. It was largely this rationalization which enabled the bulk of the Victorians to acquiesce in slums and sweated labor.

In general, however, universalist ethics has been conceived of statically, in terms of a fixed standard. In this, the imperfections of our language mechanism have materially aided. Uncritically used, an abstract noun like "the good" becomes a fictitious entity, bristling with fictitious properties, instead of a convenient pigeonhole for a variety of qualities which have in common only a certain emotive quality. A good baby gives little trouble; a good God is beneficent and moral; a good beefsteak satisfies our palate and our appetite, a good law—but why continue?

As various critical minds, from Bacon onward, have pointed out, such fictitious entities facilitate the slipping of false certitudes into reality. In the field we are considering they make it easier to conceive of universalist ethics in terms of a fixed Absolute or ideal Good, or of the eternally valid injunctions of a God.

But this, we are beginning to perceive, does not hold water. For all practical purposes the Absolute is some particular philosopher's idea of the Absolute, and God is some particular person or church's idea of God. It would be extremely salutary for the progress of clear thinking if every one invoking the support of the Deity for his beliefs would substitute for the word "God" the phrase "my idea" or "our idea of God." [3]

The so-called immutable laws and will of God, which are invoked to guarantee the principles of ethics, turn out on examination to have been extremely changeable; and the principles of ethics have changed

[3] Lord Halifax, in a speech (*The Times,* May 31, 1943), came halfway toward this view when he said that "wherever we found a false idea about men its origin lay in a false idea of God." Most modern psychologists would go further back and say that the ideas we have about God originate mainly or wholly in projections from our own ideas. Advanced theologians have, of course, for some time been concerning themselves with the facts and implications of the evolution of our ideas of God. It remains for them, however, to draw the necessary conclusion that the time has come to coin a new term which shall have the dynamic meaning of *evolving idea of God* in place of the inevitably static term *God*.

with them. So here too, in the fields where ethical certainty seems at first sight most authoritarian and most static, it is being undermined, until we are now in the midst of the complete transposition of ethics into dynamic or evolutionary terms.

To this crucial point I will shortly return. Meanwhile let us remember that in all the advanced civilizations known to history there have always been several more or less separate sets of ethics, in part competing, in part merely overlapping.

There has been the official ethics imposed by the ruling class, usually to secure stability. There has been the working moral code of ordinary citizens, and the ethics of simple everyday goodness. There has been the ethics of oppressed classes and minorities, concerned either with escape or with revolution. There has been the ethics that conduces to a sense of personal salvation, serving to escape from a too heavy load of guilt or from the squalor, violence or wickedness of current existence. There has been the true ethics of perfection, those of disciplined and developed goodness and of sainthood. There has also been what I may call the ethics of impossible perfection, which arises in part out of men's realization that there are infinite possibilities beyond the imperfect compromises of the present, in part out of their need for what in modern psychological terminology is called the ego-ideal—an idealized ethical mask, strangely compounded of moral aspiration, spiritual conceit and hypocrisy, in which we can disguise ourselves from ourselves, or which we can present to the world to enhance our self-respect and our apparent moral stature.

The actual variety is immense. The relevant fact is that all existing societies manifest considerable ethical disunity, and that this is an expression of the conflicts and contradictions inherent in the situation—conflicts between classes and groups, between long-term and short-term good, conflicts within the individual between his needs for conformity and practical action and his needs for salvation, escape or fullness of perfection. Once more, ethics is not an entity, but a loose covering term for a large number of quite different kinds of individual and social adaptations which have this alone in common—that they are concerned with the labels of rightness and wrongness. And, in all historical societies, these different kinds of adaptations may be of various degrees of efficiency, and are always to some extent in conflict.

Up to this point, increase of knowledge has produced only increase of doubt. We know more than we used to about the mechanism that affixes the labels of right and wrong: but we are as far as ever from knowing whether the labels are correctly attached. We know more about the adaptation of particular systems of ethics to particular kinds of societies; but what right have we to say that one adaptation, or one kind of society, is better than another?

However, ethics does not merely vary at random: it also evolves. That fact provides our clue. Our ethics evolves because it is itself part of the evolutionary process. And any standards of rightness or wrongness must in some way be related to the movement of that process through time.

Now that the moment has arrived when we are able to perceive evolution as an all-comprehensive process of which human existence forms a part, it is impossible any longer to rely on any static guarantees for ethics. Our fuller knowledge discloses not a set of absolute or fixed standards, but a direction of change. This is no more available to casual inspection than any other of the discoveries of science. It is one of those "secrets of excellent use, laid up in the womb of time," as Bacon called them, which are to be elicited only by the slow accumulation and distillation of tested fact.

Evolution, from cosmic star dust to human society, is a comprehensive and continuous process. It transforms the world-stuff, if I may use a term which includes the potentialities of mind as well as those of matter. It is creative, in the sense that during the process new and more complex levels of organization are progressively attained, and new possibilities are thus opened up to the universal world-stuff.

Increase in organization is for the most part gradual, but now and again there is a sudden rapid passage to a totally new and more comprehensive type or order of organization, with quite new emergent properties, and involving quite new methods of further evolution. The two major breaks that concern us here are that between inorganic matter and life and, more particularly, that between prehuman life and man.

Evolution on the inorganic level operates over an appalling vastness of space and on an equally appalling slowness of time-scale. There is continuity of bodies such as stars and nebulae, which are largely mere aggregations with a low degree of organization. It is chiefly they that show the combination of persistence with change which constitutes evolution. Here and there, however, matter was able to attain the molecular type of organization; and finally on our earth (and possibly on a few other specks within the cosmos) the world-stuff arrived at the new type of organization that we call life. This is characterized by great material complexity and by the capacity for self-reproduction, or better, self-reproductive evolution, since it includes both persistence and self-reproducing variation. On this new level, the evolutionary process was much accelerated in time, though immensely restricted in extent.

This speeding up was due to the emergence of a new method or agency of evolution—natural selection between competing variants. Natural selection automatically produces change in living matter, including change toward higher degrees of organization. The efficiency of natural selection was after a time much increased by the biological inventions of sexual fusion and Mendelian recombination. Previous to this, new mutations had to compete individually; subsequently, they could be combined, so that favorable variations could be pooled, and the speed of evolutionary change much increased.

Below the organizational level of life the world is one of mere interaction. But organizations of matter which are alive, though still interacting in what we call the balance of nature, are introduced to a new possibility—a measure of *de facto* control: they utilize other matter, both living and nonliving, in securing their own continuance and spread. Through their capacity for self-reproduction and internal adjustment they also acquire a certain independence of changes in their environment.

During the thousand million years of organic evolution, the degree of organization attained by the highest forms of life increased enormously. And with this there increased also the possibilities of control, of independence, of inner harmony and self-regulation, of experience. Compared with what a protozoan or a polyp can show, the complexity of later forms of life, like bee or swallow or antelope, is stupendous, their capacity for self-regulation almost miraculous, their experience so much richer and more varied as to be different in kind.

And finally there is, in certain types of animals, an increase in consciousness or mind. Whether mind be a sudden emergent or a gradual development of some universal property of the world-stuff, mind of the same general nature as ours is clearly present on the higher organizational levels of life, and at least in the birds and mammals we can trace its steady evolution toward greater capacities for feeling, knowing, willing and understanding.

There is thus one direction within the multifariousness of evolution which we can legitimately call progress. It consists in the capacity to attain a higher degree of organization without closing the door to further advance. In the organic phase of evolution, this depends on all-round improvement as opposed to the limited improvement or one-sided specialization which, it can be demonstrated, automatically leads sooner or later to a dead end, after which no true advance is possible, but only minor variations. Insects appear to have reached an evolutionary dead end over thirty million years ago; birds a little later; and all the main lines of higher mammals except the primates—the carnivora, ungulates, whales, bats, rodents and so forth—at about the same time, or at least no later than the early Pliocene. Most evolutionary lines or trends are specializations which either thus come to a stop or are extinguished; true progress or the unlimited capacity for advance is rare.

However, the details of biological evolution need not concern us overmuch, since during the past half million years or so a new and more comprehensive type or order of organization has arisen; and on this new level, the world-stuff is once more introduced to altogether new possibilities, and has quite new methods of evolutionary operation at its disposal. Biological or organic evolution has at its upper end been merged into and largely succeeded by conscious or social evolution.

Just as biological evolution was rendered both possible and inevitable when material organization became self-reproducing, so conscious evolution was rendered both possible and inevitable when social organization became self-reproducing. This occurred when the evolving world-stuff, in the form of ancestral man, became capable of true speech and conceptual thought. For just as animal organization, however elaborate, had been transmissible across the generations by the vehicle of the chromosomes and genes, so from then on conscious experience could be transmitted down the stream of time on the vehicle of words and other symbols and representations. And somewhat as sexual fusion made possible the pooling of individual mutations, so reason made possible the pooling of individual experiences. For the first time in evolution, tradition and education became continuous and cumulative processes.

With this, a new type of organization has come into being—that of self-reproducing society. So long as man survives (and there is no reason for thinking that he will not) there seems no possibility for any other form of life to push up to this new organizational level. Indeed there are grounds for suspecting that biological evolution has come to an end, so far as any sort of major advance is concerned. Thus further large-scale evolution has once again been immensely restricted in extent, being now, it would seem, confined to the single species man; but at the same time again immensely accelerated in its speed, through the operation of the new mechanisms now available.

From now on, it is only through social evolution that the world-stuff can realize radically new possibilities. Mechanical interaction and natural selection still operate, but are now of secondary importance. For good or evil, the mechanism of evolution has in the main been transferred onto the social or conscious level. Part of the blind struggle for existence between separate individuals or groups is transposed into conflict in consciousness, either within the individual mind or within the tradition that is the vehicle of pooled social consciousness. The slow processes of variation and heredity are outstripped by the acquisition and transmission of experience. New tools of living originated *ex post facto* as biological adaptations or unconscious adjustments become increasingly unimportant compared with those deliberately produced by human design. Physical trial and error can be more and more transposed to the sphere of thought.

And as the mechanism of evolution ceases to be blind and automatic and becomes conscious, ethics can be injected into the evolutionary process. Before man that process was merely amoral. After his emergence onto the stage of life it became possible to introduce faith, courage, love of truth, goodness—in a word, moral purpose—into evolution. It became possible, but the possibility has been and is too often unrealized. It is the business of an enlightened ethics and the new responsibility of science in this emergent civilization to help in its realization.

The attainment of the social type of organization opens a new and apparently indefinite range of possibilities to the evolving world-stuff. It can now proceed to some understanding of the cosmos that gave it birth, and of the conflicts that it must endure; it can for the first time consciously both appreciate and create beauty, truth and other values;

it becomes aware of good and evil; it becomes capable of new emotional states like love, reverence or mystical contemplation, and peace; it can inject some of its own purpose into events; finally and most significantly, many of the new experiences that are being made available have inherent value.

Even in the brief space that man has been in existence, there has been considerable evolutionary advance in the degree of social organization, considerable realization of new possibilities previously unavailable to life. What is more, the rate of advance has been growing progressively quicker as time has passed. There is every reason to believe that through the attainment of this new level of conscious and social organization the evolutionary process has taken on a new and apparently indefinite lease of life.

What guidance does all this give us in our search for independent ethical standards? There are, it seems to me, three rather separate areas in which such guidance may be found: that of nature as a whole, that of human society, and that of the human individual. All three must be considered from the dynamic angle of evolution or development; and when thus considered, all three are interlocked.

In the broadest possible terms evolutionary ethics must be based on a combination of a few main principles: that it is right to realize ever new possibilities in evolution, notably those which are valued for their own sake; that it is right both to respect human individuality and to encourage its fullest development; that it is right to construct a mechanism for further social evolution which shall satisfy these prior conditions as fully, efficiently and rapidly as possible.

To translate these arid-sounding generalities into concrete terms and satisfying forms is beyond the scope of a chapter; it is a task for an entire generation. But I must attempt a certain expansion, and some development of their implications.

When we look at nature as a whole, we find, among the many directions taken by evolution, one which is characterized by introducing the evolving world-stuff to progressively higher levels of organization and so to new possibilities of being, action and experience. This has culminated in the attainment of a stage in which the world-stuff (now molded into human shape) finds that it experiences some of the new possibilities as having value in or for themselves; and further, that among these it assigns higher and lower degrees of value, the higher values being those which are more intrinsically or more permanently satisfying or involve a greater degree of perfection.

The teleologically-minded would say that this trend embodies evolution's purpose. I do not feel that we should use the word "purpose" save where we know that a conscious aim is involved; but we can say that this is the most desirable direction of evolution, and accordingly that our ethical standards must fit into its dynamic framework. In other words, it is ethically right to aim at whatever will promote the increasingly full realization of increasingly higher values.[4]

In this aim we must reconcile the claims of the present and the future. The minimum claim of the future is that our direction of evolution (which on the human level means the direction of social change) should leave the door open for further advance in the same desirable direction—toward still higher levels of organization and as yet unrealized possibilities; its maximum claim is that future possibility should take precedence over present realization. The course of greatest moral rightness lies at a varying optimum somewhere between these two extremes.

If desirable direction of evolution provides the most comprehensive (though also the least specific) external standard for our ethics, then one important corollary at once follows: that social organization should be planned, not to prevent change, nor merely to permit it, but to encourage it. A static stability is undesirable, and a complete or static certitude of ethical belief itself becomes unethical.

In the sphere of the intellect, the past three hundred years have witnessed the reconciliation of the demands of certainty and change, through the growth of the scientific attitude and method. We have the certainty that our empirical knowledge is increasing, but we are aware that it is incomplete and imperfect. The result is not the possession of absolute Truth in relation to the processes of knowledge but a progressive advance toward the actualization of Truth. We need the same kind of reconciliation, the same facilitation of progressive change, in the sphere of religion and ethics.

[4] A mistake often made by devotees of genetic and evolutionary methods is to think that complex phenomena can be in any real sense explained in terms of their development. In point of fact, such a procedure merely explains away some of their most important characteristics. A study of the less developed will often help us to understand the more developed; but the most important subject for the evolutionist is the nature and direction of the developmental process itself, and here the more developed gives the significant clue, both to the actualities of the past and to the possibilities of the future.

Furthermore, the rate as well as the direction of change is important. Theoretically there must be an optimum rate of change, above which stability is endangered and the sacrifices of the present are excessive, below which advance is so slow that the welfare of future generations is needlessly impaired. Thus anything which retards advance below this optimum, even if it be moving in the same right direction, is wrong.

Next we have the guidance derived from an understanding of the workings of human societies. In the first place, it is clear on evolutionary grounds that the individual is in a real sense higher than the state or the social organism. The possibilities that are of value for their own sake, and whose realization must be one of our primary aims, are not experienced by society as a unit, but by some or all of the human beings who compose it.

All claims that the state has an intrinsically higher value than the individual are false. They turn out, on closer scrutiny, to be rationalizations or myths aimed at securing greater power or privilege for a limited group which controls the machinery of the state.

On the other hand, the individual is meaningless in isolation, and the possibilities of development and self-realization open to him are conditioned and limited by the nature of the social organization. The individual thus has duties and responsibilities as well as rights and privileges, or in other words, finds certain outlets and satisfactions (such as devotion to a cause or participation in a joint enterprise) only in relation to the type of society in which he lives.

In any case, the mechanism by which evolutionary advance can be produced on the human or conscious level is that of the social organization, and this operates by the pooling of experience and co-operative action in a cumulative tradition. On the biological level intraspecific competition is often not merely useless but harmful to the species as a whole. Somewhat similarly, on the social level it is clearly of evolutionary advantage that there should be a single universal pool of experience and action, not a number of isolated or even competing and hostile ones. For then evolutionary advance can be more continuous, more rapid and better consolidated.

But if unity as against multiplicity is of advantage for evolutionary advance and is therefore desirable in respect of groups, so is equality of opportunity in respect of individuals. The more individuals there exist whose desirable potentialities are fully developed, the more health, vigor, knowledge, wisdom, happiness, beauty and the rest can go into the common pool, and the better that common pool will work. That is one of the evolutionary bases for universalism in ethics.

By the unification of separate groups with their competing pools of tradition, desirable evolution can become a single joint enterprise of the human species as a whole; and the efficiency of the enterprise will rise with the degree and universality of individual development and welfare.

Unification and universality will in many minds raise the specter of regimented compulsion and uniformity; but this again is contradicted by our evolutionary standards. For one thing, the pooling of effort and experience will be more efficient if there is voluntary participation in what is felt to be a common enterprise, a plan accepted by all; less efficient if the plan is carried out under compulsion.

For another, it will be more efficient the greater the variety of skills and experiences unified in the pool. It is not uniformity which our evolutionary analysis shows to be right, but the maximum of variety-in-unity. As with the animal body, the common pool of our species becomes more efficient as it achieves greater differentiation combined with more integrated harmony of organization. This holds both for groups and for individuals. We should not aim at the spread of one uniform type of culture over the entire globe, but at what has been well described as a world orchestration of cultures. Man probably also has the highest genetic variability of any species, so that within a single group, national or cultural, there will always be an immense innate variety of temperament, capacity and talent. The more this variability can be not merely permitted but encouraged within the confines of a common pool, and the more it is integrated within those confines, the more efficient will the pool become as an agency of desirable evolution. Again it is not uniformity that is demanded, but a variety of which the components are compatible with each other and, if possible, integrated into some sort of whole.

With this we are brought into the area of the individual. The human individual is not merely inherently higher than the state, but the rightly developed individual is, and will continue to be, the highest product of evolution, even though he needs the proper organization of society to achieve his welfare and realize his development.

The phrase "rightly developed" begs a question. I would suggest that it include not only the full, all-round development of potentialities, but also the one-sided development of particular possibilities or special talents, provided always that these restrict the development or interfere with the welfare of other individuals or groups as little as possible. For instance, the new possibilities of experience that have become available on the human level include the enjoyment of great wealth or privilege built upon exploitation or oppression; such are obviously not desirable, any more than distortions like the enjoyment of sadistic torture of others.

The case is less clear when there is a conflict between the full development of a special talent, such as artistic genius or saintly and ascetic devotion to a good cause, on the one hand, and, on the other, the more ordinary but no less real duties we have to our friends or dependents. For instance, was Gauguin morally right in leaving his wife and family to devote himself to painting? There is always a price to be paid, both by oneself and by others, for bringing a talent to fruition. We must face that fact; but who is to decide if it is a just price? Some would say that the proof of the pudding is in the eating, and that the rightness of such a decision can only be judged by the quality of the results produced. Personally, I would not go so far as this, but would feel that wherever there is a genuine and informed sense of vocation, this will be a sufficient ethical sanction.

Many moralists will doubtless disagree; however, we must remember that moralists are almost certainly not a random sample of the population, but that some of them have become moralists because of an excessive load of infantile guilt, and consequent overpreoccupation with that limited sphere of morality to which the term is often but inaccurately restricted, namely, actions and beliefs which are concerned with lightening the load of guilt or escaping from the sense of sin. And through this preoccupation they are apt to attach less value to other types of achievement—artistic, intellectual or practical—and indeed often fail to realize that they enter the moral sphere at all. However, our evolutionary standards here provide definite ethical guidance; they socialize morality and enlarge the scope of its values. Thus art and science, music and philosophy, all have their ethical aspect, since they provide new possibilities of experience of value in and for themselves, and this is a desirable evolutionary outcome. Again, these activities, or their results, are capable of being shared and can go into the common pool, enhancing its efficiency by adding to its extent and variety.

If morality includes a duty of the individual to himself, or rather toward the development of that self to include as many as possible of those qualities wherein "we are greater than we know," of those potentialities which can so easily remain unrealized, it is assuredly true that it must be in the main concerned with our behavior toward others—in a word, with social relations.

If the right development of the individual is an evolutionary end in itself, then it is right that there should be universal equality of opportunity for development, and to the fullest degree. The reciprocal of this is the rightness of unselfishness and kindness, as the necessary means for realizing general well-being. Thus individual ethics will always in large measure be concerned with the conflict between the claims of self-expression and self-sacrifice, and their best reconciliation through love.

The Golden Rule, as various philosophers have pointed out, is an impossible ideal; it cannot ever be put into practice, not merely because of the imperfections of human nature, but also because it does not provide a real basis on which to make practical ethical decisions. However, it is the hyperbole beyond a perfectly practical ideal—the extension of more opportunity of fuller life to more human beings. Psychologically, this can be promoted by extending the child's love and sympathy to an ever-widening circle, and linking the idea of any and all avoidable suffering and stunting of development with his personal sense of wrong. And it can be promoted institutionally by the rational acceptance of certain moral principles, and then by laws and practical measures designed to give effect to those principles.

To accept this view is to give a new content to that sector of ethics comprised under the head of justice. The abstract term "justice" is of itself empty of meaning beyond the fact of being applied to acts which we happen to think just; its content varies from age to age with the social context. There is retributive justice, and there is distributive justice; there is justice concerned with fairness in administering existing codes of law, and justice concerned with some unrealized abstract standard. To give it the particular content implied by evolutionary ethics is to erect a new ideal of distributive justice and to assert that our laws should be modified to give effect to this ideal.

An important negative consequence of accepting the welfare, development and dignity of the human individual as a yardstick by which to measure evolutionary advance on the social level is the confirmation of Kant's insistence that it is always morally wrong to treat other human beings merely as means, since they are the embodiment of the highest ends we know. All men are of course to some extent means— for producing goods, for winning battles, for administering social functions, for creating art or knowledge or entertainment. But they should all be treated also as ends, never wholly as the tools or instruments of the ends of other individuals.[5]

Honesty and truthfulness are further implications of evolutionary ethics, since they are the intellectual lubricants of free and equal cooperation, and the basis for collective knowledge, as well as an expression of respect for one's own and others' individual integrity. Faith finds its place within the evolutionary scheme once we manage to turn society into a continuing enterprise in which ordinary men and women can believe; and self-sacrifice remains a primary virtue, though with slightly different content and connotations.

It will perhaps be objected that this elaborate detour through the realms of evolution has been quite unnecessary, as it has merely brought us back to the blend of Christian and humanist universalism characteristic of the ethics of Western civilization. The intrinsic worth of the human individual, the brotherhood of man, the universal duty of kindness and unselfishness—is not the evolutionist merely dressing up in new terminology what we have accepted for centuries?

The objection is not valid. It is of course true that the intuition and the spiritual logic of the religious moralists perceived the necessity for a universalist ethics grounded in a belief in the ultimate and intrinsic value of human personality centuries before the evolutionists were able to provide the inductive basis for this conclusion. But with this common insistence on universalism and on the value of the individual, together with their various direct consequences, the resemblance ends. For one

[5] That most men like to feel that they are serving as means to ideal and corporate ends is another matter. In such activities men find a new freedom and a further self-realization. What is immoral is the exploitation of one individual as means to another's ends.

thing, the evolutionist is able to provide new general standards or criteria for ethics when the older universalist standards, grounded in Authority, the Absolute or Revelation, were proving to be no standards at all, and to provide no guarantees against moral inflation or the debasement of ethical currency. For another, the standards are dynamic instead of static; and this fundamental fact produces many important differences in the details and indeed the principles of the resultant ethical system.

The evolutionist is not the only begetter of a dynamic ethics. Sociologists and social historians, philosophers and proponents of a dynamic or a genetic psychology, certain liberal theologians, philosophic Marxists, have all made their contribution toward the transformation of static into dynamic ethics. But the contributions from these various fields have been either incomplete (as in theology) or limited in extent. It is only in relation to the evolutionary process as a whole that our ethical standards can be fully generalized, and the new system be rounded out to completion.

Let me briefly enumerate some of the main differences that arise from acceptance of an evolutionary ethics. The first and most obvious is that our ethical yardstick is itself dynamic, and must be used for making long-term social measurements as well as immediate individual ones. The individual can always continue to make ethical progress, whether in bringing a greater range of experience into an internal harmony or in achieving a greater degree of such harmony; whether in the reconciliation of self and not-self or the synthesis of suffering and joy in a single deeper reality; whether in a further extension of love and good works or in a more perfect fruition of some special quality or talent. But around and beyond individual ethics lies social ethics, which must be judged by the direction and the rate of change in human society.

To one immediate implication of this I have already referred, namely, the ethical obligation to plan for the encouragement of social change. A further consequence is the higher ethical value set upon knowledge. Knowledge is not merely an end in itself, but the only satisfactory means for controlling our future evolution. Social morality includes the duty of providing an immense extension of scientific research and its integrated planning to provide the basis for desirable change.

If science is allotted a higher place in an evolutionary system of ethics, so too are art and certain aspects of personal religion. I have already touched on the subject of the arts. Their ethical value lies in introducing man to new possibilities of desirable experience, as well as in providing the chief means of communicating and pooling experience in the emotional as opposed to the intellectual sphere. And personal religion, in the form of a disciplined mysticism, a trained reverence aimed at enlarging and harmonizing the microcosm of the individual personality, provides the chief road to certain types of satisfying experience and desirable being.

This has its negative implications, namely, that what I may call salvationist ethics, aimed at achieving salvation in a supernatural other life, becomes redundant; indeed, if overemphasized it may itself become unethical by our evolutionary standards, by retarding or opposing right social change. The desirable sense of "salvation" can, in part, be achieved through right discipline of the soul, in part through devotion to some common continuing enterprise.

That a considerable section of the churches is aware of this latter fact is shown by the recent rapid growth of their interest in economic and political affairs; we may prophesy that, as the evolutionary concept of ethics spreads, organized Christianity will devote less attention to salvation and the life hereafter, more attention to realizing the Kingdom of God on earth.

The age-old opposition between faith and works finds a new expression in the transvaluation of values imposed by the evolutionary outlook. The aim of evolutionary "faith" consists partly in a belief in the high possibilities of man's evolutionary future, partly in achieving states of being that are of positive value in their own right, in free and satisfying activities enjoyed for their own sake, in transcendent self-dedication or sacrifice.

In place of "works" we now have the practical achievements of human society, as measured by the same criteria by which progress was measured on the biological level—greater control, greater independence or self-regulation, greater but at the same time more harmonious complexity of organization, greater range of knowledge or available experience. These trends are still desirable on the social level, but here become increasingly secondary—not ends in themselves, but means to the realization of experiences valued as ends.

This is not to say that such evolutionary works may not become short-term ethical ends. The more efficient organization of production, distribution and other physical functions of society, the abolition of insecurity, oppression, ill-health, physical underdevelopment or illiteracy —these in the long run merely provide the means by which higher or more intrinsic values may be realized, the practical foundation for a fuller and more satisfying life; but meanwhile they can provide temporary ends for our intense ethical striving. The implications of this for immediate practice will be discussed in the following paragraphs.

As regards the individual and his inescapable passage to maturity, we have already seen that degree of development, whether of a single talent, of all-round richness and fullness, or that internal harmony, which is the self-regulation of the soul, is itself a positive end, and morally right, provided it is not achieved by the exploitation or to the detriment of other human beings and their development.

Acceptance of our evolutionary ethical principles has a particular implication of some present importance: it affords a complete condemnation and refutation of totalitarian ethical principles. In providing an external sanction for universalist ethics it at once condemns any system which repudiates universalism and reverts to group ethics. The prime postulate of totalitarian ethics is the rightness of all which exalts the organized totalitarian group, preferably at the expense of any competing group. In this the totalitarian philosophy merely translates into modern terms the ethics of tribes or peoples in an early barbarous phase of the world's history.

Totalitarian ethics places the state above the individual. Being postulated on the success of a particular group, it cannot help being rooted in naked power and the use of force as a primary instrument. On the intergroup level, this results in forcible and often cruel domination and in persecution and oppression, to the denial of co-operation. It also results in the perversion of truth and the suppression of free speech and inquiry, since a naked power system cannot tolerate tolerance or face even intellectual opposition. It is unrealistic and perverted. It expressly denies the principles of the equality of opportunity and the universality of justice, and is opposed to the establishment of a single common but varied pool of human experience and effort. Its methods run counter to those which, on grounds of efficiency alone, the evolutionist demonstrates to be desirable. Furthermore, its principles run counter to those guaranteed by universalist evolutionary ethics, and their application in practice provokes immense moral indignation, which in turn provides much of the driving force that will encompass its downfall.

But to be certain that totalitarian ethics is wrong does not imply that that of the democracies is right; it may merely be less wrong. There is indeed a widespread belief in the democracies that our ethics needs reformulating. And today this can only be done in relation to general evolutionary standards.

However, this task must also be related to the needs and principles of the times. We may look forward to an eventual future in which the organization of society will be good by our evolutionary standards of goodness. But meanwhile the world in which we live is hatefully imperfect. In a rudimentary and makeshift stage of social evolution like ours, such general ethical principles as I have been sketching can only be counsels of perfection, largely inapplicable in current practice. They will therefore tend to float off and become irrelevant or even opposed to the effective social ethics of the time.

Our practical problem is thus to build a bridge of faith between the practical and the ideal, by constructing an effective ethical system which shall be adapted concretely to our age and translatable into action to meet its needs, but shall also be compatible with the general ethical standards we have been able to distil out of evolutionary fact. Here history provides us with another general conclusion. General ethical principles can be brought down to earth out of their ideal empyrean when it is possible to apply them in large-scale practice; and when it is also expedient to do so. This involves no crude materialist theory of history; on the contrary, moral principles, once conditions call for their practical application, may be powerful agencies in changing those conditions.

Slavery provides an example. The universalist principle of respect for the human individual is inherently opposed to slavery. But, over much of history, slave labor was a necessary element in production. It was no good being an abolitionist in ancient Rome; all that the most clear-sighted moralist could *do* was to demand humane treatment for slaves. But by the early nineteenth century technical advance had made it possible to put much of the mechanical drudgery of existence off the shoulders of men to where it belonged—onto machines. Further, in the new conditions free workers were on the whole becoming more efficient than slave labor. For the first time it became both possible and expedient to apply the general moral principle of human equality to the particular moral problem of abolishing slavery. And history bears witness to the practical effectiveness of the resultant moral forces in overcoming the violent resistance of the vested interests opposed to the change.

What are the special conditions of the present and immediate future that will canalize particular applications of our general ethical principles? I will instance three. For one thing, recent scientific and technical advances have, for the first time since civilization began, made it theoretically possible for every human individual, within a limited future, to be properly fed, reasonably clothed and housed, freed from the major burden of ill-health and insecurity, and provided with some opportunities for education and leisure. In the second place, communications have improved so that events everywhere are entangled; the separate regions of the world have shrunk into a single unit, though so far not an orderly but a chaotic one. And thirdly, the breakdown of the laissez-faire system has introduced the possibility of large-scale planning.

Thus the general moral principle of equality can now come down to earth in the concrete task of achieving what I may call minimum equality; it can and should now be regarded as immoral to leave any human being below certain standards of physical and mental welfare and development.[6] The general moral principle of human unity and pooling of effort can come down to earth in the concrete task of achieving a minimum co-operative organization for the world-unit; it can and should now be regarded as immoral to let anything stand in the way of producing that degree of international order which will free the world from its major burdens of disunity, as regards both war and economic competition. And finally the general moral principle of evolu-

---

[6] This implies an ethical revaluation of charity. So long as intense poverty was abundant and apparently irremediable, charitable benevolence was the only outlet for the consciences of the more fortunate, and ranked high in the moral scale of virtues. In the latter half of the nineteenth century, it began to be realized that indiscriminate or even extensive charity might do more harm than good, and that to aim at social amelioration was a higher duty. Today we realize that it is not necessary that the poor shall be always with us; poverty can perfectly well be abolished. With this realization, the ethical value of charity in the traditional sense falls below that of measures for the abolition of poverty, and it will become progressively less of a virtue as its scope is restricted.

tionary purpose can come down to earth in the concrete task of achieving minimum planning: it can and should now be regarded as immoral for society not to be at least one move ahead of events.

The tasks of increasing the amount of goodness in the world and of deciding on the rightness or wrongness of particular actions must be related to some such concrete but limited applications of general ethical principles. It is of no avail merely saying or believing that one must be as unselfish, or kind, or pure, or merciful as possible. Does unselfishness extend to providing milk for Hottentots? What is the ethics of birth control? Or of private profit? Or of the ownership of colonies? There are perhaps no correct solutions to such questions as there are to arithmetical problems in an examination paper; but there are some answers which are more right, others which are more wrong. And to work them out we need both our general principles and their special applications to present conditions.

Another moral duty of our times is that of extending and applying our new psychological knowledge so as to prevent mental and especially moral distortion and underdevelopment. If we could see minds as we see bodies, we should be astonished at their variety. But in the present state of the world we should also be horror-struck at their deformations and their dwarfish failures to develop. And there is the frightening fact that the imperfections and distortions so often manage to attach the label of goodness or rightness to themselves. Stunted spiritual growth masquerades as humility or acceptance of the decrees of Providence, sadistic projection as a crusade against evil, the excessive asceticism or moral rigor that springs from an unrealistic sense of sin and from failure to face one's own nature, as a badge of special righteousness.

According to Dr. Ernest Jones, a leading British psychologist, man is "a creature blindly resisting, with all the means at his command, the forces that are making for a higher and fuller consciousness." This cannot perhaps be maintained as a general and permanent statement; but it is undoubtedly true that resistances to mental or spiritual advance are all but universal, and that in the majority of people they are powerful. The reluctance to admit new knowledge, the refusal to acknowledge some of our own impulses, the clinging to nonrational and nonrealistic methods of thought, the tendency to put off the burdens of our conflicts and the responsibility of our choices onto the shoulders of some external authority, or to retreat within the shelter of some ivory tower—all these constitute formidable drags on our passage toward true maturity, as well as often piling up dangerous stores of guilt and pent-up aggression within the social organism.

There are several specific problems to be tackled. The most obvious is the prevention of the warping of the whole structure of personality, with accompanying primary ethical distortion, in infancy and early childhood. Another is the provision during education of outlets for repressed impulses, and of creative activities which shall be either what William James would have called the moral equivalents of antisocial action or the moral substitutes for inhibition and further distortion. This implies a greater attention to the education of the emotions—for instance, through the arts—and also to the desire of growing boys and girls to feel of use, to make sacrifices, to participate in some exciting or valuable enterprise. A more limited yet equally important problem is that of the sensitive adolescent. Too often under our present system he (or she) shrinks away from the rough school of practice, and so leaves the control of affairs increasingly to the thick-skinned, or the blatant, or the ambitious seeker after power. In existing conditions, the sensitive awareness, the unselfishness, the desire for self-dedication, which should be available to society's common pool and are needed in the highest and most responsible positions, tend to be self-defeating, by causing their owner to withdraw from the struggle.

A related subject is that of innate variations in temperament or temperamental tendencies. Our knowledge in this field is only beginning to take shape, but it appears more than probable that, for instance, certain psychophysical types are predisposed to callous and tireless aggressiveness. Here we have the reciprocal of the problem of the sensitive adolescent—how can we either prevent the innately aggressive from seizing power or, preferably, provide creative instead of antisocial outlets for him?

It is our duty to set psychologists to work studying the variations and imperfections in man's mental machinery and the obstacles to its proper development, so as eventually to overcome these resistances to his mental and spiritual growth, to provide him with understanding and the means for a rational and fruitful self-discipline, and to improve the social mechanism underlying his further evolutionary advance. For here as elsewhere it is only knowledge that will set us free. To the evolutionist, knowledge and faith are not opposites, but complements.

Faith inspires the quest for more knowledge, knowledge provides the foundation for new faith.

But in our grossly imperfect world the individual will continue to suffer painful conflict. He must reflect that this is one of the means by which we have emerged into a new and more hopeful phase of evolution. It is part of the price we pay for being men.

And society will long be faced with the conflict between the general affirmation and the particular denial of principles which we know to be right. Our ethical principles assure us that war is a general wrong; yet to urge it may still be a particular right. Tolerance and kindness are general virtues; yet ruthless suppression of opponents may be a particular duty. It is the eternal conflict between means and ends. There is a slight comfort in the reflection that fuller understanding of general principles will give us more assurance of what ends are right.

Nor will clearer ethical vision prevent us from suffering what we feel as injustice at the hands of the cosmos—congenital deformity, unmerited suffering, physical disaster, the early death of loved ones. Such cosmic injustice represents the persistence of chance and its amorality in human life; we may gradually reduce its amount but we assuredly shall never abolish it. Man is the heir of evolution; but he is also its martyr. All living species provide their evolutionary sacrifice; only man *knows* that he is a victim.

But man is not only the heir of the past and the victim of the present; he is also the agent through whom evolution may unfold its further possibilities. Here, it seems, is the solution of our riddle of ethical relativity; the ultimate guarantees for the correctness of our labels of rightness and wrongness are to be sought for among the facts of evolutionary direction. Here, too, is to be found the reconciliation of the antithesis between the ethical and the cosmic process; for the cosmic process is continued into human affairs. Thus man can impose moral principles upon ever-widening areas of the cosmic process, in whose further slow unfolding he is now the protagonist. He can inject his ethics into the heart of evolution and reiterate the truth that science without conscience is but ruin to the soul.

THE FUTURE OF THEISM
Part One—The Human Soul

THE TWO THEORIES

From the beginnings of European philosophy there have been two fundamentally opposed theories as to the nature of Mind and its relation to the perishable organism with which it is so intimately associated and upon which it is so pathetically dependent.

The first and more congenial of these theories we shall call Spiritualistic Dualism. It is the theory that the minds of men and perhaps of animals have a reality of their own that is not completely dependent upon the living bodies within which they grow and by which and through which their career is largely determined. That the mind can guide the body in the light of its memories of the past and its plans for the future seems obvious. And as the captain who guides his ship can leave it and survive its destruction so can the mind survive the body on which it has made the voyage of life. Those who hold this theory of dualistic spiritualism differ among themselves as to the nature of the mind, as it is in itself and apart from the body. Some would regard it as a pure spirit lacking all material properties but inhabiting space and time. Others would go still further and regard it as a transcendental entity outside or beyond the spatial and temporal world. I shall not deal with these questions, for I do not wish the minor disagreements among dualists to obscure the major point on which they are all agreed in their opposition to their rivals, the Naturalistic Monists.

The theory that I shall call Naturalistic Monism is the view that mind whether human or animal is an inseparable aspect of the organism and its processes, particularly those of the central nervous system. This

264

monistic conception is not so congenial to our wishes and hopes nor even to our common-sense beliefs as is its dualistic opponent. Its great and growing strength is based upon science rather than upon naïve feeling and expectation. As science has advanced, and succeeded in explaining, or at least in describing and predicting, the course of events in one domain after another without employing the conception of guidance by a spirit apart from physical phenomena, the conviction has grown that men and other living organisms are integral parts of nature, more complicated in their laws than inorganic bodies but not essentially different from them, or at least not differing from them in such a way as to require explanation by immaterial agencies such as spirits. What we experience in ourselves as mind is, then, to be conceived as the inner aspect of certain processes in our bodies, and no more separable from or independent of those processes than the shape, size or velocities of a body are separable from it. Such is the theory of naturalistic monism. It is, of course, what has been traditionally called materialism in that it regards mind as an aspect or function of the material body. But those who hold the theory today do not like to be called materialists or even mechanists because they say that such names would convey an oversimplified and distorted impression of their view. Matter at the present time is regarded as composed not of simple little elastic spheres like tiny billiard balls but of complicated clusters of waves, and its laws are not the simple mechanical laws that sufficed to explain the behavior of the old-fashioned atoms but highly complicated relations in which electrical and electromagnetic factors are at least as important as those which are mechanical. Disputes about the meaning of words are so much less interesting than disputes about the nature of things that we can afford to substitute for the labels of materialism and mechanism the labels "naturalism" and "monism" or "naturalistic monism" as acceptable names for the current theory that is opposed to spiritualistic dualism. In making this concession, however, we must be careful to remember that the new and complicated physics of the twentieth century with its concepts of relativity and quantum provides no more ground than did the older physics for the purposive or teleological type of activity that appears to be characteristic of mind. There are many contemporary theologians who have been rejoicing in the death of their ancient enemies, materialism and mechanism, because they have heard that the atoms of matter are packets of waves and that the laws of matter are at least as much electrical as mechanical. These theologians are cultivating a false hope and are doomed to disillusionment for the reason that was just stated. Nature under the new dispensation is exactly as blind or purposeless as under the old. And it is as difficult to find a place for mind and its peculiar properties in the organism as conceived today as in the organism of preceding centuries.

THE PECULIAR PROPERTIES OF MIND

Of the many characteristics of the kind of reality that we call mind or mental, I select for summary consideration those four which seem to be most fundamental and which contrast most sharply with the kind of reality that we call matter or material. They are:

1. Privacy.
2. Duration.
3. Purposiveness.
4. Integration.

Let us consider them in turn:

1. *Privacy.* Everything that is mental is "private" in the sense of not being externally observable. If you were to cut open a man's skull and examine with the most powerful conceivable microscope every cubic inch of his brain you could not imagine yourself observing any of his mental states. The simplest sensations or feelings and the most complex ideas or thoughts would be equally impossible to observe by anybody except the man who had them.

2. *Duration.* Mental states are like material or physical events in that they succeed one another in time. The experiences of Monday like the physical events of Monday are followed by those of Tuesday and of Wednesday. But between the two kinds of succession there is an extraordinary contrast. In a sequence of physical events the later moments must exclude the earlier, while in a sequence of mental events the later moments can include the earlier. The material world of Monday must be over and gone before the material world of Tuesday can exist; but the *experience* of Monday's world is contained in the experience of Tuesday. Physical time has only succession, mental time has duration as well as succession. It would be nonsense to say that in a game of bridge the later hands could include the earlier, yet the player's experience of the later does obviously include in what we call

memory the experience of the earlier. One configuration of the fifty-two cards in the pack gives place to another, and in the latter case no more than in the former is it possible for the past to be contained in the present. We are forced to conclude that the property of duration, which is the outstanding characteristic of anything that can be called mental, simply defies explanation in ordinary materialistic or naturalistic terms.

This duration is of two kinds. There is the primary or continuous duration, which is called the "specious present," and there is the secondary or discontinuous duration, which is called memory. If I make five taps on a desk, you are conscious at the moment of the fifth tap of the four that have preceded and of the interval of time which they have occupied and which is continuous with the present moment. But if I ask you to think of a certain dinner party which you attended, last week or last year, you will be conscious of it as a part of your past, but you will not have any clear or sensory consciousness of the series of events in your life intervening between then and now. This discontinuous or episodic awareness of our past is what we mean by memory or *remembering*. Henri Bergson, who was the first philosopher to emphasize the all-important factor of "duration," or *durée réelle* as he named it, believed that nothing of our past is ever really lost, though it may be buried so deep as to defy recollection at any later moment. Sigmund Freud and some other psychologists share this belief that memory is indestructible or immortal, at least during bodily life. I think they are right. We drag wtih us through time, as a comet drags its tail, the steadily lengthening and deepening totality of traces of past experience. They constitute the private hell and heaven, the shame and the glory, that we have irrevocably built into the structure of our souls.

3. *Purposiveness.* Anticipation of the future is the consequence and correlate of memory of the past. The possibilities we can imagine, and which we seek to actualize or to avoid, are but the new combinations and rearrangements of what we have already experienced, and this third peculiar property of mind which we call *purposiveness* is but another aspect of its second property of *duration.* The capacity of the present to contain and to pursue an imagined future is at least as difficult to explain naturalistically as its other capacity to contain a remembered past. And nothing in the configuration of cerebral atoms moving from place to place will in the least account for it.

4. *Integration.* This fourth and last of the distinctively mental properties which I select for the consideration of the reader might be called "organicity" as well as "integration." The mind is perpetually integrating and organizing into unified systems the new elements that come to it. Not only do we assimilate into our conceptions, our purposes and our characters the sensations that the environment presents, but we organize the environment itself. All the products of culture, such as laboratories, libraries and churches, are projections into the external world and incarnations in the matter of that world of the mind's own structures, its hopes and fears and questionings. Mind informs matter, and transforms the comparative chaos of its surroundings into a cultural cosmos nearer to its taste. And as life, once started, spreads and ramifies over the grateful earth from which it springs, so does that higher type of life which is mind wage a benign and creative war upon nature, imposing upon it its own unities of meaning and value. No greater slander of life and mind has ever been uttered than the biologist's charge that they are adaptations to environment. The truth is just the opposite. Mind and life adapt the environment to their needs and though they may stoop to conquer, and conform to things as they are, their primary intent is always conquest—conquest through a process of assimilation, organization and integration, by which what *is* becomes what *ought to be.*

THE HYPOTHESIS OF A PHYSICAL SOUL

The reader will have gathered that I believe that dualism has won its case, and that the opposing theory of naturalistic monism is quite unable to explain in its own terms the privacy, the duration, the purposiveness and the integration or organicity that are the four distinctive characteristics of the kind of reality called mental. But even if one is kind enough to agree that a victory has been achieved, the responsibilities of that victory are heavy and the real work has only just begun. For dualism, however true it may be, has always been scientifically sterile. The main work of science has been accomplished within the frame and by the methods of materialism or by what we agreed to call naturalistic monism. And for the purposes of science it is almost more important that a theory be fertile than that it be true. The soul and body of Plato and of Thomas Aquinas, the *res cogitans* and *res extensa* of Descartes, have given rise to insoluble problems as to the relation between the two opposed entities. And when we turn to contemporary dualists the case is the same. Bergson's *élan vital,* Hans Driesch's "entelechies" and William McDougall's "animistic factors" can none of them be intelligibly related to the bodies they inhabit. How can non-spatial spirit be imagined to interact with a brain spread through the space inside the skull? And worse than that, when the tried and true categories of physics are abandoned or transcended there is nothing to control or discipline our thinking. Spirits, psychoids and spooks of all kinds can be had for the asking, *ad hoc* and *ad lib,* and we are apt to find ourselves wallowing in the intellectual mud of occultism. The situation is like that which one may have experienced in playing a game of poker "just for fun." Without the sobering control of a monetary stake, however small, the bets become irresponsible and fantastic, and the whole game degenerates into childish nonsense.

Now, when we find ourselves in this impasse in which we have to choose between the fruitful falsity of monism and the sterile truth of dualism, is there anything that can be done? I believe there is, and I request the attention of the reader to a certain hypothesis which I have very much at heart and which I think will really meet the needs of our problem. It is the hypothesis of a *physical soul,* something that possesses all the four peculiar properties that we have seen to be distinctive of mind, but which at the same time is capable of being described in terms of physics and described in such a way that its own nature and its relation to the body can be clearly understood.

Let us begin by noting that energy, which is the basic category of physics, and which can be roughly defined as the quantity of motion in a system, is of two fundamentally distinct types, kinetic and potential. Kinetic energy is actual motion whose quantity is measured by the product of the amount of mass that is moving and the square of its velocity; mv^2. Kinetic energy is visible or externally observable. Potential energy is not visible or externally observable. Its amount is measured by the product of the force (ma) and the distance through which the force extends: $ma \times s$. The quantity of potential motion $ma \times s$ is algebraically equal to the quantity of actual motion, mv^2, which it is capable of producing. Now, to whatever extent a motion is changed in direction its energy passes from the visible or kinetic form into the invisible or potential form. If the question is asked, What *is* this potential energy *in itself?* a natural answer would seem to be that it is just the motion of the small particles composing the mass that had the visible motion. These motions are too small to see and in that sense their energy is invisible. This answer, however, will not do, for the simple reason that whenever the particles, be they electrons, atoms or molecules, have their motions changed in direction—their small kinetic energies will be partly or wholly transformed into small potential energies and the problem of the nature of potential energy will be back again on our hands. The answer given by the physicist is a different one. Potential energy is just the result of past motion and the possibility of future motion. In short, potential energy is *nothing but* potential; it has in itself no mysterious nature or actuality. I move a body upward or farther away from the earth, and the kinetic energy of that motion is changed into the kind of potential energy that we call energy of position. Or if I wind the stem of my watch, this motion of my winding will be changed into the kind of potential energy that we call elastic stress in the mainspring, which means only that there is the possibility that the equivalent amount of motion will slowly trickle back into the realm of external observation in the form of what to me will be the useful revolution that the hands of my watch make around its face or dial during the next twenty-four hours. But whether the potential energy is gravitational, elastic, electrostatic or magnetic, it is in any case nothing but the result of a motion that is past and the possibility of a motion that is future. If I ask the physicist whether there is not something a little queer in the fact that a good concrete thing like a motion can pass into something that in itself is nothing and then emerge from that nonentity with its quantitative identity unscathed by its period of annihilation, he will brush the question aside as inconsequential or meaningless. It's merely the way things are. A state of affairs in which motion is observed will be succeeded by a second state of affairs in which motion is not observed. And that in turn will be succeeded by a third situation in which motion is again observed. The second state is the potentiality of the third state. And that is all that potential energy means. He might be good-natured enough to add that even if there were some hidden characteristic in the state called "potential," it would not interest him, for the reason that he as a physicist is interested only in what is externally observable.

At this point I will ask the reader to consider a kind of episode which could arise in the case of two friends going out together on a hike. One of the friends is a follower of the strenuous life. He likes walking for its own sake, and he views the rests they both must take as regrettable interludes, mere potentialities of further walking. The second friend is not at all of this type. He is lazy and contemplative, and he views the actual walking as regrettable interludes, mere potentialities of the delightful rests in which one can enjoy the view. The first and more energetic friend seizes the right to christen the alternating phases of the hike, and he names the resting periods as just potentialities of walking. The other fellow, were he given the opportunity, would do the naming in reverse and characterize the walking as just the potentiality of resting.

Now to return from fable to fact—when a sensory stimulus passes from a sensory end-organ such as a retina, a basilar membrane or a patch of skin, it proceeds as a current of kinetic energy, theoretically if not actually open to external observation, to the brain, and there at the synapse the current is temporarily dammed up in the form of a potential and not even theoretically externally observable energy until it acquires sufficient intensity to spark across the gap between the neurons. Now, suppose that at the moment when the energy of the current passes from the externally observable phase into the purely internal or potential phase, the man who owns the brain exclaims, "Ouch! I've got a sensation!" I think we should all feel it was a pretty good bet that what from the external standpoint was a mere result of the past afferent current and a mere potentiality of the future efferent current of motor reaction was *in itself* the sensation. In other words, when the externally observable becomes *nothing* the internally observable becomes *something*, namely, a mental state. Now, of course, a pure physiologist would be quite indifferent to these mental states even if he were kind enough to admit their existence. For him as for the physicist it is only the stimuli and the reactions that would be of interest, for they alone can be observed from without. But the man himself who undergoes these currents of neural energy could be pardoned if he felt it a little odd to regard his sensations and his entire conscious being as nothing but the possibilities of the bodily reactions to which they gave rise.

So far I have been writing more or less in allegories and fables seeking to placate any possible opposition based perhaps on pre-existing assumptions. I wish now to abandon this policy of appeasement and proceed to a definite offensive. And to that end I ask the reader to consent to view my hypothesis, if not with actual favor, at least with an open mind and a willingness to contemplate sympathetically what I think are its implications. If he will agree to that, I can save time by stating those implications categorically or even dogmatically and without attempting much in the way of a justification of each point.

Let me begin by confessing that what I said about the transformation at the synapse of one form of energy into the other was an oversimplification. Currents of kinetic energy *are* transformed in whole or in part into states of potential energy which are experienced as mental. But there is no one synapse in which all such transformations occur. I am not attempting to revive Descartes' pineal gland as a cerebral center at which the psychophysical miracles take place. As we shall see in a moment, it is the complex field of force extending more or less throughout the brain in which and by aid of which the kinetic energies of the stimuli are changed into the potential energies that for us are actual sensations.

I think we may assume from what we know of ourselves that the intensive energy that constitutes a conscious state is not entirely expended in the motor reaction resulting from it. A specific trace appears to remain in the form of a memory image, and these traces successively superposed in an intensive hierarchy constitute the memory system. In the various forms of materialism or naturalistic monism that have been and are still being advocated, the memory system or mind is regarded as an inner aspect of the *kinetic* energies of the neural currents flowing through the brain and nervous system. The defenders of this view have recently been making quite a point of speaking not of "a mind" and "a body" but of a "body-mind," seeking to emphasize by the hyphen in this compound word the monistic identity or inseparableness of the mental and bodily components. We have pointed out the reasons why such a conception is untenable. The principal reason was that the successive moments of a sequence of motions are mutually exclusive so that there is no possibility of the later moments including the earlier and so providing for that *duration of the past in the present* which is the primary characteristic of everything that is mental.

The theory that I am proposing does something new: it identifies the mental not with the kinetic but with the *potential* energies in the brain. By so doing we can clearly see that the four peculiar properties of the mental, as revealed by introspection and seized upon by the spiritualist as justifying his dualism, can each be found to characterize a field of potential energy. Let us take each of them in turn:

1. *Privacy.* Potential energy is the only thing definable in physical terms that is private in the sense of not being open to external observation. The moment when present motion disappears from view and becomes a mere potentiality of future motion is the moment when the private or internally observable actuality of sensation makes its appearance.

2. *Duration.* Even such a simple field of potential energies as can be carried by a coiled spring can have impressed upon it a series of kinetic energies, and then can retain superposed in an intensive hierarchy the successive members of the series. The temporal order is preserved and the spring when released can regurgitate in a new series of motions of recoil the series it had received and retained. But during the period of retention the series exhibits not succession but duration, which is the presence of the past in the present.

3. *Purposiveness.* We have already seen that the imaginative anticipation of the future is, so to speak, the obverse of a memory of the past. And any field of potential energy which is the result of past motions is by the same token the anticipative possibility of future motions. And while at first hearing it might seem fanciful to attribute purposiveness or teleology to a gravitational or electric field of force, it is not fanciful to realize that such a field determines the particles that come within its scope to a predestined end. If the mind is such a field, though immeasurably more complex, then the series of actions determined by it would tend toward the ends that were in conformity with its structure.

4. *Integration.* A field of potential energy or force exhibits something of the same power of integration or organicity which we found to be characteristic of mind. Kinetic energies are passed on by "conduction." One part of space gives up the motion contained in it to other adjoining spaces. But force or potential energy can be propagated by "induction." The structure of an electric or magnetic field without itself being wasted can induce a replica of itself upon other material. The iron filings sprinkled upon a paper beneath which is a magnet are integrated or organized in conformity with the Faraday lines of force constituting the structure of the magnetic field. And if the mind is a field of force, we can see how each new sensation that it acquires is organized into

its structure, and gets stamped upon it by a kind of induction a meaning that is in conformity with the mind as a whole.

The mind as thus conceived is *an organism within an organism.* The living body takes its energies as contained in the food which it ingests and which by an activity akin to mind it builds up or anabolizes into its tissues. The brain, however, takes its most characteristic energies "neat" as pure motions of neural stimuli undiluted by matter. These energies are transformed from the kinetic into the potential type that are sensations, traces of which are integrated into the enduring fabric of memory.

The mind as constituted in this way is not an adjective of the body any more than a plant is an adjective of the soil from which and within which it grows. It is no epiphenomenal concomitant of bodily processes. It is a substantive entity existing in its own right, a veritable *soul,* which may even outlast the perishable organism on which and through which it acts and upon which it so largely depends. The theory that I offer is, then, a real dualism; but please note that it is dualism with a difference. It is not, as are the traditional dualisms, open to the charge of being methodologically sterile and irresponsible. No less than the naturalistic monism that is its rival, it interprets the mind in terms of those same physical categories which are essential to genuine progress in science.

Part Two—The Cosmic Mind

When we turn from a consideration of the nature of the human soul and its relation to the body to consider the hypothesis of a cosmic mind, we are impressed with the meagerness of evidence available to support such a hypothesis. If we lay aside the rose-colored glasses of religious tradition and look at the cosmos coldly and with the naked eye of reason, or at least of a merely secular imagination, we see a vast expanse of stars some of which like our own star, the sun, may have planets on which life as we know it could exist. Every hundred billion or so of these stars appear to be organized into what we call a galaxy, each of which rotates around its center. The galaxies, or star systems, extend through a distance of at least half a billion light years (that is, for some sextillions of miles) in every direction as so far discovered. There are certainly more beyond and their number may be infinite. Nowhere among these sprawling galaxies do we discern, nor have we the slightest reason to infer, any structure however vast that resembles the living organisms we know on our planet to be the vehicles of mind. Is it, then, more than an arbitrary fancy to suppose that the system as a whole, whether finite or infinite, could be the embodiment of a cosmic mind? I think the answer depends upon whether or not we accept as sound the theory propounded in the first part of this chapter. If mental states are identical with forms of potential energy, then the extent to which some sort of mental reality is present in the universe will be the extent to which potential energy is present—and that is everywhere. But the thought will immediately occur that the merely mental is not mind. Protoplasm is the only agency we know which acts as a trap for energy, and by means of which the traces of the kinetic currents flowing through it are preserved, accumulated and organized. In nonliving systems there is mind-stuff but not mind. Energy is dissipated almost as fast as it is received and leaves no traces of sufficient strength to propagate themselves and to determine appreciably the behavior of the system in which they may be stored. On the other hand, however, it would seem to be highly improbable that the particular combination of carbon, hydrogen, oxygen and nitrogen which constitutes our protoplasm and which can only exist under highly restricted conditions of gravity and temperature should be the only combination of atoms to serve as a vehicle for those accumulations of potential energy which mean life and mind. But whether or not there are other types of finite minds with other material embodiments than those we know on this planet, it is difficult not to believe that the cosmos as a whole possesses a completer unity than any of its parts, and thus constitutes an integrated field of energy having an organicity like that of mind and a memory from which nothing of the past could be wholly lost.

There are, however, two roads "through nature to God," and I propose now that we turn to the second of these roads and consider not the structure of the cosmos in space but its history in time in order to see whether we can there discover anything indicative of the work of mind. Does the universe show any evidence in its behavior of being created and guided by a mind that is both omnipotent and benign? To

this time-honored theological question the answer must be a flat negative. Nature is red in tooth and claw, and life is so constituted that each
creature can preserve its existence only by devouring other creatures.
The will to live is, as Schopenhauer said, a hungry will and feeds
perpetually upon itself. If there is a God, he is either not omnipotent
or not good, in any sense of the word "good" that the human conscience
can sanction. When transfixed on the horns of this ancient dilemma,
which is called "The Problem of Evil," the theologian has usually
preferred to save the omnipotence of God at the expense of his goodness. We are told that God works in a mysterious way his wonders to
perform, and that his ways are not our ways. For a being with a conscience anything like ours such a God would be regarded as diabolical
rather than divine if, *with omnipotence to draw upon,* he had made a
world in which ninety-nine per cent of His creatures were to suffer
agony and defeat in order that one per cent might thrive. And where
does a vainglorious anthropomorphism reach such a climax of im-
pudence as when the defenders of this type of theology seek to explain
and justify the misery inherent in animal life by declaring it to be
the proper result of human sin? As though anything that was done
by so recent an inhabitant of this planet as man could justify the suffering that took place in the ages that preceded man's appearance! Might
does not make right even when it is divine might. And power politics
is as ugly a thing in heaven as it is on earth. To attribute to a God of
Love the creation of the world of things as they are is blasphemy.

Suppose, then, that we purge our religion of the immoral notion of
divine omnipotence and, liberated from that embarrassment, look
again at the course of nature. At once the picture changes and brightens.
The conflict, tragedy and waste are still there, but pervading them all
we find unmistakable signs of an upward, or evolutionary, trend. As
life advances it deepens and sweetens and by the growth of sympathy
becomes broader and less discordant. Through many a setback and
defeat this Increasing Purpose runs. No aggregate of blind forces however complicated could by a miracle of chance have given us even the
life that we have, imperfect though it be. Everywhere throughout
organic nature there is the sign of something like mind dimly but
assuredly at work. And when we turn from biology to physics and from
the little oasis of organic life to the vast desert of the inorganic by
which all protoplasm is encompassed we find what is, I think, an

unmistakable echo of one of the four primary characteristics of mental reality, the one which we called "integration" or "organicity."

Science does, to be sure, record everywhere the opposite of integrations. It finds disintegrations, katabolisms and breakdowns throughout nature. Molecules disintegrate into atoms, and atoms by radioactivity disintegrate into subatomic corpuscles such as electrons, protons and neutrons. Systems tend to pass from organization and differentiation into disorganization and uniformity. Energy tends to be dissipated and lowered in grade from molar or mechanical motion to molecular motion or heat, and finally to waves of radiant energy or light which is the most "dissipated" and least organized of all. This omnipresent trend used to be called the Law of the Dissipation of Energy, and also, under another aspect, the Second Law of Thermodynamics. It is now frequently called the Increase of Entropy, where the positive-sounding word "entropy" means the amount of uniformity, extensity, scatteredness and disorganization that so far as significance and utility are concerned is very negative indeed. To congratulate a sick friend on his increase of entropy would be to congratulate him on his increase of decay and dissolution! But is it not true that this sad trend in nature must have been preceded by an opposite trend, which we can call antientropy?

Before there can be spending there must have been saving, before katabolism there must have been anabolism. In short, there cannot be death unless there has first been life. Somehow or other the corpuscles must have been organized into atoms and the atoms into molecular and supermolecular systems as a prelude to the series of breakdowns that were characterized as the dissipation of energy. I think we may say that most of the discoveries of science up to the present have pertained to the breakdowns and to the processes incidental to them. It is true that some syntheses of the less organized into the more organized have been observed and even created in our laboratories, but nothing that approaches the broad and deep integrations of nature has been accomplished by man. This is to be expected, for it is easier to destroy than to build up and far easier to understand the production of death than the production of life. Aristotle reminded us that what is last in the order of Knowledge is first in the order of Being; and there may come a time when a second volume of science is written in which not entropy but the antientropy that preceded it will be the principal theme. And yet if that second and greater volume is ever written it may be written in a different language, for the good and curious reason that the powers that make for integration and organicity are, as we have already seen, characteristic of what is essentially internal or mental, and as such not open directly to external observation any more than are the minds of other people.

All this suggests a hypothesis which I do not think is too farfetched or fanciful. It is the hypothesis that the antientropic power that must exist in nature as the cause of the organizations with which nature is filled is a mental power akin to what we find in ourselves. To call such a factor the Will of God would, then, be no empty metaphor but the very truth. For it is, in Matthew Arnold's great phrase, "a power not ourselves that makes for righteousness." That it is not an omnipotent power is all too sadly obvious. Everywhere there is the conflict of wills and tendencies that makes for disorganization and pain. But among these varied tendencies, and leavening the chaos that they constitute, is the tendency to higher organization and to a higher harmony.

But now in conclusion there is a final question that must be asked. If the cosmic mind, or God, is not omnipotent, does that mean that the chaos of nature is something outside God and menacing him with a more or less unpredictable fate? The brave Zoroastrians and after them William James, John Stuart Mill and many others who have preferred to save God's goodness at the expense of His traditional omnipotence have seemed to think so. With all respect to the great leaders of that school of thought, I cannot believe that in this point they are right. If there is a cosmic mind, or God, then everything moves and has its being within that mind. I prefer to think of the chaotic tendencies of nature as what Boehme or Meister Eckhart characterized as "that in God which is not God." Cosmic evolution could then be regarded as the work of organizing the independent centers of activity in the divine mind that constitute its contents taken distributively and as a plurality, and informing them more and more with the harmony characteristic of that mind when considered in its collective unity.

When viewed in this way and interpreted in the language of the noblest of the legends of ancient Greece, the Will of God would not be the analogue of any omnipotent Zeus but rather of the Prometheus, the Divine Rebel, whose heart was directed singly to the good and who waged an unyielding war against the Tyrant's claim that Right be sub-ordinated to Might.

If such a Promethean Spirit is indeed a reality, he should be thought of not as a King of kings but as a Comrade of comrades, needing our aid as we need his in that unending pursuit of the ideal which for God no less than for Man makes up the meaning of existence.

A NEW APPROACH TO GOD

1   If civilization is to survive, if the emergent civilization is to achieve the fulfillment of its potentialities, the coming age must be an age of spiritual as well as social integration.

Today the human mind is torn and divided between positivism and irrationalism. The endeavors of pragmatism succeeded in making important discoveries concerning a number of basic attitudes in thought and morality, and in what might be called the sociology of knowledge. As a universal system of knowledge and life, as a philosophy, however, pragmatism has been a failure.

What is essentially needed is a renewal of metaphysics. The conceptions of modern science—the unification of matter and energy, physical indeterminism, the notion of space-time, the new reality recognized both as to quality and duration—are invaluable means of deciphering material phenomena. A cosmos of electrons and stars in which the stars are the heavenly laboratories of elements, subjected everywhere to genesis and transmutation, a universe which is finite but whose limits cannot be attained because of the curvature of space, and which dynamically evolves in a definite direction, namely, toward the highest forms of individuation and concentration and toward a simultaneous degradation of the quality of its total energy—all this is external description and scientific imagery rather than ontological insight. Such knowledge can never directly serve the purpose of any philosophical or metaphysical extrapolations. Yet all this constitutes at the same time a basic representation of the world incomparably more favorable to the edification of a philosophy of nature and more open to the deepening labor of metaphysical reason than the old Newtonian physics. The opportunity is now given for that reconciliation between science and wisdom for which the human mind thirsts. What the emergent civilization is anticipating, nay, presenting to the world as a tangible possibility and necessity, is a rediscovery of Being, and by the same token a rediscovery of Love.

This means axiomatically a rediscovery of God. The *existential* philosophies which are today in fashion are but a sign of a certain deep want, an inability to find again the sense of Being. This want is now unfulfilled, for these philosophies are still enslaved by irrationalism and seek for the revelation of existence, for ontological ecstasy, in the breaking of reason, in the experience of Despair and Nothingness, of Anguish or Absurdity. True existentialism is the work of reason. The act, by virtue of which I exist and things exist, transcends concepts and ideas; it is a mystery for the intellect. But the intellect lives on this mystery. In its most natural activity it is as ordinary, daily and vulgar as eating or drinking. The act of existing is indeed the very object of every achieved act of the intellect, that is, of judgment. It is perceived by that intellectual intuition, immersed in sense experience, which is the common treasure (all the more precious since it is natural and imbues the depths of our thought) of all our assertions, of all this mysterious activity by means of which we declare either *ita est* or *fiat!* in the face of the world or at the moment of making a decision. Now, when the intellect passes the threshold of philosophy, it does so by becoming aware of this intellectual intuition, freeing its genuine power, and making it the peculiar weapon of a knowledge whose subject matter is Being itself. I do not here refer to Platonic essences. I refer to the act of existing in so far as it establishes and centers the intelligible structure of reality, as it expands into activity in every being; and as, at its supreme plenitude, it activates and attracts to itself the entire dynamism of nature. At their ontological peak, in the transcendence of the Pure Act and the Absolute, Being, Reason and God are one and the same reality. In the created realm Reason confronts Being and labors to conquer it, both to transfer Being into its own immaterial life and immaterially to be or become Being. In perceiving Being Reason knows God, in an enigmatic but inescapable manner.

Yet my thesis does not deal only with philosophers and philosophy, but with the mental behavior of the common man. Werner Sombart used to say that the "bourgeois," the man of the "capitalistic" era, was *neither "ontological" nor "erotic,"* had lost the sense of Being and the sense of Love. Torture and death have made us aware of the meaning

of ontology. Hate has awakened an awareness of the meaning of eros.
Let us emerge from sleep, cease to live in the dream or magic of images
and formulas, well-systematized words, practical symbols and world-
festering kabbala! Once a man is awakened to the reality of existence
and the true life of Reason, to the intelligible value of Being, once he
has really perceived this tremendous fact, sometimes exhilarating, sometimes disgusting and maddening in the knowledge that *I exist,* he is
henceforth taken hold of by the intuition of Being and the implications
it involves.

Precisely speaking, this prime intuition is both the intuition of *my*
existence and of the existence of things; but first and foremost of the
existence of things. When it takes place, I suddenly realize that a given
entity, man, mountain or tree, exists and exercises that sovereign
activity *to be* in its own way, totally self-assertive and totally implacable,
completely independent from *me.* And at the same time I realize that
I also exist but as thrown back into my loneliness and frailty by such
affirmation of existence in which I have positively no part, to which
I am exactly as naught. So the prime intuition of Being is the intuition
of the solidity and inexorability of existence; and, secondly, of the
death and nothingness to which *my* existence is liable. And thirdly,
in the same flash of intuition, which is but my becoming aware of
the intelligible value of Being, I realize that the solid and inexorable
existence perceived in anything whatsoever implies—I don't know in
what way, perhaps in things themselves, perhaps separately from them
—some absolute, irrefragable existence, completely free from nothingness and death. These three intellective leaps—to actual existence as
asserting itself independently from me; from this sheer objective existence to my own threatened existence; and from my existence spoiled
with nothingness to absolute existence—are achieved within that same
and unique intuition which philosophers would explain as the intuitive
perception of the essentially analogical content of the first concept, the
concept of Being.

Then a quick, spontaneous reasoning, as natural as this intuition
(and, as a matter of fact, more or less involved in it) immediately
springs forth, as the necessary fruit of such primordial apperception
and as enforced by and under its light. I see that my Being, first, is liable
to death; and, second, that it depends on the totality of nature, on the
universal whole whose part I am; and that Being-with-nothingness, as

my own being is, implies, in order to be, Being-without-nothingness. It implies that absolute existence which I confusedly perceived as involved in my primordial intuition of existence. The universal whole, whose part I am, is Being-with-nothingness, from the very fact that I am part of it; so that finally, since the universal whole does not exist by itself, there is another, separate, whole, another Being, transcendent and self-sufficient and unknown in itself and activating all beings, which is Being-without-nothingness, that is, Being by itself.

Thus the inner dynamism of the intuition of existence, or of the intelligible value of Being, causes me to see that absolute existence or Being-without-nothingness transcends the totality of nature, and compels me to face the existence of God.

This is not a new approach to God. It is the eternal approach of man's reason to God. What is new is the manner in which the modern mind has become aware of the simplicity and liberating power, the natural and somehow intuitive characteristics of this eternal approach. The science of the ancients was steeped in philosophy. Their scientific imagery was a pseudo-ontological imagery. Consequently there was a kind of continuum between their knowledge of the physical world and their knowledge of God. The latter appeared as the summit of the former, a summit which was to be climbed through the manifold paths of the causal connections at play in the sublunar world and the celestial spheres. The sense of Being that ruled their universal thought was for them a too usual atmosphere to be felt as a surprising gift. At the same time the natural intuition of existence was so strong in them that their proofs of God could take the form of the most conceptualized and rationalized scientific demonstrations, and be offered as an unrolling of logical necessities, without losing the inner energy of that intuition. Such logical machinery was quickened instinctively by the basic intuition of Being.

We are in a quite different position now. In order to solve the enigma of physical reality and to conquer the world of phenomena, our science has become a kind of Maya—a maya which succeeds and makes us masters of nature. But the sense of Being is absent from it. Thus when we happen to experience the impact of Being upon the mind it appears to us as a kind of intellectual revelation, and we realize clearly both its liberating and its awakening power and the fact that it involves a knowledge which is separated from that sphere of knowledge peculiar to our science. At the same time we realize that the knowledge of God, before being developed into logical and perfectly conceptualized demonstrations, is first and foremost a natural fruit of the intuition of existence, and forces itself upon our mind in the imperative virtue of this intuition.

In other words, we have become aware of the fact that human reason's approach to God, in its primordial vitality, is neither a mere intuition, which would be suprahuman, nor is it that artlike philosophical reasoning by which it is expressed in its achieved form, each step of which is pregnant with involved issues and problems. Human reason's approach to God in its primordial vitality is a *natural* reasoning, that is, intuitive-like or irresistibly vitalized by and maintained within the intellectual flash of the intuition of existence. Then the intuition of existence, grasping in some existing reality Being-with-nothingness, makes the mind grasp by the same stroke the necessity of Being-without-nothingness. And nowhere is there any problem involved, because the illumining power of this intuition takes hold of the mind and obliges it to see. Thus it naturally proceeds, in a primary intuitive flash, from imperative certainty to imperative certainty. I believe that from Descartes to Kierkegaard, the effort of modern thought —to the extent that it has not completely repudiated metaphysics, and if it is cleansed of the irrationalism which has gradually corrupted it— tends to such an awareness of the specific *naturality* of man's knowledge of God, definitely deeper than any logical process scientifically developed. It tends to the awareness of man's knowledge of God, and of the primordial and simple intuitivity in which it originates. Availing itself of any true progress achieved by the critique of knowledge, and realizing its own existential requirements, philosophy must enforce this new awareness and make clear in this way the manner in which the eternal approach of man, of the common man, to God proceeds.

On the other hand, becoming aware of the subconscious life of the spirit, and considering not only our theoretical but also our practical approach to God, philosophy must lay stress on the following fact. When a man experiences, in a primary act of freedom, the impact of the moral good, and is thus awakened to moral life, and directs his life toward the good for the sake of the good, then he directs his life, even without knowing it, toward the absolute Good, and in this way knows God vitally, by virtue of the inner dynamism of his choice of the good, even if he does not know God in any conscious fashion and by means of any conceptual knowledge. Thus Conscience, with its practical intuition of the moral good, and with a practical and preconscious knowledge of the supreme existing Good, has its own approach to God, just as Reason has its own approach with its speculative intuition of existence and with the theoretical and conscious knowledge of the supreme existing Being.

Finally, the rediscovery of the value of existence not only means the rediscovery of God. It also means the rediscovery of Love. For when the intuition of Being and Existence takes place in me, it normally carries along with itself another intuition, the intuition of my own existence or my Self, the intuition of Subjectivity as subjectivity. Now Subjectivity, in so far as it is subjectivity, is not an object presented to thought but rather the very wellspring of thought—a deep, unknown and living center which superabounds in knowledge and superabounds in love, attaining only through love its supreme level of existence, existence as giving itself.

This is what I mean: Self-knowledge as a mere psychological analysis of phenomena more or less superficial, a wandering through images and memories, is but an egotistic awareness, however valuable it may be. But when it becomes ontological, then Knowledge of the Self is transfigured, implying intuition of Being and the discovery of the actual abyss of subjectivity. At the same time it is the discovery of the basic generosity of existence. Subjectivity, this essentially dynamic, living and open center, both receives and gives. It receives through the intellect, by superexisting in knowledge. It gives through the will, by superexisting in love; that is, by having within itself other beings as inner attractions directed toward them and giving oneself to them, and by spiritually existing in the manner of a gift. And "it is better to give than to receive." The spiritual existence of love is the supreme revelation of existence for the Self. The Self, being not only a material individual but also a spiritual personality, possesses itself and holds itself in hand in so far as it is spiritual and in so far as it is free. And to what purpose does it possess itself and dispose of itself, if not for what *is better,* in actual existence and absolutely speaking, or to give of itself? Thus it is that when a man has been really awakened to the sense of being or existence, and grasps intuitively the obscure, living depth of the Self and subjectivity, he discovers by the same token the basic generosity of existence and realizes, by virtue of the inner dynamism of this intuition, that love is not a passing pleasure or emotion, but the very meaning of his being alive. He becomes both an "ontological" and an "erotic" man, he is a man renewed.

And not only does he know, by virtue of his primordial intellectual grasping of existence, that God exists and is absolute Being, is self-subsisting *Esse*. He also knows that because of this very fact God is absolute ontological generosity, self-subsisting Love; and that such transcendent Love inherently causes, permeates and activates every creature, which in answer loves God more than itself. Thus love for God, the natural and universal eros, is the very virtue and innermost vitality in which all beings desire and love, act and strive.

2   In the preceding pages I have emphasized our new awareness of the eternal approach to God. Summing up what I have often tried to point out, I should like now to outline what may be called, properly speaking, a new approach to God, not in the field of knowledge but in the field of culture and in the historical life of man.

Every great age of culture receives its deepest meaning and direction from a particular constellation of spiritual factors or dominating ideas; let us say, from a particular historical heaven. And the most significant factor to be considered in such moving appearances of the Zodiac of history is the peculiar approach to God characterizing a given period of culture. What are, from this point of view, the main characteristics of the human approach to God, or of the human attitude toward God, in the new age of civilization that is emerging?

The Medieval Age was a humble and magnanimous period of history. I would say that at the end of this *sacral* era man experienced not humility but humiliation. Whereas new forces awakened in history, he felt distressed and crushed by the old structures of a civilization which had considered itself as God's stronghold built up on earth. From the Renaissance on, he endeavored to become aware of and establish his own dignity by the sole effort of his own reason liberating itself both from the old structures of the world and from all sorts of disciplines and authorities which were in the name of God the keystone of these structures. He isolated himself progressively from God. God, the heavenly God of Christianity, or the immanent and evolving God of pantheism, was but the supreme assurance of his own greatness and power. He expected progress and happiness from the effort of man centered upon himself and set apart from God. He realized his dignity; he became the master of nature. But he was alone. The age was an age of anthropocentric humanism. It ended in human devastation.

If civilization is to be saved, the new age must be an age of theocentric humanism. Today human dignity is everywhere trampled down. Still more, it crumbles from within, for in the mere perspective of science and technology we are at a loss to discover the rational foundations of the dignity of the human person and to believe in it. The task of the emergent civilization consists in refinding and refounding the sense of that dignity, in rehabilitating man in God and through God, not apart from God. This means a complete spiritual revolution. Then all the conquests of the preceding epoch will be both purified and saved, redeemed from the errors of this epoch and transfigured, brought to a new flowering. The age will be an age of dignification of the creature, in its living relation with the Creator; as vivified by Him, and as having in Him the justification of its very existence, its labor on earth, its essential claims and its trend toward freedom. It will be again, at least for those capable of understanding, an age of humility and magnanimity, but with a new awareness of human potentialities and of the depth, magnitude and universality of human problems. The new approach to God will be a new approach to the true God of the Judaeo-Christian tradition, the true God of the gospel, whose grace perfects nature and does not destroy it, transcending reason in order to strengthen, not to blind or annihilate, it; making moral conscience progress in the course of time and leading human history, that is, the ceaseless and ceaselessly thwarted effort of mankind toward emancipation, in the direction of its supratemporal accomplishment. This new approach will proceed neither in the adoration of creatures, which was the foolishness of our time, nor in that bitter contempt which too many Christians mistake for the divine madness of the saints. It will manifest itself in a deeper respect for and understanding of the creature and a greater attention will be given to the discovery in man of every vestige of God.

Hence there are a number of consequences which I should like merely to enumerate. Doubtless metaphysical anguish, the great anguish of Augustine and Pascal, will always play its part in the human search for God. Yet it seems that in the present situation of mankind it is rather through the practical effort to rediscover man, through the actual experience of the basic conditions of personality, justice, freedom, respect and love for our fellow men, that we shall be led to the rediscovery of God. On the other hand, it appears that the controversial emphasis of religious thought has now shifted from humbling to promoting reason. Religious thought will have to defend itself not so much against philosophical (critical) reason, as at the time of the Enlightenment, as it will have to defend philosophical (ontological) reason against sheer irrationalism and a metaphysics of despair and also against such ultimate fruits of rationalism as old pseudo-scientific positivism and dialectical materialism. It will have to defend the existence of supernatural reality less against naturalistic exaltation than against naturalistic destruction of nature. In the structure of human knowledge theology occupies and will always occupy the highest position. Yet with regard to the role played by it, in fact, in the inner stimulations of culture, it is through Christian philosophy, in addition to the irrefragable ontological truth promulgated by every great religion, that the new civilization will be spurred, at least to the extent that it will be inspired by the spirit of Truth. The momentous question will be more than ever: What is man? I mean man not only essentially, but existentially. In the very perspectives of religious thought there must be developed a philosophical ethics, as distinguished from moral theology and as encompassing anthropology as well as sociology. The notion of natural law, cleansed of the spurious interpretations that preyed upon it, will be re-examined and restored. Whereas for centuries the most crucial issues for religious thought were the great theological controversies centered on the dogmas of faith, these most crucial issues will now deal with political theology and political philosophy.

Yet, since the preaching of the gospel, what has had, in the supreme regions of knowledge, and will always have, a characteristic and all-pervading significance for a given period of civilization, is the peculiar way in which the human mind is able to grasp the mystery of human freedom and divine grace. I think that the emergent civilization will not fail to have its say in the matter. At the same time the reverse mystery, which displays the power of refusal and nothingness, the problem of evil, will be scrutinized anew in its metaphysical and psychological recesses and implications.

Finally, we are searching for the deepest characterization, from the spiritual point of view, of the new age we are considering. It is necessary to make clear that the spiritual dynamism at work in human culture implies a twofold movement. First, there is the movement of descent, the movement by which the divine plenitude, the prime source of existence, descends into human reality to permeate and vivify it. For God infuses in every creature goodness and lovability together with being and has the *first* initiative in every good activity. Then there is the movement of ascent, which is the answer of man, by which human reality takes the *second* initiative, activates itself toward the unfolding of its energies and toward God. From the point of view of the Absolute, the first movement is obviously what matters most; to receive from God is of greater moment for man than to give to God, and man can only give what he has received.

Thus we shall observe that the great error of modern times, from the Renaissance on, has been to believe that the second movement matters more than the first, or to expect from man the *first* initiative; let us say to forget that the word of God precedes man's answer, and perversely to consider the answer to be the first utterance.

And we shall conclude that the emergent civilization will realize again that the descent of divine plenitude into man matters more than the ascent of man toward self-perfection. In this new age the movement by which the human being answers God's movement of effusion will not take place, as in the Middle Ages, in a childlike, ignorant-of-itself humanity. Its new simplicity will be a mature and experienced, self-awakened simplicity, enlightened by what might be called a free and evangelical introspection.

Such will be the new approach to God peculiar to this age, the age of the spiritual revolution. Man will understand that he ascends toward his own fullness and toward God all the better because he himself espouses the movement of descent of the uncreated Love and in so doing reveals all that he is and possesses. He will understand that he must edify himself in order to receive such an effusion. Gospel generosity, by accustoming human life to the divine ways, appears at the same time as a manifestation of the "philanthropy of our God," as St. Paul puts it, and corresponds to that rehabilitation and dignification of the creature in God of which I spoke above. Man will find anew his internal unity by definitely preferring the evangelical loss of himself which is produced by love—that readiness to give everything, the mantle and the tunic and the skin—to the rationalist self-achievement which is the conquest of illusion and delusion, and to the irrationalist self-achievement which is dissolution in the sea of despair and absurdity.

3   The dialectics of anthropocentric humanism developed within three centuries. Man's approach to God changed accordingly. For the notion of God—to the extent that it ceases to be encompassed and kept pure by revelation—is linked to culture and its fate is conformable to that of culture. At the first moment of humanistic dialectics, God, as we noted above, became the assurance of man's domination over matter. He was a transcendent God, but closed up in His transcendence and forbidden to interfere in human affairs. He became a decorative God, the God of the classical bourgeois world. At the second moment, with romanticist philosophy and the great idealist metaphysicians, God became an idea. He was an immanent God, engulfed in the dialectical progress of the self-asserting Idea and the evolving world. This God of pantheism and of the romanticist bourgeois world was but the ideal borderline of the development of mankind. This God was also the absolute, basic and unbending justification of good and evil, of all crimes, oppressions, iniquities, as well as of conquests and the money-making progress of history.

At a third moment, Feuerbach was to discover that God—such a God—alienates man from himself. Marx was to declare that He is but an ideological mirror of the alienation of man accomplished by private property. And Nietzsche was exhilarated by the mission with which he felt himself endowed; namely, to proclaim the death of God. How could God still live in a world from which His image, that is, the free and spiritual personality of man, seems definitely destined to vanish away? God as dead, God in the grave, was the God of the final agony and self-destruction of an age of civilization which is now at its end. Atheism is the final end of the inner dialectics of anthropocentric humanism.

Thus we are confronted with the problem of atheism, the significance of which for culture and for the emergent civilization must be scrutinized. There are many kinds of atheism. There are pseudo atheists who believe that they do not believe in God and who in reality unconsciously believe in Him, because the God whose existence they deny is not God but something else. There are practical atheists who believe that they believe in God but who in reality deny His existence by each one of their deeds. Out of the living God they have made an idol. There are absolute atheists who actually deny the existence of the very God in whom the believers believe and who are bound to change their entire scale of values and to destroy in themselves everything that connotes His name.

Practical atheism does not pose any special problem for the philosopher, except the problem of the possibility of cleavage between the intellect and the will, theoretical belief and actual behavior, or, in theological terms, between faith (dead faith) and charity. Dead faith is faith without love. The practical atheist accepts the fact that God exists—and forgets it on all occasions. His case is a case of voluntary, stubborn forgetting.

Quite different is the case of the absolute atheist. He does not forget God, he steadily thinks of Him—in order to free himself from Him. When he has acquired the intellectual persuasion that God does not exist, his task and endeavor is not finished; this very negation delivers him over to an inner dialectic which obliges him ceaselessly to destroy any resurgence in himself of what he has buried. For in denying God he has explicitly denied Transcendence. But in actual fact the good which everyone desires, even without knowing it, is finally self-subsisting Good; and thus, in actual fact, the dynamism of human life, because it tends toward good and happiness, even if their true countenance is not recognized, tends implicitly toward Transcendence. Doubtless the absolute atheist may ascribe to superstition or human stupidity or human "alienation" every vestige or trace of Transcendence he contemplates in the common behavior and beliefs, individual or social life, of men. Yet within himself is the real drama. In proportion as the dialectic of atheism develops in his mind,—each time he is confronted with the natural notion of and natural tendency to an ultimate End, or with the natural notion of and natural attention to absolute values or unconditioned standards, or with any metaphysical anxiety—he will discover in himself vestiges of Transcendence which have not yet been abolished. He must get rid of them. God is a perpetual threat to him. His case is not a case of practical forgetting, but a case of deeper and deeper commitment to refusal and fight.

What is the meaning of this absolute atheism? It is in no way a mere absence of belief in God. It is rather a refusal of God, a fight against God, a challenge to God. And when it achieves victory it innerly changes man, it gives man a kind of stolid solidity, as if the spirit of man had been stuffed with dead substance, and his organic tissues turned into stone. Atheism begins with a kind of new start in moral activity, a determination to confront good and evil in an absolutely free experience by casting aside any ultimate end—a determination which is mistaken for moral maturity and boils down in reality to the complete giving of self to some human, concrete "Great Being." For Auguste Comte it was Mankind; for others a Work to be done or a Party to serve. At the same time the relation to the absolute Good which the moral good essentially implies is abolished, and as a result the very nature of the moral good vanishes away. In the true atheist, duty or virtue necessarily becomes a requirement of his own perfection accepted as a supreme cult, or as a hopeless rite of his own greatness, or as an attribute of his deified will. The thunderlike appearance of absolute atheism in human history has been the conclusion of a progressive degradation of the idea of God and has meant the beginning of a new age in which the process of death and the process of resurrection will develop together, confronting each other and struggling with each other.

With regard to culture, atheism is a mirror, a true and faithful mirror, of the state to which the human being has been reduced. For man being the image of God, he naturally thinks of Him according to the state in which the image presents itself at a given moment of culture. Absolute atheism means that the personality of man is definitely endangered; and that all the masks, the words, the façades, the palliatives, the plasters and cosmetics with which human conscience tries to deceive itself and to give us the appearance of man are henceforth useless and will be cast away. Picasso's art, in its present character, is the true art of atheism; I mean of that thorough defacement of contemporary man, which is mirrored in atheism. We are no more persons than the distorted, imbecile faces of those ferocious females. We no longer possess true, human faces.

Absolute atheism is also a translation into crude and inescapable terms, a ruthless counterpart, an avenging mirror, of the practical atheism of too many believers who do not actually believe—Christians who keep in their minds the stage-set of religion, especially because of the class or family advantages that religion seems to them to protect.

But they deny the gospel and despise the poor. They pass through the tragedy of their time only with resentment for the loss of their social and political privileges and fear for their own prestige or possessions. They contemplate without flinching every kind of injustice or atrocity if it does not threaten their own way of life. They scorn their neighbor, scorn the Jew, scorn the Negro, scorn their own nation if it ceases to be the "good nation" of their old dreams, worship force and brand as "subhuman" the peoples, races or classes they fear or do not understand. They have a clear conscience and live and act as if God did not exist. Such men and women invoke the name of God and do not really believe in Him. They live on empty formulas and stereotyped phrases, on mental clichés. They cherish every kind of sham that will soothe and deceive them. They await the deceivers. They are famished for deception.

In their own existence absolute atheists have dehumanized life and the claims of the soul. They have replaced human receptivity to transcendence and the vital, unsatisfied needs of personality by the cosmic dynamism of nature. They present the appearance of corpses. In some of them, moreover, the process of death is not achieved; there still remains a hidden germ of life, a living thirst. And this subsisting germ, thwarted, denudated, stripped of every rational support, becomes all the more genuine and alive as it resists the destruction and havoc which atheism has brought on all sides into the spiritual substance of man. Such atheists, if they receive the grace of faith, will become men for whom nothing is of account except God and the gospel. For them atheism has been a sort of hellish purification.

Practical atheists also have dehumanized life and the claims of the soul in their own existence. They nurture nothingness. But they have the appearance and colors of life although they are dead within. They are whited sepulchers. They are perfumed with all the fragrance of self-righteousness; there is no substance in them. It would be too optimistic to pretend that their time has passed. Yet it seems probable that they will be of no use in the new age of civilization, in the emergent civilization of revolution and change that is already upon us.

Atheists and believers will live together in this new age. They will walk a long way, each asserting his own position against the other, each endeavoring to have the human mind and civilization inspired by his respective philosophy. Under penalty of spiritual death civilization will have to overcome atheism and free itself of its inspiration. This cannot be done by machine guns, police forces and dictators. If it is true that absolute atheism is primarily the fruit and condemnation of practical atheism and is its reflected image in the mirror of divine wrath, then it must be said that the only way of getting rid of absolute atheism is to get rid of practical atheism. Decorative Christianity is nowadays not enough. Living Christianity is necessary to the world. Faith must be actual, practical, existential faith. To believe in God must mean to live in such a manner that life cannot be lived if God does not exist. Gospel justice, gospel attentiveness to everything human must inspire not only the deeds of the saints, but the structures and institutions of common life, must penetrate to the depths of social, terrestrial existence.

This is not possible, even in the imperfect ways of humanity and among the hard conflicts of the coming age, if in those who believe in God the true sources are not alive, and if the life they must give to the world does not flow down into them from the heights of God-given wisdom. A great deal of wisdom, a great deal of contemplation will be required in order to render the immense technological developments of the emergent civilization truly human and liberating. At this point one should recall Henri Bergson's observations on the mutual need which "mystics" and "mechanics" have of each other, and on the *supplément d'âme* that must vivify the body, now become too large, of our civilization. Contemplative life, perhaps in new forms, and made available not only to the chosen few but to the common man if he actually believes in God, will be the prerequisite of that very activity which tries to spread the gospel leaven all over the world.

As I have endeavored to emphasize for many years, the deepest requirement of a new age of civilization will be the sanctification of secular life. For pagan antiquity, *holy* was synonymous with *sacred;* that is, with what had been set apart to be physically, visibly, socially at the service of God. And it was only to the extent that sacred rites and symbols ruled human life that the latter could externally please God. The gospel has deeply changed all that by interiorizing moral life and the sanctity in the hearts of men, in the secret of the invisible relations between the divine Personality and the human personality.

Henceforth what is secular or "profane" is not to be distinguished from what is sacred in the sense that what is impure is differentiated from what is pure; but rather as a certain order of human activity, the aim of which is temporal, is distinguished from another order of human activity which is socially constituted to assure spiritual aims by preaching the Word of God and ministering to the soul. And both, the one involved in the secular or temporal order and the other involved in the sacred order, must tend to the perfection of human life; that is, to inner sanctity.

Now it can be observed that this evangelical principle has been progressively realized and manifested in human conscience and behavior, but that its process of spiritual development is far from being achieved on earth.

In these perspectives we may understand that a new "style" of sanctity, a new step in the sanctification of secular life, will be demanded by the new age. Not only will the spirit of Christ spread into secular life, seek for witnesses among those who labor in yards and factories, in social work, politics or poetry, as well as among monks dedicated to the search for perfection; but a kind of divine simplification will help people to realize that the perfection of human life does not consist in a stoical athleticism of virtue nor in a bookish and humanly calculated application of holy recipes, but rather in a ceaselessly increasing love, despite our mistakes and weaknesses, between the Uncreated Self and the created Self. There will be a growing consciousness that everything depends on that descent of the divine plenitude into the human being of which I spoke above, and which performs in man death and resurrection. There will be a growing consciousness that man's sanctification has its touchstone in neighborly love, requiring him to be always ready to give what he has, especially himself, and finally to die in some manner for those he loves.

THE EMERGENCE OF THE NEW IDEALS

"Thou hast seen the kettles of thought a-boiling. Consider also the fire." Man belongs now to one single world community and all the world belongs to all mankind. Personal liberty and social justice must now become part of man's experience on earth. Man must finally learn that the meaning of each individual existence rises above the socio-historical process and has a direct kinship with universal truth. And in overcoming the dichotomy between *individual* and *social* he must know that the denigration of humanity that has taken place affects the human being in his entirety. For *individual* and *social,* although characteristics of unitary human beings, are so integral and indivisible that they are but two characteristics of man in his actual existence as a member of society. And the events of history constituting man's denigration are characteristics of the violation and dissolution of the inherent interrelationship correlating man and society. The social bonds and identities inhere integrally in human beings in their very humanity. Their relation with the characteristics that distinguish one man from another is so intrinsic and permeative that the individual cannot be either comprehended or fruitfully evaluated unless the social is included in the examination.

The contributors to this volume have endeavored to point out the one inexpugnable fact of contemporary society, the fact that if civilization is to survive, not in a rhetorical sense but actually, man must cultivate the art and the science of human relationships. For what matter most are not empirical relations between causes and effects, but the intensity and depth with which human relations are felt. Man must finally accept the necessity of living together and working together with all peoples of all kinds in the same world, at peace. The contributors to this book have endeavored, with unity of purpose, to reveal the fundamental truth in the life of modern man, to point out the changeless in the changing, the one in the many. They hope they have succeeded in indicating that the intellectual and moral solidarity of humanity is now a practical possibility and that it can be achieved without attempting to obliterate or surrender variations in belief, culture or institutions which bestow upon mankind its pluralism, richness and vigor.

They have endeavored to show that democracy, from which the *demos* has not been removed, once the most revolutionary of forces, is now the greatest conservative power on earth, conservative in the deepest and best sense of the term, because it is the only defense and support of the ethical foundations of the world now almost blotted out in the miasma of doubt, ignominious defeat and despair. The contributors to this book have pointed out that human culture is not the firmly established, eternal and unassailable thing we once supposed it to be. Our science, our art, our poetry and our religion are only the upper layer of a much older stratum that reaches down and penetrates to a great depth, and we must always be prepared for violent concussions which may shake our cultural world and our social order to their very roots. These contributors have reiterated the demand of our modern society that in order to do justice to our new responsibility and to prove ourselves worthy of it we must restore to democracy its pristine revolutionary character. Democracy cannot merely *be*; it must *do*. For without doing, it will cease to be, is in fact on the verge of imminent destruction. The truth itself is not enough. A way to the truth must be found. To say that man lives for the mere sake of action as action, irrelevant of the thought it carries out, would of course be to say that no rational purpose is possible. Thought and action must be reunited. Therefore this apostrophic plea has been made to the conscience of modern man—a plea to re-evaluate the fundamental premises of democracy, to restore the nexus between being and doing, between spirit and matter. A passionate and purposeful desire and will must begin to evolve out of the anxiety and confusion of the moral abnegation of our time; the will to concentrate and resist; the will to call a halt, to *command* a halt; the will to defend civilization against the corrupting onward march of force, tyranny and fear. The *ecclesia militans* always preceded the *ecclesia triumphans*. And so democracy, if it is to triumph, must revivify itself, even though it has long lost the habit and the attitude of life-giving authority. A vital, militant, revolutionary social democracy is our plea, a democracy liberated from self-doubt and vacillation, a democracy cognizant of its own indispensable ends, cognizant of its universal applicability and of its necessity to foster the growth of an integrated, intrepid, creative human society.

Humanity, true humanity which democracy makes possible, moreover, has combined the individual and the social principles in a manner that is irrefutable and wholly natural. Democracy makes clear that no act of submission can exist, no *pactum subjectionis* by which man is able to renounce his condition of being a free agent and enslave himself. For by such an act of repudiation he would abandon that very character which constitutes his essence and nature: he would abandon his very humanity. The value in dignity, which democracy bestows upon the individual being and upon the human soul in its immediate relationship to absolute truth, is not contradicted by the principle of the equality of all men. It is in the statute of human rights, this Christian heritage of the great bourgeois revolution, that both principles, the individualistic and the social, freedom and equality, are combined, interrelated and mutually justify each other. It cannot be denied that all collectivity tends to exaggerate the mechanization, the bureaucratization, the regimentation of man and to submerge the individual and the group in a pragmatic uniformity, even in a conformity, and in mass movements. There is a certain fear for the disappearance of human liberty and individual values in the deep and often unnavigable waters of collectivity. One may say that it is "democracy's fear of itself"—a fear potently conducive to the spiritual distress and moral emasculation from which democracy has suffered. There would be no hope for democracy if it had to choose between anarchy, chaos and the extreme collectivization, or exaggerated socialization, that destroys personality.

But this is not the meaning of a socialism, as the authors of this book have pointed out, that recognizes democracy as its native soil, and demands an equalizing justice in the name of freedom. Socialism implies a quickened consciousness to a socially minded way of thought and action. It is the recognition that man is a social being and cannot exist without social forms, without society, which is so inherent in his nature. And society existing within each of its members has claims which express the totality of its vigor. Socialism implies that a purely individualistic personal and spiritual humanity is incomplete and dangerous to human culture; nay, is not even possible. Socialism implies that political, economic and social responsibilities are essential demands of man's existence and moral life, and that these may not be separated from spiritual and cultural activities.

We have uttered a plea to man's conscience to renounce his past compromising ways and to stand forth in an abandoned and morally leaderless world as the strong and unswerving protector of the good and godly in humanity. Such an awakening will mean the spiritual rejuvenation of society and its moral vindication. Conscious, responsible leadership is the only hope against destruction. Blind leadership will be our doom. For "if the blind lead the blind, both will fall into the ditch."

Further, we have tried to point out that there must be a re-evaluation of the "common man." The *communis homo* referred originally not to the man in the street, to the amorphous, inarticulate, anonymous man, but to the immanent deity, the very *man* in every man. What we demand also is something other than a quantitative standard of living. We demand a reinterpretation of democracy which recognizes that an evaluation of equality and justice must be made in accordance with proportionate and analogical truth rather than merely in numerical terms. We demand a form of society in which all work has an inherent dignity and a close relation with the perfection of the personality. We demand a *basis* for communication, understanding and agreement, for effective co-operation in the application of the commonly recognized spiritual values to the solution of contingent problems of organization and conduct. We demand that our decaying civilization be "renewed in knowledge," as St. Paul declared; not in reference to the facts of science exclusively but in reference to our Self as the only hope of restoring meaning and value to a world of impoverished reality. We demand a world in which the concept of vocation is revitalized, not as a mere matter of arbitrary choice, or of passive determination by pecuniary needs, but of occupation to which one is ineluctably summoned by one's own nature and in which each man can develop not only the perfection of his product or profession but his very entelechy itself. Work is made for the man; not man for the work. The primary purpose is to provide simultaneously for the development and the fulfillment of the workman's potentialities and for the needs of society. In the final analysis, this is the meaning of justice and equality: that every man should do that work for which he is by nature fitted, thereby enriching his own growth and thereby

perfecting himself and society. The highest justice is that which dis-
tributes to each in accordance with his own nature, permitting of
course equal access to all to the sources of economic wealth and
spiritual fulfillment; a natural equality, a political justice which mankind requires if anarchy is to be avoided. For when work is divorced
from culture in the highest spiritual sense, when the nexus between
them is destroyed, nothing but the task remains and leisure and high
wages will not compensate for what has been lost by man's spirit, dignity and integrity in hours of unintelligent, meaningless labor to which
an exclusively industrial society condemns and relegates the majority
of men. This is the answer to the dehumanized industry, misery and
prostitution of contemporary man, and the only hope for achieving a
morally unified society and the restoration of man to a common humanity.

Long ago Plotinus declared, perhaps anticipating the ultimate, inevitable unity of mankind, that there is nothing strange in the reduction of all selves to the one; although it may be asked how there can
be only one, the same in many, entering into all, but never itself divided
up. The emergence of the new ideals evokes the recognition that there
can be no liberation for individual man if there is no liberation for
all mankind. Liberation is not for our self, for this specific man, but
for *that* Self which never becomes anyone; that is, only for us when
we are no longer our subjective selves, but have verified the dictum
"*That* art thou." In dividing effect from cause we impose the finiteness
of our duration upon the eternity of the soul. For there is nothing
whatever that I might obtain that I am not already possessed of. Man
is what he knows. When this immanent body-dweller is released from
the body, from the bonds of materialism, what actually survives? "That
art thou." This is what exists if we include in our individualism all that
is not-self; for our end is to exchange our own limited manner of being
subjective, isolated, abandoned for the universal's unlimited manner of
simply *being,* and thereby identifying ourselves with humanity. And
this is perhaps the only meaning of immortality. It exists when we cease
to identify our self with the perishable psychophysical self and when
we recognize ourselves in all mankind.

The pragmatic ideals and theories with their confusion of ends and
means have given way to the ultimate ideals about man and society,
ideals which recover at last the truth about man's nature, namely, that

the man who knows himself must see himself in everyone and everyone in himself. One may say it is a kind of unified man as everywhere seeing the same God universally hypostatized, the Self established in all beings and all beings in the Self. Were it not that whatever we do to others is thus really done to our Self which is at the same time their Self, there would be no metaphysical basis for any doing to others as we would be done by. The principle is implicit in the rule, and only more explicit elsewhere. This is the spirit of truth immanent in the new civilization, the divine *Eros* upon which our very life depends, making possible not only the enjoyment of *eros* but also the fecundity of *agape*. Ignorance itself is nothing more than the inability or unwillingness to see things as they really are and the consequent attribution of substantially to what is merely phenomenal; the seeing of Self in what is not-Self.

> I was the Sin that from Myself rebell'd,
> I the remorse that tow'rd Myself compell'd. . . .
> Pilgrim, Pilgrimage and Road
> Was but Myself toward Myself; and Your
> Arrival but Myself at my own door.

Man has passed through the straits. He knows that he is adapted by his congenital constitution to the apprehension of natural laws which cannot be proved by experience, although experience is in conformity with them. He has passed beyond the Charybdis of false rationalism which attempted to deduce particular existence from misconceived universals and he has left behind him the Scylla of blind positivism and empiricism which denied genuine universals or by dubious induction tried to deduce from them mythically self-sufficient particulars. He begins to demand the universal truth that gives meaning and purpose and moral integrity to his existence. He begins to recognize that the autonomous will is self-legislating and exercises its causality uninfluenced by anything except itself. It is *free*. Freedom, man begins to learn, is not lawlessness, arbitrariness or caprice but the ability of the will to consent to and accept universal law. And the free will is always the moral will. In so far as we act reasonably and morally we act as free men, since our reason cannot regard a moral judgment as inspired by anything except itself. Thus deterministic acts must be recognized for what they are: an interference with reason on the part of impulse. This realization of the universal truth of reason can now be restored to us. Everything that we loved in the past has betrayed us. And our last love—the love that makes us acknowledge it, our love for Truth, in spite of a certain reluctance to accept it, let us take care that by virtue of our own blindness we do not in turn betray it. And even if finally because of our blindness Truth is impossible for contemporary man to achieve, then at least let there be truthfulness, for this may be the only honor and the only moral integrity left to his conscience.

Today it is not only the abstract principle of the moral and ethical truths of Christianity, of democracy, that must be saved as well as reexamined in new forms, made to live as a noetic force in the life of man, since the dogma of Christianity is dead. The increasing demand for social justice has to be met if we wish to guarantee the efficacy of the new social order. Predatory attacks on the liberal intelligence are designed to annihilate the last remnants of Christianity and humanism (in which *humanitas* is still preserved) and to frustrate all efforts to bring peace and social stability to the world. If the new society is to last and if it is to be worthy of the efforts of humanity made thus far, the new leadership must be blended with the spiritual truths of the past. Together they can bring about a revitalization, a rejuvenation of the valuable elements in tradition, continuing them in the spirit of creative evolution without abandoning them to the liberalism that has languished and grown apathetic, the liberalism of the deontologized man.

Such an apathetic liberalism misinterpreted the meaning of tolerance. It mistook neutrality for tolerance. Yet, neither democratic tolerance nor scientific objectivity means that man should refrain from assuming the responsibility for what he believes to be true, should avoid taking a stand, or should repudiate the advantages of an analysis of the final values and objectives in life. The meaning of tolerance is that everyone should be given a just opportunity to present his case, but not that nobody should passionately and uncompromisingly believe in and be devoted to and be responsible for his cause. This attitude of apathy and ennui in modern democracy went so far that man ceased to believe, out of mere fairness, or fatigue, in his own objectives. Man no longer believed that moral objectives or adjustments were desirable, that freedom, like love and friendship, must be won again and again, at every moment of man's existence, through nurture and understanding; and that the goals of a social democracy must never be eclipsed. The challenge of the totalitarian systems more than anything else evoked in man the consciousness that socially democratic societies have a set of basic values in common, inherited from classical antiquity and even more from the Judaeo-Christian tradition, and that they must be stated and agreed upon. Although tolerance epitomized the liberation from dogmatic authority, it nevertheless axiomatically achieved that static attitude of neutrality in relation to the life of the spirit which inevitably substitutes a relativist rationalism for universal, objective truth and reason.

The common fear on man's part of his fellow man, the horizontal fear so characteristic of man's immediate past and present history, a fear which had its prototype in the vertical fear of previous history, the fear of God, of punishment after death, must be dissolved. The ethos and the ethnos must be transcended and must become one universal whole. The essential character of human life, the thing that constitutes its humanness, is the self-discovery of man and the inherent unity of man. This in the final analysis is the meaning of personality, denoting the general character that distinguishes human life from all other forms of life. To recognize that human life is personal is primarily to deny that human life is merely physiological, or that it can be treated as differing from animal life only in degree and not in kind. It is to recognize that the essence of human life is radically different from the essence of organic life, and that the relations that constitute the totality of human life are radically different from those which form a unity of the organic world.

In the Gospel, St. John declares, "*This* is the condemnation, that light is come into the world, and men loved darkness rather than light, because their deeds were evil." It is here that the unity of thought and action may be revealed. The discovery of self necessarily involves a choice in the sphere of action. And the choice hitherto has been preponderantly evil. Actually, it must be said that it is not so much the atomizations of science during the past two hundred years that have produced the contemporary chaos, the evil, in society but rather the atrophy of morality, ethics and religion. It was not that science was so strong but that morality was so weak. And finally, the secularization of the spirit and of values has resulted in the deepest tragedy of all. Man has almost lost the capacity to love and to be loved, and therefore to know the good. And in order to be restored he must reinstitute the most significant and nonmaterial of human hierarchies: the order of intellectual and spiritual values and disciplines. To achieve this man must learn that hate is a part of love, the negation of love; and that evil must be abhorred as a negation of the good.

Thus again man is confronted with the necessity of responsibility, of choice. And if this choice involves a refusal to act in terms of the newly discovered truth, then it axiomatically involves a refusal to believe the truth, and this can only exist through the intellectual effort to repudiate the truth. The truth of the wholeness of life must be restored, a wholeness which counteracts the divisive tendencies of the mind. This intuitive organic wholeness expresses itself in the mythopoeic faculty of man and is a defensive reaction of nature against the dissolvent power of the intelligence. Contemporary man must become his own prophet. He must become the prophet and the architect of the new world social democracy. At one period of its history democracy was as restricted in its vision and as narrow in its application as the Hebrew religion at the time of King David. Now the fetters of an established aristocracy, an established church and an established ignorance have been broken. We begin to believe in the potentialities of black men and of men of other cultures as well as of white men. Even as the apostle Paul was driven by the universal implications of the Christian religion, so today we must be driven by the universal implications of a social democracy.

Nevertheless, in order to remain dynamically alive, in order to be able to state and solve the problems that perpetually arise in human existence, in order to permit the growth and expansion of human personality, Truth must not only be sought for but passionately defended when found. For example, the basic discrepancy between social fact and social theory must be recognized, treated and resolved. Man must not only seek freedom from want and from ignorance, but he must demand that the new social structure provide freedom for the full realization of human potentialities. In this way the danger of the utter destruction of man by turning him into a destroying force himself need never again be part of his experience. He must at last know that he is implacably and inevitably committed to the thesis that there is a common world which we must all understand, a common human nature which we all share, a common history which we all inherit.

By placing co-operative social action regarding the basic social categories of man's interest at the very apex of the hierarchy of values as the potential synthesizer and builder of the new world order, man will hold the hope of giving to society and to himself, who is the potential artist-philosopher, the key tool by which he may exercise a measure of control over his own destiny. All existing societies are societies imperfectly, since society is a movement toward a goal. And progress consists in the enlargement of the area of rational personality so that it will comprise all colors, all religions, all economic stratifications; in other words, all cultural diversities under the aegis of an immutable human nature and common humanity.

But there is another consideration, the consideration of highly wrought emotions and acquisitive designs. Such emotions and designs are a continual threat to the common good that unites individuals in a society. And this is precisely the need for the existence of an international state. Such a state is endowed with the power to curb such prerogatives. The abandonment of parochialism, of power worship, of apathetic fear, of a relativism of moral and ethical values, and the embrace of the law of the primacy of the common good over the individual good since the individual personal good *is* the common, universal good; the embrace of the noumenal power in man by the milking of an inner prescience, this is the fortification of our life, our humanity, our international human society. Human society requires government, but government can claim no end of its own. It exists for man. It is his instrument. It only serves to implement the ends of society. Therefore government must serve as a moral tool.

Thus it follows that if peace is to be assured, moral controls born out of the deepest spiritual and religious needs of man's nature must be enacted. Recognizing the necessity of the universal approach in the affairs of men in our shrunken world, we must demand that the new universal ethical controls are universally applicable and based upon humanistic principles acceptable to all mankind. Scientific universalism has made possible scientific humanism, a system which lacks, however, the messianic power of emotional interest. The universal ethical creed must contain the fervor, almost the ebriety, of a religious pursuit. By enforcing virtue, the state will tend to elevate society to a condition of creative nature. The effect of governmental participation and delegation is to transform a moral law into a natural law—what ought to be into what will be.

The principle underlying the new ideals will be not individualism but humanism which, since the time of Varro and Cicero at least, possessed a nobler and severer meaning in addition to its early vulgar meaning of humane behavior. The principle underlying the new ideals will be the teleological power directing the education of man into his true form, the real and genuine human nature. It will derive its inspiration not from the individual alone but from the ideal, from the synthesis of the subject and the object, the individual and the person. And this ideal of human character which it must be the aim of the new civilization to educate each man to achieve is not an empty abstract pattern existing beyond time and space. It is a living, life-giving dynamic force. Above man as an integral aspect of the horde and man as a supposedly independent personality stands man as an ideal, the fulfillment of a prophecy. For when considered merely as an individual, as has been said before, man becomes isolated, desolate in his atomization of the organic unity of his spirit, violated by empirical rationalism. But when considered as a person, metaphysically bound to his individuality from which in truth he cannot be separated, then is he led directly to the absolute, since only in this, his spiritual homeland, can man experience his full sufficiency and transcend the existential world, thereby attenuating its limitations, cruelty and despair.

What is the ideal man? It is the universally valid model of humanity which all individuals are bound to emulate. It is the recognition that man must be inspired by a philosophy which moves from the problem of the cosmos to the problem of man. And thus the unity of nature will find its counterpart in the unity of the community. Man will find his superior strength in the fact that his mind and spirit will be deeply rooted in the life of the community. We must begin to look at the world with the steady gaze that does not see any part of it as separate and cut off from the rest, but always as an element in a living whole. This sense of the natural and mature structure of life must be intimately connected with the desire to discover and formulate the laws governing reality—the reality of the new universal man. The one law of universal justice and truth must pervade the new civilization, and life and thought must be made to harmonize with this law.

The contemporary intellectual interest in the state, particularly in the international or universal state, has quickened man's consciousness to the fact that responsible, moral men without state are as impossible as a state without responsible, moral men. Thus it is that the state, the international or universal state, must compel a choice in man's thought and action, must compel a moral choice, for there is grave danger that if this were not so, there would be no moral choice at all in any realm. The instrumental state is a certain benignant compromise between the ideal society and the actual one. And while there is tension between state and society, there is no necessary or inevitable opposition. They serve to complement each other and to overcome certain divergent tendencies by a superior moral force which binds them together and directs them to a common center.

A tremendous *bouleversement* has dislodged the concept of independent, autonomous states. A universal, social democracy is the new kinetic power of civilization. The values of individual liberty, of ethnic, cultural autonomy, are recognized and admitted, but the shrinking world, the totalitarianization of war, the acceleration of change, and the rise of a conscious democracy have created universal conviction that when these values epitomize separatism and exclusiveness they can only breed greater and greater evils. In a severely crowded, vertiginously changing, highly powered world, if each part attempts to regulate its own affairs and destiny irrespective of a consideration for the whole, only responsive to its own wishes and its own internal conditions, conflicts will be frequent and ultimate disaster inevitable. The freedom of the individual and the nation must not be permitted to destroy such universal and indispensable values as peace, stability, prosperity, progress and justice experienced on a universal scale.

We are in the midst of a world revolution to which nothing can compare since the Reformation or the febrile forty years which inaugurated the Revolutionary War, the publication of the *Wealth of Nations* and the *Decline and Fall*. We are in the vortex of a world maelstrom analogous to the fall of Turgot and the end of any fundamental hope of reform by consent in France, culminating in the categorical surrender of Napoleon at Waterloo. This revolution is crystallizing the manifold potentialities of human society. It is slowly clarifying the principles of international law which, in fact, have been gestating in the womb of history for centuries, and which are awakening man to the necessity of establishing at last an equilibrium between national, cultural autonomy and the unity of world order.

From the heritage of Aristotle, we learn the ontological truth that man's essence consists in being rational, social, free; that acts compatible with man's essential nature are good, and those incompatible are bad. This brings us to the question of natural law (and must be considered in relation to international law) which is inherently reason, a rule of reason for rational beings.

The imperishable words of Cicero found in his *De Legibus* reveal the true meaning of law. "Of all these things respecting which learned men dispute there is none more important than clearly to understand that we are born for justice, and that right is founded not in opinion but in nature. There is indeed a true law, right reason, agreeing with nature and diffused among all, unchanging, everlasting . . ." *Jus naturale* was for Aristotle, Justinian, St. Thomas Aquinas and other moral leaders of history the principles of reason and justice indigenous and intelligible to man, "an ordinance of reason made for the common good," "divine law revealed through natural reason": *participatio legis aeternae in rationali creatura,* and man's necessity to conform to natural law is a command laid upon him by his own nature as a rational being.

Law depends upon morals and morals on God. Finding his intellectual inspiration in the laws of Hamurabi and the Mosaic code, Blackstone in his *Commentaries* declared: "Man, considered as a creature, must necessarily be subject to the laws of his Creator . . . This law of nature, being co-eval with mankind, and dictated by God Himself, is of course superior in obligation to any other. It is binding all over the globe, in all countries, and at all times; no human laws are of any validity if contrary to this; and such of them as are valid derive all their force, and all their authority, mediately or immediately, from this original." Just as there is in the universe a physical order governed by physical law, so there is a moral order intelligible to human reason and governed by moral law.

Objective norms of right and wrong can no longer be abandoned in order to pamper the caprice of a dominant group, either national or international, possessing the power to act. Ultimate reason can no longer be abrogated in favor of "experience," or history, the pragmatic test, or efficiency. Law must be based on reason, not on arbitrary will. For if law is founded essentially on arbitrary will, no legal provision or decision can ever be unjust, since the lawgiver has the power, i.e., the physical force, to actualize his desired ends. And this presents an inherent, if aberrated, logic whether the lawgiver is a majority, a group or a tyrant. An objective, moral criterion of right and wrong must be embraced, a criterion which evokes the reverence not only of the ruler but of the ruled. There must in addition be a limitation of the power of the national or international state over the community, else law degenerates into a mere arithmetical evaluation of majority or physical force. Finally, man must refresh himself in the wellsprings of his spiritual and moral origins, the ultimate source of objective truth and universal law, or he will perish.

The establishment of such moral and spiritual law will be one of the manifold changes wrought by the moral and spiritual revolution through which contemporary man is passing, changes which first must be actualized by the recognition of a common humanity among peoples since we are all bound together by a more primitive and fundamental unity than any unity of thought and doctrine; we all possess the same human nature, the same primordial tendencies, and the nature we hold in common is a rational nature subject intellectually to the attraction of the same fundamental objects. Secondly, in the economic realm, a choice must be made, a choice indicating whether the immense productive capacity that science has placed at our disposal is to be operated through a system which affords abounding wealth to a few and condemns the overwhelming majority of mankind to live on a standard which denies them adequacy, both in material comfort and in spiritual fulfillment, or whether it is to be operated through a system of non-anarchic production for community consumption. The latter is the obvious choice. Thus there can emerge the gradual freedom of the individual and of society and the realization of their deepest potentialities. Man's social life is not a mere aggregate of incoherent and accidental facts. It is dependent upon judgments which are of the same objective validity as any mathematical proposition. For they are not the result of haphazard empirical observations; they possess the dignity of universal truth. Freedom itself seems to lie in some ratio between our desires and our capacities to satisfy them; between what we can intend and what we can achieve. Freedom depends upon the character of the nexus of relations: personal relations, international relations, man in relation to himself, his work, society, the cosmos. And if this nexus is not a valid one, if it is artificial and predatory, the end can only be one of sterility, frustration and failure. Man must be rooted in truth; he must be needed and wanted; he must participate; he must realize his own indispensability.

The old forms have died, died an ignominious death on the battle-field of human indignity and human suffering. What are now being challenged are all the basic hypotheses of that bourgeois civilization which had its genesis at the time of the Reformation. It is no longer possible to superimpose the faith that the mere conflict of private interests, the all too simplified system of the natural liberty of Adam Smith, will produce a systematic, well-integrated commonwealth. We are on the threshold of a new world, a new civilization is in the pangs of birth. We are witnessing the creation of the world. Our decision will determine whether the result will be one of liberation or suffocation. We can no longer demand without challenge that the principle be supported which permits the white man's burden to be tolerated without complaint or revolt by the yellow races and the black. We must concede that during the course of the various stages of historical development the objective requirements of universal reason and natural law should themselves appear to human beings in a way at first shadowy and dim as the twilight. But little by little these requirements appear to lay a command upon man's conscience, they become more perfect in accordance with the development of the moral conscience and the moral will. This apperception has now permitted the full flowering of that objective reality which bestows upon all men the light and efficacy of universal justice and universal equality. These are the new directives. Man must accept this new teleological destiny if he is to master all the potentialities of the new civilization and not be mastered by them. The leaven of equality and justice directs human history toward the ideal of respect for the rights of each human person, and this leaven will continue to work until the end of time in human history in order to eliminate at last every form of servitude.

Scientific cruelty has reached its apex. For good or for evil, science has become the master warmaker, developing new techniques of mass destruction, unlocking the atom to forge out of the energy that holds the earth together the weapon that gives man the final godlike power to tear it apart. Man is at once more powerful than he has ever been before and more helpless in the face of his own power. It would be futile to pretend that the disappearance of historic landmarks and the evidence of the impermanence of all his works will not affect man's relation to life, to the national community, and to the earth itself. It will be long indeed, if ever again, before any political organization will be able to restore the sense of terrestrial security and social equilibrium for mankind. Man has emerged from the Second World War torn and humiliated, his soul lost, shaken to the roots, diminished as a human being in his own eyes and filled with a mortal fear.

> Art after art goes out, and all is night,
> See skulking Truth to her old cavern fled,
> Mountains of casuistry heaped o'er her head!
> Religion blushing veils her sacred fires,
> And unawares morality expires.

If man is to recover the force of religious truth and the transforming, restoring power of love, if he is to regain moral integration without which life is not life and not even death, he must re-evaluate the fundamental law of human nature and demand that it never be broken again, the law that "he that saveth his life shall lose it," that the will to power is self-frustrating, that the fearless and the upright will inherit the earth. He must know that the truth that "all men are created equal" is a political formulation having its genesis in Judaeo-Christian ethics, that the only community in which problems pertaining to diverse ethnic cultural groups can be solved is a community of humanity in which race is no longer a principle of unity, that the profound social affirmations in the Emancipation Proclamation are both political and religious, that the new civilization must concern itself with both religion and democracy, with the individual's relation to the universe as well as to society. An acute awareness must be maintained of the tensions between good and evil both within man and in the external world, and there must be a recapturing of the living truth in such terms as sin and grace, collective guilt and individual redemption. The profound struggle between reason and impulse in existence, this powerful duality, is not to be overcome by the speculative dialectic of idealism but can only be unified in the vital, dynamic process of creativity, a creativity in which all mankind must and can at last participate.

The fate of man depends mainly on the ability to create a universe of discourse—a communal basis—which is paradoxically against the grain of self-assertive tendencies. But one must be aware of this paradox, of the inherent tragedy of human life, without letting that awareness destroy one's courage and one's will. Although Kant, who vitalized the formalization of the new ethics, the attempted reconciliation of individualism and collectivism, was himself unaware of the sociological foundations of his thought, we may say that he arrived at the formalizing concept of the categorical imperative mainly because he recognized that the predetermination of the relevant patterns of action could only result in the limitation of the freedom of the pioneering individual. The demand that man revise his moral and ethical standards is therefore not so unprecedented as it would seem. What were the Reformation and the Puritan movements if not a penetrating purge of the animistic, magical elements within the Roman Catholic religion in order to achieve a more rational morality? It is a logical and inevitable continuity of this tendency when we begin to demand a collective philosophy which must be functional rather than formal, comprehensible rather than arbitrary, and vitalizing rather than apathetic.

In the common-experience philosophy of the future the spirit of community, solidarity and co-operation will be the ideal. Not authoritarianism and the concept of irreconcilable differences, but responsible participation and mutual understanding. And these ideals will differ from the decadent ideals of the past, ideals which were conducive to a *laissez-faire, laissez-aller, sauve qui peut* philosophy, in this respect that they will substitute for misguided tolerance and apathy a categorical recognition of right and wrong. The new social democracy will differ from the age of Cartesian, atomistic individualism in that it will finally establish genuine powers and possibilities of group life. It will become the meaning of a world-wide Oriental as well as Occidental movement to destroy the frustration that comes from isolation, excessive privacy and sectarianism, and to integrate instead the forces of community life in the service of a social and humanistic ideal. This will be accomplished in spite of the seeming contradiction that the Spirit speaks to the Spirit in the inner silence of individual conscience and that any externalization of the message alters and diminishes its essence.

We are with certainty and celerity moving toward an era in which the relations of property must be defined in the interest of the masses of people everywhere on earth, the only alternative of which in every organized society being violent conflict. One of the manifold results of World War II has been to attenuate the authority of the men who had been accustomed to exercise it, even to deprive these men of their psychological hold over the masses of people who had previously respected and even feared it. The people of the world are demanding economic and social reorganization, although the custodians of the *status quo* are anxious, but equally ineffectual, to curb the tides of history.

The ideals of the new civilization will permit, nay, even demand, the re-evaluation of freedom. The revolution embracing these ideals has already begun to exert its compelling force among the masses of most countries, of India, China, Europe and Australia. The bitter experience and the long agony of war have awakened the consciousness of peoples everywhere to their *right* to freedom. This freedom, as Heine declared in his deep awareness, "which has hitherto only become man here and there, must pass into the mass itself, into the lowest strata of society and must become people." The change to a conscious value appreciation and acceptance of freedom for all mankind is analogous to a Copernican change on the social plane in man's history, and if permitted its necessary growth and expansion can only result in the amelioration of the sufferings and deprivations of the masses of men on this earth. Thus new forms of individual and collective responsibility will emerge and men will be given at last the opportunity to assume the responsibility for their efforts and will no longer be denied the experience of self-respect derived from the skill invested in these efforts, a denial which has produced the bitter frustration and depression of modern man and precluded the adequate formation of his personality. The educational tradition and the system of values adapted to the needs of a provincial, parochial world must be relegated so that man may be permitted to function on the broad life-fulfilling plane of international unity and co-operation, and thus of individual spiritual worth.

In the early Renaissance, mystical and voluntaristic tendencies prevented the full realization of the human spirit, while Cartesian dualism precipitated the loss of the idea of spirit completely and even of the word "spirit." In Anglo-Saxon culture, spirit became intellect, thus divesting it of its essential meaning and inherent potentialities. Spirit is *energy* and *mind*; *life* and *reason*. And this recognition must be restored to man's consciousness. Hegel's concept of "Geist" in his early fragments meant life which separates itself from itself and then reunites itself with itself. Later, in his *Phenomenology of Spirit,* he is driven, alas, to the rationalization of spirit. In Thomas Aquinas, spirit is also intellect, while in Duns Scotus it is will. Anaxagoras was the first to emphasize the supremacy of mind over matter and for him power and mind are synonymous. And finally, and most important, for Plato Logos and Eros are united. It is this synthesis, this unity, which modern man must reconquer. He must return to the dynamic unity of power and mind, universality and personality. This is his only salvation. For the essence of spirit is to think, to love, to be conscious, watchful, transitive. The Logos, the *Word,* must be spoken, must be transmitted, and such utterance cannot be either momentary or endlessly repeated. It must progress, it must vary, completing itself in endless and multiple ways. This is the immortality of spirit; this is its infinity, the infinity of that which can be renewed. And out of spirit, as the fountain source, will ultimately emerge the wisdom and self-knowledge for which the world thirsts, a fountain source at which man may drink in solitude but at which mankind must drink in society. One cry of moral actuality breaking from the heart of man is his final glory and his final hope.

There is no depth of life without *a way* to depth, no truth without *a way* to truth. There is no intellectual and moral meaning in life without an economic and social basis. A social philosophy based upon reality must assert itself against two antagonistic fallacies. It must renounce the pseudo idealism that stems from Rousseau to Lenin, that nourishes man with false hopes and that perverts the emancipation to which he aspires while pretending to achieve it. And it must also renounce the predatory pseudo realism that stems from Machiavelli to Hitler, that distorts man under the terror of violence while apotheosizing the animality that enslaves him. Human life depends upon ideas and co-operative social life, permitting each human person to reach his highest heights; human life depends upon a community of ideas. With correct judgment, correct action will ensue. How profoundly applicable are Pascal's words: *"Travaillons donc à bien penser!"* Tyranny and slavery entered man's existence hurling him into a vacuum of despair when he failed to accept the responsibility of the indispensable moral, economic and political planning for his future. If such responsibility is assumed within the tradition of freedom and with the moral passion to permit man to be free, we shall then realize the new ideal —the creed of the new liberalism. The deep sense of causality, of solidarity, the awareness of values, the spectacle of profound spiritual struggle (and not merely sensitive concern), which the greatest experiences of existence reveal, will be conveyed through the massive, reverberative maturity of the fulfilled and emancipated personality of man.

Peace in the world can endure if the peoples of the world share with one another their common inheritance of art, knowledge and skill and if they communicate back and forth among themselves the new experiences of their lives. Peace in the world can endure if international anarchy can be avoided, if enforceable international law can be established predicated upon the unity, the federation of peoples, not governments. Peace in the world can endure if human society can finally become as revolutionary in its political and social adaptation as it has been in its scientific adaptation. Woodrow Wilson was the spirit of the League of Nations but one of the most salient influences was Lord Robert Cecil. When the Covenant was finally completed, Hugh Cecil, the brother of Lord Robert, asked, "Will your League work?" And Sir Robert replied, "Think again, Hugh. Does a spade work?" Not an instrument, not a mechanism, but the spirit and will of the people will prove the accuracy or the fallacy of Kant's grim prophecy that the world will be "the graveyard of the human race."

Peace in the world can endure if the propinquity and interrelation of human interests that hold the world together are encouraged; if new areas and techniques of co-operative action, rallying points of unity and centers around which men of different cultures and faiths can combine, are made available. All the products of the mind and spirit: mathematics, medicine, machinery, art, ideas about social progress, the best that every individual or group has produced anywhere in the world, all this must be accessible to the race of mankind.

In his *Reflections on the French Revolution,* Edmund Burke declared:

Society is indeed a contract. Subordinate contracts, for objects of mere occasional interest, may be dissolved at pleasure; but the state ought not to be considered as nothing better than a partnership agreement in a trade of pepper and coffee, calico or tobacco . . . to be taken up for a little temporary interest, and to be dissolved by the fancy of the parties. It is to be looked on with other reverence; because it is not a partnership in things subservient only to the gross animal existence of a temporary and perishable nature. It is a partnership in all science; a partnership in all art; a partnership in every virtue, and in all perfection. As the ends of such a partnership cannot be obtained in many generations, it becomes a partnership not only between those who are living, but between those who are living, those who are dead, and those who are to be born.

If from the principles contained in these words an extrapolation in international terms can be made of a concrete program of action for a true unity of society, man will not have lived and suffered in vain. In order to achieve this, the term "politics" must be re-evaluated. For Aristotle, for the Greeks, the Romans, and for the people of the Middle Ages, the term "politics" related to institutions, laws, customs, moral and religious ideas which inspired men and influenced their community. The analysis of politics as propounded by Machiavelli, the dissolution of the relationship between morality, ethics and political philosophy, must give way to a new ideal, a new morality, one based upon the right of the human person to have a part, both spiritual and material, in the elementary goods of civilization and the right to demand its effectuation by a responsible world government.

History must not repeat itself. The Enlightenment, that intellectual movement of the eighteenth century, in which the ideals of a liberal democracy for all men had their genesis, although the particular individualism of that period is no longer valid, was in the universality and in the unity of its concepts essentially international. The doctrine of national rights imputed to all men the same rights, and the form of government indispensable to the establishment of these rights had to be the same for all peoples and all nations. However, more tragic and invidious than the defeat of Napoleon was the defeat of the spirit of internationalism, of universality. An aversion developed among the peoples of Europe to any universalism, accompanied by a passionate, if insular, preference for their own respective governments whether they were salutary, expressing the will of the people, or not. The world again became parochial. The particular preempted the hierarchical place of the universal.

The doctrine of socialism formulated by Karl Marx in the nineteenth century likewise possessed in its universality and in the logic of its ideas an international rather than a national philosophy. The emancipation of the masses, of the industrial worker particularly, the freedom from exploitation by the "capitalist" class everywhere in the world, was the demand of this doctrine. And these revolutionary international ideas took strong root, precipitating a profound appeal to and a last hope for the economic liberation of mankind from his everlasting slavery. But this socialist solidarity was a hollow thing, posited upon the frail foundations of incomplete abstract principles and conclusions, upon hypotheses which took into account only one aspect of man's nature and needs. And finally, since the devotion to these principles had not been, and could not be, translated into an allegiance to a pattern of conduct, the allegiance of the workers of the world found itself more potent in relation to their respective nationalities than in relation to their international socialist ideals.

And society has witnessed, also, during the past few years, the decline of international communism in Russia. It is this sentiment of nationalism, of ethnocentrism, as the prime mover and principal political force of our age which has now become an anachronism. But this spirit of nationalism cannot be attenuated one iota unless the people of the world will summon the necessary intelligence and moral responsibility to *demand* their own *common good*, the good of the social body as the *exclusive* aim of society.

Thomas Paine, one hundred fifty years ago, said, "We have it within our power to begin the world over again." The twentieth century, it is true, is the bloodiest in human history, but it still can be retrieved. Man can now produce, if he will, a world-wide flowering of the human spirit, a flowering which society has not known since the twelfth century, a flowering which would be fecundated by the sorrow and tears of these last fatal years. Man can now, with conscience and intelligence, make gigantic strides in social evaluation and control, concentrating the predatory weapons of society within the orbit of a world authority and legislating their powers in order to augment the tranquillity and to enhance the dignity of the human person. Man must now move quickly, for the universal brotherhood to which his philosophy and religion have summoned him has become the condition of his survival.

The human adventure comes to be dignified and serious because it demands communication, and communication is impossible in the fear and isolation of the human being, in the repudiation of universal brotherhood. Our fates are not soliloquies. In the pregnant words of St. Paul, we are "all members of one another." The mystical sense that once declared us all children of God can now find realization in the awareness of our common humanity. As individuals, each of us is one fragment of a species, one aspect of the universe, enjoying a unique position and bound by the laws of historical, ethnic and cosmic forces. Thus we are all subject to the determinism of the material and the physical world. But the *mind* is not a *tabula rasa,* "conditioned" by external circumstances. The perceptive organs are themselves creative and it is not the mind but the world that is conditioned. As persons, we possess spirit subsistent in us which is an ever fecund source of liberty and creative unity. Thus the command is laid upon us to understand the organicity and unity of the human personality with its unending demand to be renewed in the organicity and unity of spiritual, moral, economic, political and social life.

A new and great opportunity has been opened to modern society and all future society, an opportunity unprecedented in the history of the world, the opportunity to produce a fundamental change in the vital basis of civilized life without resort to violence. Man, now conscious of his rights, with an immutable faith in freedom and democracy, must demand a world constitutional government to enforce and assure these rights. A great, new energy must begin to influence the thoughts of men and become a powerful impulse of human action, a Platonic idea of the state whose thesis is that the first and principal task of the state, international as well as national, is the maintenance of justice. This must be the very focus of the political philosophy of the new civilization, for justice is the foundation of law and of organized society, and where there is no justice there is no confederation of peoples. The idea of justice is an end in itself. It exists and subsists by itself; it has an objective, absolute validity. The dignity and justice of man issue from moral thought translated into relevant action. The elevation of man issues from this and not from time and space which he cannot fill. Man must then labor to think morally and act morally. This will secure his freedom.

Man has no homogeneous nature. He is a strange, paradoxical mixture of being and nonbeing. And he must choose which will preponderate. For in the words of Pico della Mirandola: Man is neither earthly nor divine, neither mortal nor immortal, but has the power to form himself into whatever shape he may desire as a free former and sculptor of himself. He can degenerate into the lower things which are brute or can be regenerated by the very sentence of his soul into the higher things which are divine. And it is the latter which alone will inspire a spiritual reconstruction of society, if it is embraced with *enthusiasm* which is essential to man's creativity, enthusiasm meaning that God is in him who is enthusiastic.

Life itself is changing and fluctuating. Even the belief in the immutability of the atom has been destroyed, causing man to pause and say, in awe of the profound cosmic creativity of his mind, *"Le silence éternel de ces espaces infinis m'effraye."* But the true value of life is sought in an eternal order that admits of no change. It is not in the world of our senses, it is only by the power of our judgment that we can grasp this order. For judgment is the central power in man, the common source of truth and morality.

Let us not be oblivious to the warning that a people preserves its vitality only as long as it engenders a genuine contrast between what has been and what may be, and is attuned to adventures beyond the securities of the past. But even if the germ of decay has already set in, inevitably toward the end of such a historical period when thought and custom have petrified into rigidity and when the elaborate machinery of civilization opposes and represses man's heroic qualities, life stirs again, must stir again, palpitating pitifully but persistently beneath the hard crust.

It is this more than anything else that affords the spirit of man its greatest consolation—the gentle assurance of its own immortality; it is this that gives man the resurrected hope to be found in knowledge and in will and the deep realization that there are no remedies which can take the place of the intellectual and moral conscience or that can be of help to that conscience if it is incapable of being of help to itself. The emergent civilization contains a promise: a promise to restore to man his ethical dignity, a dignity which cannot be lost for it does not depend upon an external revelatory gnosis or upon any dogmatic creed. It depends exclusively upon the moral will, on the worth that man attributes to himself, and on his refusal to live an unlived life, the ultimate source of all destruction. It depends upon the comprehension that infinity is mere vacancy when separated from its embodiment of finite values. The notion of understanding requires some grasp of how the finitude of an entity in question requires infinity for its actualization and also some notion of how infinity requires finitude. For example, Buddhism in emphasizing the sheer infinity of the divine principle robbed its practical influence of energetic, originative value and activity. And every concrete unity of experience must be fecundated by the rediscovery of the generative principles of knowledge, worth, beauty, love, salvation.

The world of activity is emphasized by the multiplicity of mortal things. It is creative, originative. It anticipates the future, transforms the past, originates the present. But the continuity and transition must never be omitted, for if this is done, mere immediate creation loses its meaning, destroys the existence of value and the absence of value obliterates any possibility for the exercise of reason. Value demands persistence. In its very essence value is timeless and immortal. It is not rooted in any ephemeral occasion, and the value intrinsic to the universe has an inherent independence of any moment of time; yet is divested of any authority or meaning when separated from its essential relevance to the immediate world of transient fact.

The primary metaphysical nature of being is the convergence of potentiality and actuality, the interpenetration of spirit and nature. It is the originative source of the qualitative variations and differentiations among all possible forms; and thus of value. Even the contention of natural science asserting the primacy of nature at once establishes the absolute sovereignty of spirit, since it is spirit that has conceptualized this primacy of nature thereby rendering all things subservient to the noumenal power of spirit. Yet any attempt to hypostatize the polarity of spirit and nature precipitates man into a dualistic world of absolute spirit manifesting itself in idealism, or some form of mythology, on the one hand; or absolute nature manifesting itself in naturalism, or some form of materialism on the other. And this postulate of an ultimate duality, this contradiction, is untenable by virtue of the very content of these concepts. Although they are not absolute antinomies, they yet exist in an antinomic world. At the same time they cannot be reduced to each other or to any monistic principle. They are simply intertwined with each other, inseparably related, and every spiritual act implies some form of nature, of matter.

The function of philosophy is to evoke the recognition of this truth in man's consciousness. In this sense philosophy is like art in that it reflects passion through language thereby illuminating the sphere of memory and experience, epitomizing through language the inherent crisis in which the permanent merely ostensibly, not actually, is opposed to the transient, being to becoming, and spirit to nature. The longings of the oppressed mind and the "escape from the loneliness of a closed consciousness" are reflected in the universal medium of language which holds indisputable preeminence in the hierarchy of generative principles.[1]

In thus rediscovering a conceptual frame of reference, man will re-experience his capacity for originative value by re-experiencing simultaneously what is universally good through the actualization of his uncreated perfection and through the realization in each being of a plan immanent in its substance. Man will no longer be absorbed with the mere sterile enunciation of abstract principles and doctrines but his existence will be suffused with the implicit suggestion of the concrete unity and organicity of all experience whereby every abstract principle derives its vitality and life. A new concept of man has been born, a new hope for unity and fulfillment, a hope which can now lead him over the Jordan into the Promised Land, into the calm serenity of the rising sun, and the hope of a new day. Man has met man at Golgotha. Let there not be another Crucifixion!

[1] Cf. *Work and History: A Study in the Structure of Civilization;* forthcoming book by Paul Schrecker, Princeton University Press.

BIOGRAPHICAL NOTE

BRAND BLANSHARD, Professor of Philosophy in Yale University

GEORGE E. G. CATLIN, Professor of Politics in Cornell University, and Lecturer in Yale, Columbia and Calcutta Universities

F. S. C. NORTHROP, Professor of Philosophy and Master of Silliman College in Yale University

HARRY W. LAIDLER, Executive Director, League for Industrial Democracy

ROBERT M. MacIVER, Lieber Professor of Political Philosophy and Sociology in Columbia University

JOHN M. CLARK, Professor of Economics in Columbia University

ANANDA K. COOMARASWAMY, Fellow for Research in Indian, Persian and Muhammadan Art, Museum of Fine Arts, Boston, Massachusetts; Fellow of University College, London, England

WERNER JAEGER, Professor of Classical Philology in Harvard University

GEORGE PLIMPTON ADAMS, Mills Professor of Mental and Moral Philosophy and Civil Polity in the University of California; Dean of the College of Letters and Science in the University of California

FRANK H. KNIGHT, Professor of Economics in the University of Chicago

JULIAN HUXLEY, Secretary, Zoological Society of London; Vice-President, Eugenics Society, London, England

WM. PEPPERELL MONTAGUE, Professor of Philosophy in Barnard College, Columbia University

JACQUES MARITAIN, French Ambassador to the Holy See

RUTH NANDA ANSHEN, Editor, Science of Culture Series

INDEX